Transnational Organised Crime
A Comparative Analysis

Organised crime covers a wide range of activities, including drug trafficking, illegal trafficking of people, and fraud. The existence of a land border does not impede these operations; instead in many cases it is used to their advantage. In response, law enforcement strategies must include a transnational, multi-agency approach.

This book critically analyses the extent to which Northern Ireland and the Republic of Ireland have been successful in implementing effective action against transnational organised crime. It explores the adoption of key law enforcement strategies and measures in these jurisdictions, and evaluates how regional (EU law) and international (UN Convention) standards have been implemented at the national level. Drawing on interviews with over 90 stakeholders including the Department of Justice Northern Ireland, the Department of Justice and Equality in Ireland, the Police Service of Northern Ireland and An Garda Síochána, Tom Obokata and Brian Payne discuss the factors affecting the effective prevention and suppression of organised crime, particularly in relation to cross-border cooperation.

In exploring challenges of transnational crime and cooperation, this book will be of great use to students and researchers in international and transnational criminal law, criminology, and crime prevention.

Tom Obokata is a Professor of International Law and Human Rights at Keele Law School. Previously he taught at Queen's University Belfast (2006–2012) and the University of Dundee (2004–2006). He is an expert on transnational organised crime and has published and consulted widely on this topic.

Brian Payne is a Senior Lecturer of Criminology at the University of Gloucestershire. Brian's primary research interests lie in the areas of transnational organised crime, community policing, and restorative justice. Prior to taking up this post, Brian was a Research Fellow for the research project 'North–South Irish Responses to Transnational Organised Crime'.

Routledge Research in Transnational Crime and Criminal Law

Available titles in this series include:

Cross-Border Law Enforcement
Regional Law Enforcement Cooperation – European, Australian and Asia-Pacific Perspectives
Saskia Hufnagel, Clive Harfield and Simon Bronitt (eds.)

Combating Economic Crimes
Balancing Competing Rights and Interests in Prosecuting the Crime of Illicit Enrichment
Ndiva Kofele-Kale

Transnational Organised Crime

A Comparative Analysis

Tom Obokata and Brian Payne

Routledge
Taylor & Francis Group
LONDON AND NEW YORK

First published 2017
by Routledge
2 Park Square, Milton Park, Abingdon, Oxon OX14 4RN

and by Routledge
711 Third Avenue, New York, NY 10017

First issued in paperback 2018

Routledge is an imprint of the Taylor & Francis Group, an informa business

British Library Cataloguing in Publication Data
A catalogue record for this book is available from the British Library

Library of Congress Cataloging in Publication Data
Names: Obokata, Tom, author. | Payne, Brian (College teacher), author.
Title: Transnational organised crime : a comparative analysis / Tom Obokata and Brian Payne.Description: Abingdon, Oxon; New York, NY: Routledge, 2017. | Series: Routledge research in transnational crime and criminal law | Includes bibliographical references and index.
Identifiers: LCCN 2016010434| ISBN 9781138934504 (hbk) | ISBN 9781315677958 (ebk)Subjects: LCSH: Organized crime—Law and legislation. | Organized crime—Law and legislation—Ireland. | Organized crime—Law and legislation—Northern Ireland. | Organized crime–Prevention.
Classification: LCC K5240 .O255 2017 | DDC 345–dc23
LC record available at http://lccn.loc.gov/2016010434

ISBN 13: 978-1-138-61856-5 (pbk)
ISBN 13: 978-1-138-93450-4 (hbk)

Typeset in Galliard
by Keystroke, Station Road, Codsall, Wolverhampton

Contents

Acknowledgements

This book is based on the research project 'North–South Irish Responses to Transnational Organised Crime' conducted between 2012 and 2014. We would like to thank the Arts and Humanities Research Council for giving us the opportunity to carry out this research. The successful completion of this project would not have been possible without the valuable contributions of a host of other individuals and organisations. We would like to acknowledge the support and expert advice provided by Professor John Jackson (University of Nottingham) who served as a consultant for this project. We also wish to express our immense gratitude to the following members of the advisory board of stakeholders who have guided the research team throughout the research cycle: Eugene Corcoran (An Garda Síochána), Brian Gormally (Committee on the Administration of Justice), Claire Hamilton and Mark Kelly (Irish Council for Civil Liberties), Robert Kidd (Department of Justice – Northern Ireland), Philip Marshall (Police Service of Northern Ireland), Roy McComb (Police Service of Northern Ireland/ National Crime Agency), Deirdre Meenan (Department of Justice and Equality – Republic of Ireland), Tricia Roulston (Organised Crime Task Force), and John Whiting (HM Revenue & Customs). Finally, we would like to thank over 90 interviewees, representing the law enforcement agencies, the civil society sector, the legal profession and the European Union agencies, who have kindly provided valuable insights into the action against transnational organised crime in Northern Ireland and the Republic of Ireland.

Abbreviations

CAB	Criminal Assets Bureau
CAJ	Committee on the Administration of Justice
CHIS	Covert Human Intelligence Sources
CPS	Crown Prosecution Service
DPP	Director of Public Prosecutions
EAW	European Arrest Warrant
ECHR	European Convention on Human Rights 1950
ECtHR	European Court of Human Rights
ECJ	European Court of Justice
EEW	European Evidence Warrant
EIO	European Investigation Order
EU	European Union
GCHQ	Government Communications Headquarters
GRETA	Group of Experts on Action against Trafficking in Human Beings
HMRC	HM Revenue & Customs
ICCL	Irish Council for Civil Liberties
ICCPR	International Covenant on Civil and Political Rights 1966
JIT	Joint Investigation Team
NCA	National Crime Agency
NPS	New Psychoactive Substances
OCTF	Organised Crime Task Force
PII	Public Interest Immunity
POCA	Proceeds of Crime Act 2002
PPS	Public Prosecution Service (Northern Ireland)
PSNI	Police Service of Northern Ireland
REFCO	Network of Prosecutors against Organized Crime
RIPA	Regulation of Investigatory Powers Act 2000
SCC	Special Criminal Court
SOCA	Serious Organised Crime Agency
TEU	Treaty on European Union
TFEU	Treaty on the Functioning of the European Union
UNODC	United Nations Office of Drugs and Crime
UNTOC	United Nations Convention against Transnational Organised Crime 2000

Table of cases

International & regional cases

UN Human Rights Committee

European Court of Human Rights

European Court of Justice

Inter-American Court of Human Rights

National cases

Republic of Ireland

United Kingdom

United States

Table of international and regional instruments

International treaties

Regional treaties

European Union instruments

Treaties

Directives

Framework decisions

Others

Tables of national legislation

The Cook Islands

Extradition Act 2003 32

Croatia

Criminal Code 1997 49

Czech Republic

Criminal Code 1961

Denmark

Criminal Code 1930 13

Egypt

Law No. 64 Regarding Combating Human Trafficking 2010 13

Estonia

Criminal Code 2001 48–9

Fiji

Extradition Act 1977 32
Extradition Act 2003 25
Mutual Assistance in Criminal Matters Act 1997 26

Finland

Criminal Code 1889 49

France

Criminal Code 1994 .... 17, 49

Germany

Criminal Code 1971 48
Criminal Procedure Code 1950 82

Ghana

Human Trafficking Act 2005 13
Mutual Legal Assistance Act 2010 27

Greece

Criminal Code 1950 48

Hong Kong

Interception of Communications and Surveillance Ordinance 2006 85
Mutual Assistance in Criminal Matters Ordinance 1997 32
Mutual Legal Assistance in Criminal Matters (Australia) Order 1999 25

United Arab Emirates

United Kingdom

United States of America

Vanuatu

Introduction

Background

Transnational organised crime is a serious international problem that affects every single State either as a source, transit or destination for illicit cash, goods, services and even people. According to the United Nations Office on Drugs and Crime (UNODC), global opium production reached 7,554 tons in 2014 alone, and approximately 120,000 hectares of land were used for the cultivation of coca leaf in 2013.[1] Human trafficking has also become an important modern issue. Thousands of people are trafficked each year and may often be held in debt bondage, slavery and subjected to forced labour against their will.[2] The criminal proceeds generated from these and other forms of organised crime are laundered and reinvested in the licit and illicit economies for the maximisation of long-term profits for criminals. Estimates suggest that between $2.17 and $3.61 trillion is laundered each year, which is equivalent to between 3 per cent and 5 per cent of global GDP.[3] These examples amply demonstrate the serious scale of transnational organised crime.

The picture is similar within Europe. Major crimes committed in the region include the production and trafficking of drugs; the counterfeiting of currencies; human trafficking; and environmental crimes such as illicit waste trafficking and dumping.[4] In addition, fiscal/excise fraud such as tobacco smuggling has become more prominent in recent times as this is regarded by criminals as a good alternative due to lower penalties and higher profits.[5] It is worth highlighting here that the annual losses to the Member States of the European Union (EU) due to cigarette

1 UNODC, *World Drug Report* 2015, xiii and xv.

2 US Department of State, *Trafficking in Persons Report 2015*; and UNODC, *Global Report on Trafficking in Persons* (2014).

3 U.S. Department of State, Anti-Money Laundering/Terrorism Financing, <www.state.gov/j/inl/c/crime/c44634.htm>. The UNODC similarly has estimated that the laundered proceeds amounted to 3.6 per cent of global GDP. See UNODC, *Estimating Illicit Financial Flows Resulting from Drug Trafficking and Transnational Organised Crimes* (Vienna 2009).

4 Europol, *EU Serious and Organised Crime Threat Assessment 2013*, 18–31.

5 Europol, *EU Serious and Organised Crime Threat Assessment 2011*, 32.

smuggling amount to €10 billion.[6] Whilst these States constitute the major destination for illicit goods, services and people due to, among other things, their strong economic status and high demand, some are also source countries. In this regard, it has been reported that the majority of victims of human trafficking within the EU Member States are their own nationals and not foreign victims.[7] There is also evidence to suggest that new psychoactive substances, many of which are still classified as legal, are produced and trafficked by organised criminals and groups within this region.[8]

These global and European trends are reflected in the island of Ireland (Northern Ireland and the Republic of Ireland) which is the main focus of this book. The latest threat assessment published by the Organised Crime Task Force of Northern Ireland (OCTF) has identified a range of crimes in this jurisdiction, such as tiger kidnapping, drug offences, currency counterfeiting, human trafficking and money laundering.[9] Tobacco smuggling and fuel laundering have also been recognised as serious threats.[10] For instance, over 3 million cigarettes with an estimated tax value of £958,000 and 600,000 litres of illegal fuel were confiscated between 2014 and 2015.[11] In the Republic of Ireland, organised crime also covers a wide range of activities, including drug and human trafficking, counterfeiting, organised vehicle crime and tiger kidnapping.[12] According to An Garda Síochána, the Irish national police, illegal drugs worth €698 million were seized and over 600 organised criminal gangs were targeted in 2014.[13] It is also worth highlighting that €4.3 billion was estimated to have been laundered in this jurisdiction during the same year.[14] Although it is impossible to present accurate statistics on the extent of organised crime due to its sophisticated and clandestine nature, these figures at least demonstrate that transnational organised crime is widespread. It is also important to emphasise a strong cross-border element in the activities of organised crime groups in the island of Ireland. For instance, counterfeit tobacco products are known to be smuggled into Northern Ireland from the Far East by sea via ports in the Republic of Ireland.[15] Criminals involved

6 Directorate-General for Internal Policies, *Workshop on Cigarette Smuggling* (January 2014), 18.
7 Eurostat, *Trafficking in Human Beings: 2015 Edition*, 11.
8 See, for instance, European Monitoring Centre for Drugs and Drug Addiction, *New Psychoactive Substances in Europe: An Update from the EU Early Warning System* (March 2015).
9 OCTF, *Annual Report & Threat Assessment 2015*.
10 Northern Ireland Affairs Committee, *First Special Report, Fuel Laundering and Smuggling in Northern Ireland, Third Report of Session* (2012).
11 OCTF, *supra* n 9, 18.
12 See Police Service of Northern Ireland (PSNI) and An Garda Síochána, *Cross-Border Organised Crime Assessment 2014*
13 An Garda Síochána, *Annual Report 2014*, 1.
14 *Supra*, n 12, 26.
15 HM Revenue & Customs (HMRC), *Tackling Tobacco Smuggling – Building on Our Success, A Renewed Strategy HM Revenue and Customs and the UK Border Agency* (2011), 13.

in this and other criminal activities are said to be based around the border on both sides which allows them to coordinate their operations efficiently. The existence of a land border, therefore, does not impede the operations of organised criminal networks but rather, in many cases, it is used to their advantage.

Wherever transnational organised crime is committed, the involvement of highly sophisticated criminal groups cannot be ignored. The best-known criminal groups in the world include the Mafia (Italy),[16] Triad (Hong Kong),[17] Yakuza (Japan),[18] Sinaloa Cartel (Mexico)[19] as well as mafias/criminal syndicates in Russia[20] and West Africa.[21] It has been estimated that approximately 3,600 groups of varying sizes and structures actively carry out a variety of criminal activities within the territories of the EU Member States.[22] This, however, is a conservative estimate as it has recently been suggested that approximately 5,800 criminal groups are operating in the United Kingdom alone.[23] Of particular concern in recent times has been the nexus between organised crime and terrorism. There is sufficient evidence to suggest that terrorists are increasingly committing various forms of organised crime in order to finance their activities globally. Criminal groups such as Al-Qaida and the Revolutionary Armed Forces of Colombia are known to profit from drug cultivation and trafficking[24] whilst the so-called Islamic State actively engages in human trafficking and extortion among other things.[25] This organised crime-terrorism nexus is also a serious concern in the island of Ireland.[26] Both Republican and Loyalist paramilitary groups are said to be involved in crimes such as drug trafficking, human trafficking and fiscal/excise fraud in order to finance terrorist activities or purely for personal gain.[27] Therefore, any

16 Europol, *Threat Assessment: Italian Organised Crime* (2013); and Federal Bureau of Investigation, *Italian Organized Crime: Overview*, <www.fbi.gov/about-us/investigate/organizedcrime/italian_mafia>; Letizia Paoli, *Mafia Brotherhood: Organized Crime, Italian Style* (Oxford University Press 2003); and Letizia Paoli, 'Italian Organised Crime: Mafia Associations and Criminal Enterprises' (2004) 6 *Global Crime* 19.

17 Yiu Kong Chu, *The Triads as Business* (Routledge 2008).

18 David Kaplan and Alec Dubro, *Yakuza: Japan's Criminal Underworld* (University of California Press 2003).

19 June S. Beittel, *Mexico: Organized Crime and Drug Trafficking Organizations* (US Congress Research Service 2015).

20 Federico Varese, *The Russian Mafia: Private Protection in a New Market Economy* (Oxford University Press 2001).

21 UNODC, *Transnational Organized Crime in West Africa: A Threat Assessment* (2013).

22 Europol, *supra* n 4, 32.

23 National Crime Agency (NCA), *National Strategic Assessment of Serious and Organised Crime 2015* (June 2015), 8.

24 John Rollins, Liana Wyler and Seth Rosen, *International Terrorism and Transnational Crime: Security Threats, U.S. Policy, and Considerations for Congress* (Congressional Research Service 2010), 9.

25 Financial Action Task Force, *Financing of the Terrorist Organisation Islamic State in Iraq and the Levant* (February 2015), 12.

26 See, for instance, Independent Monitoring Commission, *Twenty-Sixth and Final Report of the Independent Monitoring Commission, 2004–2011: Changes, Impact and Lessons (2011).*

27 OCTF, *Annual Report & Threat Assessment 2014*, 23.

response to organised crime in these and other jurisdictions must be able to address this organised crime-terrorism nexus sufficiently.

The transnational nature of organised crime means that domestic efforts alone are not sufficient for its prevention and suppression. Closer and more effective bilateral, regional and international law enforcement cooperation are necessary. A number of initiatives have been taken to achieve this. At the international level, one of the most important measures in recent times has been the adoption of the United Nations Convention against Transnational Organised Crime in 2000 (UNTOC).[28] This treaty provides for relevant international standards ranging from the enhancement of domestic criminal law provisions, the use of special investigative techniques and confiscation of criminal proceeds, to international cooperation measures such as joint investigation, extradition and mutual legal assistance in criminal matters. Unlike subject-specific treaties, such as the United Nations Convention against Illicit Traffic in Narcotic Drugs and Psychotropic Substances 1988[29] and the Convention on International Trade in Endangered Species of Wild Fauna and Flora 1973,[30] the scope of the UNTOC is wider as it covers a broad range of organised crime and related conducts.

At the European level, the EU and its Member States have long recognised the need to promote integrated responses to transnational organised crime, and a wide variety of legal and non-legal measures have been implemented.[31] The EU legal order has been restructured by the Lisbon Treaty[32] which has strengthened the so-called 'Area of Freedom, Security and Justice' to include measures against this type of crime. Of particular importance is the stronger emphasis on the core principles of approximation of national criminal laws and procedures and mutual recognition of judicial decisions which are designed to make cross-border cooperation much easier. Many important international standards under the UNTOC have also been transposed into the EU legal order, thereby demonstrating a degree of synergy between the different levels of governance. Together, these international and regional standards not only provide broad frameworks for States to enhance their individual and collective responses to transnational organised crime but also serve as the benchmarks against which State practice can be evaluated.

The aim and scope of this book

Although the importance of these international and European standards should be recognised, the extent to which they are being implemented and are making a

28 2225 UNTS 209. It entered into force on 29 September 2003. As of January 2016, there were 186 State Parties.

29 1582 UNTS 95.

30 993 UNTS 243.

31 Tom Obokata, 'Key EU Principles to Combat Transnational Organised Crime' (2011) 48 *Common Market Law Review* 801.

32 [2007] OJ C 306/1.

tangible difference at the national level is not entirely clear. The main aim of this book is to explore this question through the case studies of Northern Ireland and the Republic of Ireland. It is based on a two-year research project entitled 'North–South Irish Responses to Transnational Organised Crime' (2012–2014) funded by the Arts and Humanities Research Council. Its main objective was to critically analyse the extent to which Northern Ireland and the Republic of Ireland have been successful in implementing effective action against transnational organised crime, with particular reference to cross-border cooperation as well as the protection and promotion of human rights. In order to achieve this objective, the project identified and analysed relevant legislative frameworks for substantive offences, criminal procedures and international law enforcement cooperation. In so doing, the project looked at how international and regional standards as represented by the UNTOC and EU law have been implemented there.

This book does not provide a detailed account of all domestic criminal laws and procedures relevant to action against transnational organised crime as this has been done elsewhere.[33] Rather, it focuses on several key areas in the investigation, prosecution and punishment of transnational organised crime identified as part of the aforementioned research project and aims to advance knowledge in this field. Prior to this book, there has never been comprehensive academic research on action against transnational organised crime in Northern Ireland. In particular, it closely analyses the impact of devolution of policing and criminal justice on responses to transnational organised crime in this jurisdiction. A number of statutes passed by Westminster are applicable in Northern Ireland for crimes which are regarded as 'reserved matters', such as drug offences and fiscal/excise fraud. However, Northern Ireland has begun to enjoy a margin of appreciation in implementing some measures. This book therefore analyses whether this has made any difference on the ground.

Another important aspect of this work is its focus on the cooperation of cross-border law enforcement between Northern Ireland and the Republic of Ireland. As stressed above, domestic efforts alone are not sufficient in combating transnational organised crime. Thus, this book presents interesting case studies of measures, such as extradition, mutual legal assistance, joint investigations and customs cooperation, which have not been studied thoroughly in the existing literature. Furthermore, there will be an assessment of the extent to which the relevant international and regional standards on law enforcement cooperation are implemented by both jurisdictions. Typically, formal requests for cooperation are transmitted through the so-called 'Competent Authorities' designated by the central governments. This means that the law enforcement agencies in Northern Ireland usually transmit their requests through the Home Office in London. However, the aforementioned research project also discovered that more informal arrangements for cooperation exist between Northern Ireland and the Republic of Ireland which are supported by their shared history, culture and legal

33 Liz Campbell, *Organised Crime and the Law: A Comparative Analysis* (Hart 2013).

traditions. This book will highlight examples of good practice as well as areas of concern in this regard.

The value of this book has been greatly enhanced by interviews conducted with the relevant stakeholders in Northern Ireland and the Republic of Ireland as part of the research project. The research team was granted unprecedented access to key law enforcement agencies (PSNI, An Garda Síochána, Public Prosecution Service of Northern Ireland, the Office of the Director of Public Prosecutions, HMRC, Revenue, Irish Tax & Customs, the Departments of Justice and the Serious Organised Crime Agency – now the National Crime Agency), human rights NGOs and the legal profession (defence lawyers and judges) in both jurisdictions. This enabled the research team to interview over 90 individuals during the research cycle. As such, in addition to primary and secondary research materials, this book reflects the real voices of those with experience in dealing with transnational organised crime. In summary, this book not only complements the existing literature but also contributes to the advancement of knowledge and ongoing policy discussions in the field.

The book is structured as follows. Chapter 1 begins with an illustration of relevant international standards which focus on organised crime with particular reference to the UNTOC. The key obligations related to the criminalisation of organised crime and related offences, special investigative techniques, confiscation of criminal proceeds as well as international cooperation including extradition and mutual legal assistance in criminal matters will be analysed in great detail. Examples of State practice around the world will be presented in order to demonstrate the extent to which these standards have been implemented at the national level. The UNTOC facilitates a criminal justice response to transnational organised crime but does not focus enough on the protection and promotion of the human rights of suspects and defendants as well as victims of organised crime. Therefore, this book will also explore applicable norms and principles under international human rights law which will be expanded further when discussing the case studies of Northern Ireland and the Republic of Ireland.

Chapter 2 provides an overview of regional standards which focus on action against transnational organised crime as developed by the EU and its Member States. This analysis is relevant as the United Kingdom (UK), including Northern Ireland, and the Republic of Ireland are bound by many measures which they have decided to opt in to. Compared to other regions of the world, legal and other developments are far more progressive within the EU. This being the case, the present analysis can provide a framework for a comparative analysis. The core EU principles are the approximation of national criminal laws and procedures, and a mutual recognition of judicial decisions. It is evident that these have played, and continue to play, an important role in encouraging Member States to strengthen their individual and EU-wide responses to transnational organised crime. In addition, the relevant human rights provisions under EU law as well as those of the European Convention on Human Rights 1950 (ECHR)[34] will be explored.

34 ETS No. 5.

The remainder of the book will present case studies of action against transnational organised crime in Northern Ireland and the Republic of Ireland. Chapter 3 highlights the legislative frameworks on substantive offences in both jurisdictions. It explores the definitions of an 'organised criminal group' in an attempt to understand the extent to which the international/European definitions previously explored reflect these. It continues with an analysis of legislative frameworks for core offences examined for the purpose of this book: participation in activities of organised criminal groups; drug offences; human trafficking; and fiscal/excise fraud. Both jurisdictions are based on the common law tradition, and there are similarities in the way some offences are defined in their respective legislations. However, differences are also recognised, particularly in relation to the punishment regimes. This demonstrates that the seriousness of various forms of organised crime are understood differently at the national level in practice. It also underscores the importance of the margin of appreciation in implementing domestic responses to transnational organised crime.

Chapter 4 examines how Northern Ireland and the Republic of Ireland investigate and prosecute transnational organised crime, including cross-border cooperation. In terms of criminal investigations, the focus of this chapter is on the use of special investigative techniques such as surveillance, interception of communications and the use of covert human intelligence sources (CHIS). It will also highlight practical issues that arise from criminal investigations. The chapter then discusses the prosecution of transnational organised crime. The issues covered in this regard are legal guidance; immunity granted to criminals to facilitate prosecution; and obstruction of justice (intimidation of witnesses). Although the procedures are quite similar in Northern Ireland and the Republic of Ireland, some variations are nevertheless evident. The final part of this chapter focuses on cross-border cooperation in investigation and prosecution. Both jurisdictions have good legislative frameworks to facilitate this in areas such as joint investigation, cross-border surveillance, extradition and mutual assistance in obtaining evidence. It is also evident that these largely reflect the international and regional standards explored earlier in the book. In addition to formal cooperation, the law enforcement communities in both jurisdictions promote informal cooperation through regular communication, meetings and coordination of activities. Institutional mechanisms, such as a cross-border taskforce on human trafficking, further complement smoother cooperation between the two jurisdictions. However, issues have been identified in some areas, such as the establishment of joint investigation teams and the role of the EU agencies such as Eurojust. This once again highlights the differences in attitude towards cross-border cooperation. An overarching theme is the promotion and protection of human rights and, in connection with this, the relevant norms and principles are identified and analysed.

Finally, Chapter 5 presents an analysis of criminal proceedings against transnational organised crime and the confiscation of criminal proceeds generated from it. One important issue is the non-jury trial. Whilst trial by jury is a fundamental aspect of the criminal justice system in Northern Ireland (as in the rest of the UK) and the Republic of Ireland, non-jury trial can be instituted particularly when there is a risk of the administration of justice being undermined due to intimidation of witnesses and juries. Although these arrangements have been regarded as useful by the law enforcement communities in both jurisdictions, and as being in conformity with human rights principles by the domestic courts and the ECHR, serious concerns have been expressed by civil society organisations and defence lawyers. The chapter also looks at evidential matters, including disclosure; public interest immunity; the use of opinion evidence and intercepts; and problems arising from sentencing. In addition, the use of both conviction-based and non-conviction-based confiscation is explored. These key issues are analysed in the context of cross-border cooperation, and their implications for human rights are also highlighted throughout.

1 International standards on action against transnational organised crime

1.1 Introduction

This chapter explores important international standards concerning transnational organised crime with particular reference to the UNTOC. It begins by identifying the definitions of organised crime, and then highlights core obligations imposed upon States, such as prohibition of organised crime and related crimes; establishment of criminal jurisdiction; the use of special investigative techniques; confiscation of criminal proceeds; and international cooperation. It will be shown that the overarching principles reflected in these obligations are the harmonisation of national laws and criminal procedures as well as mutual recognition of judicial/law enforcement decisions as these are designed to facilitate more effective international law enforcement cooperation. In addition, the protection and promotion of the human rights of victims and perpetrators of organised crime is discussed. The UNTOC is very weak in this regard. Therefore, reference will be made to international human rights law which imposes additional obligations upon States and supplements international law on transnational organised crime.

1.2 International standards on action against transnational organised crime

1.2.1 Defining organised crime

The most comprehensive treaty on transnational organised crime is the UNTOC which came into force in September 2003. According to Article 1, the main purpose of this instrument is to promote cooperation in order to prevent and combat transnational organised crime. The UNTOC has created a number of relevant standards and obligations to achieve this. The first important aspect is the stipulation of various definitions that should be adopted by States. The UNTOC does not provide a definition of 'organised crime' *per se* but rather it is to be understood as a 'serious crime' committed by an 'organised criminal group' and is defined as:

> [A] structured group of three or more persons, existing for a period of time and acting in concert with the aim of committing one or more serious crimes

> or offences established in accordance with this convention, in order to obtain, directly or indirectly, a financial or other material benefit.[1]

Among the general public, the popular perception of organised crime has long been associated with the Italian Mafia. This was and still is a large, hierarchical criminal organisation that has been particularly evident in the United States (US) where it was known as La Cosa Nostra.[2] This idea of organised crime has been strongly influenced by the so-called 'alien conspiracy theory' that portrayed the Italian Mafia as 'a coherent and centralised international conspiracy of evil' which threatened the political, economic and legal systems of the US.[3] It is worth noting that the term 'organised crime' was coined in that country at the end of the nineteenth century when the New York Society for the Prevention of Crime used the term to describe gambling and prostitution.[4] At that time, the term referred to 'illegal business deals involving politicians, police officers, lawyers or professional thieves' and not to gangsters or Mafia-type criminal groups.[5] This changed in the 1950s when the term began to be used to describe the Italian Mafia. It is evident that the above definition of an 'organised criminal group' under the UNTOC does apply to this type of criminal organisation as it refers to a structured group of multiple individuals existing for a certain period of time. Another example is the Japanese Yakuza. These groups have hierarchical structures with the bosses (*oyabun*) at the top, assisted by lieutenants (*wakagashira*) in the middle and lower ranking criminals at the bottom (*kobun*) of the pyramid.[6]

During the drafting stage of the UNTOC, however, it was decided that the term would also apply to non-hierarchical groups.[7] Article 2(c) in this regard stipulates that a structured group does not have to have formally defined roles for its members nor does a group need to have continuity of its membership or a developed structure. This also seems to be in line with the scholarly debates, particularly within anthropology and political science, which took place in the

1 Art 2(a).
2 For discussions on criminal organisations, see Donald Cressey, *Theft of the Nation* (Harper Collins 1969); A.K. Cohen, 'The Concepts of Criminal Organisation' (1977) 17 *British Journal of Criminology* 97; Cyrille Fijnaut, 'Organized Crime: A Comparison Between the United States of America and Western Europe' (1990) 30 *British Journal of Criminology* 321; and Letizia Paoli and Cyrille Fijnaut (eds.), *Organised Crime in Europe: Concepts, Patterns and Control Policies in the European Union and Beyond* (Springer 2006).
3 Michael Woodiwiss, 'Transnational Organised Crime: The Global Reach of an American Concept' in Adam Edwards and Peter Gill (eds.), *Transnational Organised Crime: Perspectives on Global Security* (Routledge 2005), 15.
4 Michael Woodiwiss, 'Transnational Organised Crime: The Strange Career of an American Concept' in Margaret Beare (ed.), *Critical Reflections on Transnational Organized Crime, Money Laundering and Corruption* (University of Toronto Press 2003), 5.
5 Paoli and Fijnaut, *supra* n 2, 24.
6 Kaplan and Dubro, *supra* intro n 18, 115–116.
7 *Travaux Préparatoires of the Negotiations for the Elaboration of the United Nations Convention against Transnational Organized Crime and the Protocols Thereto* (2006), 7–18.

1970s outside the US.[8] It was argued that the perception of organised criminal groups as being hierarchical was too simplistic and did not reflect the reality of contemporary organised crime.[9] These scholars advocated a so-called 'network model' in which organised crime is understood to be carried out by a collection or network of individuals, small groups or departments collaborating with each other to varying degrees.[10]

Some examples indicate that many groups are indeed not hierarchical. Contrary to popular belief, the Medellin and Cali cartels in Colombia in fact consisted of 'loose combinations of relatively small, family-based cocaine manufacturing firms that merely joined forces in the early 1980s'.[11] The network model also seems to be the dominant form of organised crime in European States such as the Netherlands[12] and Germany.[13] Furthermore, it has also been argued that Triads (Hong Kong) and Snakeheads (China) operate largely through informal networks rather than formal structured organisations.[14] In this respect, it can be concluded that the network model is equally important in understanding organised crime, and that the definition in the UNTOC is broad enough to cover a wide range of criminal groups.

A few more points should be highlighted in relation to this definition. According to Article 2(b), a 'serious crime' means conduct constituting an offence punishable by a maximum deprivation of liberty of at least 4 years. The UNTOC also defines 'criminal offences' as those that are committed for financial or material benefit. This is an important aspect because what distinguishes organised crime from ordinary crime generally is the generation of longer-term, as opposed to immediate or one-off, profit or benefit.[15] This means that criminal proceeds are normally diversified and reinvested in legal/illegal enterprises for the generation of sustained income for criminals.[16] Therefore, organised criminal groups are

8 Jeffrey S. McIllwain, 'Organized Crime: A Social Network Approach' (1999) 32 *Crime, Law and Social Change* 301, 303.

9 Phil Williams and Roy Godson, 'Anticipating Organized and Transnational Crime' (2002) 37 *Crime, Law and Social Change* 311, 332.

10 Gerben Bruinsma and Wim Bernasco, 'Criminal Groups and Transnational Illegal Markets' (2004) 41 *Crime, Law and Social Change* 79, 79.

11 Letizia Paoli, 'The Paradoxes of Organised Crime' (2000) 37 *Crime, Law and Social Change* 51, 68.

12 Williams and Godson, *supra* n 9, 332; and Peter Klerks, 'The Network Paradigm Applied to Criminal Organisations: Theoretical Nitpicking or a Relevant Doctrine for Investigators? Recent Developments in the Netherlands' in Edwards and Gill, *supra* n 3,101.

13 Paoli, *supra* n 11, 67.

14 Sheldon Zhang and Koh-Lin Chin, *Characteristics of Chinese Human Smugglers: A Cross-National Study* (U.S. Department of State 2003); Sheldon Zhang and Koh-Lin Chin, 'Snakeheads, Mules and Protective Umbrellas: A Review of Current Research on Chinese Organized Crime' (2008) 50 *Crime, Law and Social Change* 177; and Chu, *supra* intro n 17.

15 Tom Obokata, *Transnational Organised Crime in International Law* (Hart Publishing 2010), 22.

16 Andreas Schloenhardt, 'Organised Crime and the Business of Migrant Trafficking: An Economic Analysis' (1999) 32 *Crime, Law and Social Change* 203; and Cressey, *supra* n 2, 72.

comparable to legitimate corporations and businesses except that they mainly operate in illegal markets.

One of the key benefits of providing these and other definitions under the UNTOC is the facilitation of harmonisation of national criminal laws and justice procedures among State Parties. If organised crime offences and their serious nature were understood in the same way by all States, this would naturally lead to smoother international cooperation and would also help reduce safe havens for criminals[17] as punishments for transnational organised crime could be aligned. Harmonisation could also bridge diverse gaps in legal traditions among State Parties. Whilst it may be easy to support this in theory, in practice each State defines an offence according to its own political, cultural and social traditions. To illustrate this with some examples, an examination of State practice reveals that the definitions of an 'organised criminal group' vary between State Parties. For instance, the Crimes Act 1961 of New Zealand (as amended) gives the following definition:

> A group is an organised criminal group if it is a group of 3 or more people who have as their objective or one of their objectives –
>
> (a) obtaining material benefits from the commission of offences that are punishable by imprisonment for a term of 4 years or more.[18]

This definition is broadly in line with the UNTOC. In contrast, the Australian definition refers to a group as one which consists of 2 or more people who if prosecuted can be imprisoned for at least 3 years, without any material or financial benefit.[19] This makes the Australian definition much wider as it can apply to a variety of ordinary crimes such as theft and criminal damage if committed by 2 or more individuals. The Malaysian Criminal Code also refers to a group of 2 or more people, and defines a 'serious crime' as any offence punishable with imprisonment of 10 years or more.[20] The principle of State sovereignty, therefore, has taken precedence over the implementation of international standards.

However, these discrepancies should not be used to dismiss the value of international law on transnational organised crime. As succinctly put by one of the working groups of the Conference of Parties to the UNTOC, harmonisation is not a one-off thing. Rather, it is an ongoing process which all State Parties should respect and implement to strengthen their action against organised crime.[21] The sensitive nature of the subject matter means that it naturally takes time to develop

17 Working Group on Technical Assistance, *Assistance in Harmonising National Legislation with the United Nations Convention against Organised Crime and Protocol Thereto: Discussion Paper by the Secretariat*, CTOC/COP/WG.2/2013/4, para 6.

18 S 98A.

19 Criminal Code Act 1995 as amended, s 390.4.

20 Criminal Code 1936 as amended, s 130U.

21 Working Group on Technical Assistance, *supra* n 17, paras 30–41.

a common understanding on all issues. Therefore, patience is key in the successful implementation of this instrument. Nevertheless, it is encouraging to see that harmonisation is gradually being accepted in some areas. The prosecution and punishment of human trafficking is a case in point. The Protocol to Prevent, Suppress and Punish Trafficking in Persons 2000, attached to the UNTOC,[22] provides the following definition of this crime:

> Trafficking in persons shall mean the recruitment, transportation, transfer, harbouring or receipt of persons, by means of the threat or use of force or other forms of coercion, of abduction, of fraud, of deception, of the abuse of power or of a position of vulnerability or of the giving or receiving of payments or benefits to achieve the consent of a person having control over another person, for the purpose of exploitation.[23]

A number of States, such as Bhutan,[24] the Czech Republic,[25] Denmark,[26] Egypt,[27] Ghana,[28] India,[29] Kenya,[30] Myanmar,[31] Oman,[32] Serbia,[33] Singapore,[34] South Africa,[35] Thailand[36] and the United Arab Emirates,[37] have incorporated this definition or amended their legislation accordingly. In addition, despite varied legal traditions and perceptions of organised crime, States have been able to come to a general consensus on key definitions stipulated in Article 2 of the UNTOC. This shows that it is possible to find some common ground and that international law on transnational organised crime continues to play an important role in achieving a degree of harmonisation among State Parties.

1.2.2 Prohibition of organised crime

The first important obligation under international law on transnational organised crime is undoubtedly the prohibition of organised crime. In addition to serious crimes, as noted above, the UNTOC obliges States to criminalise participation in

22 2237 UNTS 319.
23 Art 3.
24 Criminal Code 2004 as amended, s 154.
25 Criminal Code 1961 as amended, art 232a.
26 Criminal Code 1930 as amended, s 262a.
27 Law No. 64 Regarding Combating Human Trafficking 2010.
28 Human Trafficking Act 2005.
29 Criminal Code 1860 as amended, s 370.
30 Counter-Trafficking in Persons Act 2010.
31 Anti-Trafficking in Persons Law 2005.
32 Royal Decree 126/2008 Promulgating the Law Combating Trafficking in Persons.
33 Criminal Code 2005 as amended, art 388.
34 Prevention of Human Trafficking Act 2014.
35 Prevention and Combating of Trafficking in Persons Act 2013.
36 Anti-Trafficking in Persons Act 2008.
37 Federal Law 51 (2006) on Combating Crimes of Human Trafficking.

organised criminal groups.[38] The rationale for this provision is to prosecute and punish those who contribute to the operations of organised crime groups without directly committing substantive offences themselves.[39] This can therefore be used to target Mafia bosses who simply order their subordinates to commit various crimes. There are two possibilities provided in Article 5. The first is to criminalise an agreement to commit crimes. This is also known as 'conspiracy' and is widely accepted by common law jurisdictions. The key aspect is that a person can be prosecuted even if an offence has not actually been committed. However, this is not supported universally, in particular in civil law jurisdictions, because it breaches the principle of *nullum crimen sine actus* which provides that the actual commission of an offence is necessary for prosecution and punishment.[40] In order to accommodate these States, Article 5 provides for another possibility: the criminalisation of participation in the activities of organised criminal groups, which requires actual conduct. In addition to 'criminal activities', participation also covers 'other activities' which may not be criminal in nature on their own but still contribute to the achievement of a criminal aim. For instance, arranging transportation and purchasing property can fall under this. The ambit, therefore, is wide, and this raises an issue of legal certainty. A mitigating factor here is the requirement of 'knowledge' by the participant that his/her participation will help a group to achieve its objectives. Therefore, acts such as carrying illegal goods without knowledge are not criminalised. Finally, so-called secondary participation (e.g. aiding and abetting) is punishable under Article 5.

The UNTOC also obliges States to address risk-averting strategies employed by criminals. Money laundering is one example.[41] Proceeds obtained as a result of organised crime are diversified and reinvested through this method. There are three stages in the money laundering process. The first is placement; this is where illegal proceeds enter into the financial system. A technique known as 'smurfing' (or 'structuring') – dividing the proceeds into smaller bundles – is used in order to avoid detection through reporting or record-keeping by financial institutions. The second stage is laying; this is where proceeds are moved from one place to another so as to conceal their origin. Overseas offshore banks, which do not always have strict regulations, are often used for this purpose. The final stage is integration; this is where the proceeds are returned to the financial system. It is extremely difficult, if not impossible, to take action at this stage as the proceeds appear legitimate. Therefore, it is essential that State Parties establish sufficient legal and administrative frameworks to detect and prosecute this offence. States must also address other risk-averting strategies such as corruption and obstruction of

38 Art 5.

39 UNODC, *Legislative Guides for the Implementation of the United Nations Convention against Transnational Organised Crime and Protocols Thereto* (UNODC 2004), 21.

40 Obokata, *supra* n 15, 40–42. See also, Chris Harding, 'The Offence of Belonging: Capturing Participation in Organised Crime' (2005) *Criminal Law Review* 690.

41 Art 6.

justice.[42] Bribery and the threat or use of violence against victims, witnesses and jurors in criminal proceedings are common tactics used by criminals to avoid law enforcement.[43] In addition to criminalising these practices with dissuasive punishments, States should tackle the culture and the root causes of corruption, such as low salaries, and provide sufficient protection to victims and witnesses so that administration of justice is properly conducted.

Aside from these offences under the UNTOC, other subject-specific international treaties impose a duty on States to prohibit various forms of organised crime, such as migrant smuggling;[44] the trafficking of firearms,[45] drugs,[46] cultural property,[47] endangered species[48] and nuclear materials;[49] illicit trade in tobacco products;[50] child pornography;[51] cybercrime;[52] counterfeiting;[53] and slavery/forced labour.[54] In view of these, it seems reasonable to conclude that international law on transnational organised crime as represented by these legal instruments establishes a clear obligation to criminalise organised crime and related conducts. In particular, the UNTOC is broad enough to cover the existing as well as new and emerging criminalities as it is not subject-specific. At the national level, although flexibility is necessary in order to allow States to formulate domestic criminal laws in accordance with their legal, political, social and cultural traditions,

42 The UNTOC, Arts 8 and 23. See also the United Nations Convention against Corruption 2003, 2349 UNTS 41.

43 See, for instance, UNODC, *The Role of Corruption in Trafficking in Persons* (UNODC 2011); Maurice Kugler, Thierry Verdier and Yves Zenou, 'Organised Crime, Corruption and Punishment' (2005) 89 *Journal of Public Economics* 1639; and Stuart Mass, 'The Dilemma of the Intimidated Witness in Federal Organised Crime Prosecution: Choosing among the Fear of Reprisal, the Contempt Powers of the Court, and the Witness Protection Programme' (1981–1982) 50 *Fordham Law Review* 582.

44 Protocol against the Smuggling of Migrants by Land, Sea and Air 2000, 2241 UNTS 507.

45 Protocol against the Illicit Manufacturing of and Trafficking in Firearms, Their Parts and Components and Ammunition 2001, 2326 UNTS 208.

46 The 1988 Narcotics Trafficking Convention.

47 Convention on the Means of Prohibiting and Preventing the Illicit Import, Export and Transfer of Ownership of Cultural Property 1970 (UNESCO Cultural Convention), 823 UNTS 231; Convention Concerning the Protection of the World Cultural and Natural Heritage 1972, 1037 UNTS 151; and Convention on the Protection of the Archaeological, Historical and Artistic Heritage of the American Nations 1976, 15 ILM 1350.

48 The Convention on Endangered Species 1973.

49 Convention on the Physical Protection of Nuclear Material 1979, 1456 UNTS 101; and European Convention on the Protection of Environment through Criminal Law 1998, ETS No. 172.

50 Protocol to Eliminate Illicit Trade in Tobacco Products 2012 to the WHO Framework Convention on Tobacco Control, Decision FCTC/COP5 (1).

51 Optional Protocol to the Convention on the Rights of the Child on the Sale of Children, Child Prostitution and Child Pornography 2000, 2171 UNTS 227.

52 European Convention on Cybercrime 2001, ETS No. 185.

53 International Convention for the Suppression of Counterfeiting Currency 1929, 112 LNTS 371.

54 Slavery Convention 1926, 60 LNTS 254; and ILO Convention (No. 29) Concerning Forced and Compulsory Labour 1930, 39 UNTS 55.

it is just as important that the principle of legality is fully observed in defining and establishing organised crime offences, which is also a well-established principle under international law.[55]

Finally, it is important to remember that the application of the UNTOC, including against the offences stipulated within this instrument, is limited by the requirement of transnationality. In this regard Article 3(2) provides that an offence is transnational in nature if:

> (a) It is committed in more than one State;
> (b) It is committed in one State but a substantial part of its preparation, planning, direction or control takes place in another State;
> (c) It is committed in one State but involves an organized criminal group that engages in criminal activities in more than one State; or
> (d) It is committed in one State but has substantial effects in another State.

It is apparent that the transnationality principle applies not only to criminal activities but also to criminals and groups. This provision in effect excludes crimes committed purely by local groups which do not operate beyond national borders. For instance, organised robbery committed by a local gang falls outside of the UNTOC. Whilst it might make sense to treat this type of crime as purely domestic, the same may not be said for other crimes such as trafficking of a State's own nationals from one city to another within its domestic borders or domestic production and distribution of narcotics by local gangs. As will be shown throughout this book, in practice, States punish all types of organised crime equally regardless of whether they are purely domestic or transnational. Therefore, this requirement under the UNTOC does not have a major impact on actual law enforcement.

1.2.3 Establishment of criminal jurisdiction

Another important obligation imposed upon States is the establishment of criminal jurisdiction over organised crime. The transnational nature of organised crime means that multiple States are affected. Article 15 of the UNTOC provides some guidance on which State can and should take a lead in prosecution, thereby contributing to smoother international cooperation and administration of justice. Consistent with the principles of international law, particularly State sovereignty, the main basis for the exercise of jurisdiction is territory.[56] In other words, the State in which the organised crime is committed has the primary jurisdiction to

55 See, for instance, art 15(1) of the International Covenant on Civil and Political Rights 1966 (ICCPR), 999 UNTS 171, which provides that 'no one shall be held guilty of any criminal offence on account of any act or omission which did not constitute a criminal offence, under national or international law, at the time when it was committed. Nor shall a heavier penalty be imposed than the one that was applicable at the time when the criminal offence was committed.'

56 M. Cherif Bassiouni, 'Universal Jurisdiction for International Crimes: Historical Perspectives and Contemporary Practice' (2001) 42 *Virginia Journal of International Law* 81, 90.

prosecute and punish.[57] An extension of this is the flag principle which allows a State to exercise jurisdiction over a vessel or aircraft flying its flag as if it formed part of its territory.[58] This is relevant, for example, when aircrafts and ships are used to traffic narcotics and people. As the term 'shall establish' suggests, the exercise of criminal jurisdiction on these bases is mandatory, and therefore ensures primacy over others.

It is often difficult to establish criminal jurisdiction solely on the territorial and flag principles as organised crime also occurs in areas outside a State's jurisdiction, such as the high seas, airspace or even cyberspace. In order to ensure that criminals are prosecuted and punished appropriately, other types of jurisdiction have been recognised under the UNTOC. There is, for instance, the passive personality principle where a State can exercise jurisdiction if a crime is committed against its nationals.[59] This has been recognised, for example, in Argentina, Ecuador, Egypt, Indonesia and Sweden.[60] Another relevant principle is that of nationality (also known as the active personality principle). This allows States to try their own offending nationals.[61] The exercise of jurisdiction on this basis is recognised in States such as Albania,[62] Azerbaijan,[63] France,[64] Poland[65] and the UK[66] in relation to some offences.

There is another dimension to the exercise of jurisdiction. Article 15(2)(c) of the UNTOC provides that:

> 2. Subject to Article 4 of this Convention, a State Party may also establish its jurisdiction over any such offence when:
>
> *(c)* The offence is:
>
> (i) One of those established in accordance with Article 5, paragraph 1, of this Convention and is committed outside its territory with a view to the commission of a serious crime within its territory;
>
> (ii) One of those established in accordance with Article 6, paragraph 1 *(b)* (ii), of this Convention and is committed outside its territory with a view to the commission of an offence established in accordance with Article 6, paragraph 1 *(a)* (i) or (ii) or *(b)* (i), of this Convention within its territory.

57 Art 15(1)(a).
58 Art 15(1)(b).
59 Art 15(2)(a).
60 *Implementation of the United Nations Convention against Transnational Organised Crime: Consolidated Information Received from States for the First Reporting Cycle*, CTOC/COP/2005/2/Rev.2 (2008), para 31.
61 Art 15(2)(b). This article also allows prosecution of a stateless person whose habitual residence is located in the State concerned.
62 Criminal Code 1995 as amended, art 6.
63 Criminal Code 2000 as amended, art 12(1).
64 Criminal Code 1994 as amended, art 113.
65 Criminal Code 1997 as amended, art 109.
66 Modern Slavery Act 2015, s 2.

In a sense, this is similar to the 'effect principle' where criminal jurisdiction may be established if an act committed abroad has some kind of impact on a given State. This is recognised in a number of countries, such as Angola, Brazil, Cyprus and Kazakhstan.[67] It should be noted, however, that Articles 5(1) and 6(1)(b)(ii) relate to inchoate offences and secondary participation in an organised criminal group and money laundering. Therefore, the principle does not apply to the actual commission of serious crimes or money laundering. One difficulty of applying this type of jurisdiction is that the harm may be intended but no harmful effect actually occurs in relation to inchoate offences.[68] This raises the issue of *nullum crimen sine actus.*

Finally, universal jurisdiction may be relied upon. Simply put, universal jurisdiction allows any State to apply its laws to punish an offence even when the State has no territorial or nationality links with the offence in question.[69] Whilst the exercise of this jurisdiction over international crime has been established as a matter of customary law, this principle is also important for organised crime because of its transnational nature. Indeed, the UNTOC does not deny the possibility of universal jurisdiction. Article 15(6) stipulates in this regard that it 'does not exclude the exercise of any criminal jurisdiction established by a State Party in accordance with its domestic law'. Bassiouni explains that a provision such as this, which is also found in other international instruments,[70] implicitly authorises the exercise of universal jurisdiction.[71]

A State may also exercise universal jurisdiction on the basis of the presence of foreign suspects who commit crimes outside its territory. This is regarded as 'universal jurisdiction' in the sense that a State in which the suspect is found has no territorial or nationality connections with the offences in question. In the modern context, the exercise of universal jurisdiction on this basis is reflected in the principle of *aut dedere aut judicare*.[72] This phrase is a modern version of that used by Hugo Grotius: '*aut dedere aut punire* (extradite or punish)'[73] and is useful

67 Consolidated Information Received from States, *supra* n 60, para 34.

68 Christopher L. Blakesley, 'United States Jurisdiction over Extraterritorial Crime' (1982) 73 *Journal of Criminal Law and Criminology* 1109, 1145.

69 American Law Institute, *Restatement of the Law (Third), Foreign Relations Law of the United States, 2 American Law Institute* (1987), para 404.

70 Single Convention on Narcotic Drugs 1961, art 36(4), 520 UNTS 151; and Convention on Psychotropic Substance 1971, art 22(5), 1019 UNTS 175.

71 M. Cherif Bassiouni, *International Extradition: United States Law and Practice* (Oceana Publications 1987), 125.

72 Edwin D. Dickinson, 'Codification of International Law: Part II: Jurisdiction with Respect to Crime' (1935) 29 *American Journal of International Law Supplement* 435, 574. See also A.R. Carnegie, 'Jurisdiction over Violations of the Laws and Customs of War' (1963) 39 *British Yearbook of International Law* 402, 405; and Antonio Cassese, 'Is the Bell Tolling for Universality? A Plea for a Sensible Notion of Universal Jurisdiction' (2003) 1 *Journal of International Criminal Justice* 589, 592–593.

73 Edward M. Wise, 'The Obligation to Extradite or Prosecute' (1993) 27 *Israel Law Review* 268, 276.

in prosecuting and punishing crimes at the national level.[74] This principle holds that if a State does not extradite an offender to a requesting State, then this State must exercise its jurisdiction to prosecute him/her. This is regarded as a subsidiary form of universal jurisdiction as its application is limited to cases where the surrender of a suspect to the territorial/nationality State is not possible.[75] In any event, the principle of *aut dedere aut judicare* is recognised under Articles 15 and 16 of the UNTOC and in other suppression conventions.[76] It is worth noting that the nature of the obligation depends on the nationality of the offender. Under Article 15(3), if a State does not extradite its own nationals, then it must establish criminal jurisdiction over them. This, in effect, is the exercise of the nationality principle as noted above and the use of 'shall' illustrates that the principle has a stronger legal force. Nevertheless, Article 15(4) provides that States 'may' establish criminal jurisdiction over foreign nationals which suggests that prosecution is not mandatory. Such a provision can also be seen in other treaties.[77]

Some examples of State practice indicate that domestic legislation does allow the exercise of universal jurisdiction for some crimes. The Austrian Criminal Code provides for universal jurisdiction over offences such as human trafficking, counterfeiting, participating in criminal organisations, child pornography and other offences established in accordance with international treaties.[78] Similarly, the Azerbaijan Criminal Code establishes universal jurisdiction over terrorism, narcotics trafficking and counterfeiting of currencies.[79] In addition, the Japanese Criminal Code 1907 as amended provides for universal jurisdiction over counterfeiting of currencies and official documents and offences established by an international treaty.[80] Finally, the Criminal Justice (International Co-operation) Act 1990 of the UK allows the authorities to exercise jurisdiction over foreign ships which traffic drugs at sea.[81] All of these examples show that universal

74 M. Cherif Bassiouni, 'The Penal Characteristics of Conventional International Criminal Law' (1983) 15 *Case Western Reserve Journal of International Law* 27, 35.

75 Dickinson, *supra* n 72, 574; and Carnegie, *supra* n 72, 405.

76 International Counterfeiting Convention; Convention for the Suppression of the Illicit Traffic in Dangerous Drugs 1936, 198 LNTS 301; International Convention for the Suppression of Unlawful Seizure of Aircraft 1970, 860 UNTS105; Convention for the Suppression of Unlawful Acts against the Safety of Civil Aviation 1971, 974 UNTS 178; Convention on the Prevention and Punishment of Crimes against Internationally Protected Persons 1972, 1035 UNTS 167; International Convention against the Taking of Hostages 1979, 1316 UNTS 205; Convention on Nuclear Material; Convention against Torture and Other Cruel, Inhuman or Degrading Treatment or Punishment 1984, 1465 UNTS 85; Convention for the Suppression of Unlawful Acts against the Safety of Maritime Navigation 1988,1678 UNTS 221; and International Convention against the Recruitment, Use Financing and Training of Mercenaries 1989, 2163 UNTS 75.

77 Wise, *supra* n 73, 274.

78 Criminal Code 1974 as amended, s 64.

79 *Supra* n 63, art 12(3).

80 Arts 2 and 3.

81 Ss 19–21.

jurisdiction is often relied upon by States in prosecuting and punishing transnational organised crime.

1.2.4 Intelligence-led law enforcement

The sophisticated nature of organised crime and the *modus operandi* means that proactive intelligence-led law enforcement must be facilitated for successful prevention and suppression. Article 20 of the UNTOC is important as it provides for measures to be taken in this regard. For instance, it touches upon controlled delivery which is defined in Article 2(i) as:

> the technique of allowing illicit or suspect consignments to pass out of, through or into the territory of one or more States, with the knowledge and under the supervision of their competent authorities, with a view to the investigation of an offence and the identification of persons involved in the commission of the offence.

Controlled delivery is often employed in the investigation and prosecution of drug-related offences.[82] Article 20 also encourages States to consider other techniques such as electronic surveillance and undercover operations. The obligations under this Article are not strong as it uses phrases such as, 'if permitted by the basic principles of its domestic legal system' and 'within its possibilities'. Indeed, the interpretative note on this Article makes it clear that it 'does not imply an obligation on State Parties to make provision for the use of all forms of special investigative technique' and a degree of reluctance to be bound by hard obligations was also evident during the drafting stage.[83] While many States, including Algeria, Benin, Kuwait, Spain and Turkey, have established legislative frameworks on special investigative techniques,[84] others do not provide for these measures.[85] This raises a great deal of concern from the point of view of legality, accountability and human rights. It is, therefore, imperative that these States put in place adequate legislative frameworks that govern their use. Article 20 also encourages States to facilitate international cooperation in using these techniques through bilateral or multilateral arrangements.[86] This is supplemented by Article 28 which touches upon collection, analysis and the sharing of intelligence on organised crime.

82 See the 1988 Narcotics Trafficking Convention, art 11; and Gregory D. Lee, *Global Drug Enforcement: Practical Investigative Techniques* (CRC Press 2004), 255.

83 *Travaux Préparatoires*, *supra* n 7, 205–206.

84 *Implementation Report 2008 of the United Nations Convention against Transnational Organized Crime: Consolidated Information Received from States for the Second Reporting Cycle*, CTOC/COP/2006/2/Rev.1 (2008), para 27.

85 Ibid.

86 See the 1988 Narcotics Trafficking Convention, art 11.

1.2.5 Confiscation of criminal proceeds/asset recovery

Another important obligation to be implemented at the national level is the confiscation of criminal proceeds. An effective regime of confiscation can send a strong message to criminals that they are not able to benefit from their criminal activities, and this may be to some extent a deterrent. It can also significantly disrupt criminal activities or even dismantle criminal organisations.[87] The first international instrument that touched upon this was the 1988 Narcotics Trafficking Convention.[88] The UNTOC now uses it for different forms of organised crime. To begin with, Article 12 obliges States to take necessary measures to confiscate criminal proceeds or property whose value corresponds to that of such proceeds. Although it was highlighted during the drafting stage that the domestic legal systems of some States did not allow confiscation of the latter, this was ultimately retained in line with the 1988 Narcotics Convention.[89] The common law jurisdictions also seem to support this.[90] Furthermore, States have to target other property converted from criminal proceeds as well as income and other benefits generated from such proceeds. In addition, Article 12 makes it clear that States are not able to rely on bank secrecy to evade their obligations. Finally, they are allowed to require offenders to prove the lawful origin of alleged proceeds, shifting the burden of proof from the prosecution.

The State practice of confiscation of criminal proceeds can be divided roughly into two categories. The first is conviction-based confiscation. As the name suggests, a confiscation order is issued after a person is convicted of organised crime. In this sense, such confiscation can be seen as an additional form of punishment. In addition, some States, such as Australia, Canada, Colombia, Ireland, Italy, the Netherlands, the UK and the US,[91] also rely on non-conviction-based confiscation. This can be facilitated through civil proceedings using the 'balance of probabilities' as the standard of proof without conviction. For this reason, non-conviction-based confiscation is sometimes referred to as 'civil asset recovery' in some jurisdictions, such as the UK and the Republic of Ireland. There, the guilt is associated with property and not offenders. A practical implication of this divergence in confiscation regimes is that it can make international cooperation somewhat difficult because many States, particularly civil law jurisdictions, do not rely upon non-conviction-based asset recovery.[92] Therefore, a high degree of mutual respect and recognition is needed among State Parties in facilitating cross-border confiscation of criminal proceeds. It is worth highlighting here that although Hong Kong and Jersey do not allow non-conviction-based confiscation

87 Barbara Vettori, *Tough on Criminal Wealth: Exploring the Practice of Proceeds from Crime Confiscation in the EU* (Springer 2006), 3.

88 Art 5.

89 *Travaux Préparatoires, supra* n 7, 110.

90 Arvinder Sambei, *Civil Forfeiture (Confiscation in Rem): Explanatory and Impact Study* (Council of Europe 2012), 8.

91 Ibid., 5.

92 See ch 2.

domestically, they have legal frameworks in place to enforce foreign non-conviction-based recovery orders.[93] Given that this respects the principle of State sovereignty, this seems to be a good example of mutual respect and recognition in operation, and the UNTOC can make further contributions in this regard.

Finally, Article 14 touches upon the disposal of confiscated proceeds. Whilst each State can decide their use in accordance with their domestic legal and administrative frameworks, this Article additionally provides that such proceeds should be given to international organisations which specialise in the fight against organised crime. This is important as organisations such as the UNODC have been instrumental in promoting international standards related to action against transnational organised crime and enhancing domestic capacity of States to combat it by implementing a variety of projects on the ground. Further, it is submitted that confiscated proceeds can and should be used for other important purposes such as the protection of victims and witnesses of organised crime; provision of compensation; and education of the general public although these are not clearly stipulated in the UNTOC.

1.2.6 International cooperation

As the core aim of the UNTOC is to facilitate international cooperation in the prevention and suppression of transnational organised crime, it contains a number of provisions for this purpose. In addition to the harmonisation of national criminal laws and procedures, another important principle which facilitates international cooperation is mutual recognition of law enforcement and judicial decisions. This generally means that decisions made by the law enforcement or judicial authorities in one State are to be recognised and executed in another. Whilst the harmonisation of national criminal laws and procedures will naturally make it easy for States to facilitate mutual recognition, the latter is not contingent upon the former. In other words, the mutual recognition principle can operate despite the diversity in legal traditions, thereby preserving and respecting State sovereignty. As will be shown in Chapter 2, this principle has long been recognised within the EU legal order as a useful tool to combat serious crime with cross-border dimensions, including organised crime. Although specific references are not made, the UNTOC also encourages States to respect each other's law enforcement or judicial decisions with a view to facilitating more effective international cooperation.

1.2.6.1 Extradition

One of the important measures in international criminal justice cooperation is extradition. This is the process of transferring a suspect or criminal from one

93 Kevin M. Stevenson *et al.*, *Barriers to Asset Recovery: An Analysis of Key Barriers and Recommendations for Action* (The International Bank for Reconstruction and Development/The World Bank 2011), 68.

jurisdiction to another for the purposes of prosecution and punishment. This is facilitated mainly by bilateral and/or multilateral treaties. International instruments that touch upon various types of organised crime such as counterfeiting and drug trafficking also have provisions on extradition.[94] The UNTOC, as the consolidated version of these instruments which relate to organised crime, provides detailed guidance on extradition under Article 16. The benefit of this provision is that it applies to all regions of the world unlike the geographically limited regional treaties.[95] Furthermore, it applies to almost all instances of organised crime, and therefore does not limit itself to particular crimes stipulated under the subject-specific conventions. At the time of ratification or accession, States can choose to use the UNTOC as a legal basis to facilitate extradition in the absence of pre-existing treaties. It is worth pointing out here that in 2008, 59 Member States stated that the UNTOC was to be used as the legal basis for extradition.[96] This demonstrates that this instrument is valued by a number of States in facilitating international cooperation.

There are several key principles related to extradition. The first is the principle of reciprocity. This means that a State will honour a request for extradition if others honour the same request.[97] Whilst Article 16 of the UNTOC does not specifically provide for this, it can be inferred because the instrument is designed to promote mutual recognition and confidence as noted above. Indeed, regardless of the existence of bilateral or multilateral treaties, States such as Djibouti, El Salvador, Guinea-Bissau, Latvia, Madagascar, Mexico, the Philippines, South Africa, Switzerland and Turkey implement extradition on the basis of reciprocity alone.[98] The second principle is double criminality. It provides that the conduct for which extradition is sought must be an offence both in the requesting and requested States. This reflects the principle of *nulla poena sine lege* and is recognised in Article 16(1) of the UNTOC although some States do not recognise it at all.[99] The third principle is the political offence exception which provides for the refusal of extradition if the offence in question is political in nature.[100] This principle is recognised in countries such as Brazil, China, Congo, Iceland and

94 The 1988 Narcotics Trafficking Convention, art 6; the Optional Protocol to the CRC, art 5; the UN Corruption Convention, art 44; and the Protocol on Illicit Trade in Tobacco Products, art 30.

95 See for instance, Inter-American Convention on Extradition 1981, 20 ILM 723; European Convention on Extradition 1957, ETS No. 24; and Economic Community of West African States Convention on Extradition 1994, A/P.1/8/94.

96 *Information Submitted by States in their Responses to the Checklist/Questionnaire on the Implementation of the United Convention against Transnational Organised Crime for the First Cycle*, CTOC/COP/2008/CPR.7, 17–20.

97 Geoff Gilbert, *Aspects of Extradition Law* (Martinus Nijhoff Publishers 1991), 17–19.

98 Information Submitted by States, *supra* n 96.

99 Consolidated Information Received from States, *supra* n 60, para 61.

100 See, for instance, the European Convention on Extradition, art.3. For the discussion of this concept, see Chris van den Wyngaert, *The Political Offence Exception to Extradition* (Kluwer Law International 1980).

Tunisia.[101] Whilst the notion of political offence is vague and varies between States,[102] it suffices to note that this should not apply to organised crime as it is committed mainly for economic reasons. Even where organised crime has a strong nexus with terrorism, it is widely accepted that the latter is not regarded as a political offence.[103] To strengthen this, Article 16(3) makes it clear that each offence covered in the instrument is to be regarded as extraditable. Finally, there is the rule of speciality under which a person who has been extradited may be prosecuted but only for the offence listed in the extradition request.[104] It is clear that these principles are designed to protect the rights of suspects and defendants as well as mutual recognition.

Several aspects of extradition under Article 16 should be expanded upon. The principle of *aut dedere aut judicare* is explicitly recognised. This principle becomes relevant particularly when States do not extradite their nationals.[105] This is common in civil law jurisdictions whilst common law States such as the UK allow for the extradition of their own nationals. The facilitation of expedited procedures for extradition is also provided for.[106] It is worth highlighting that some States in Asia-Pacific, particularly in the Pacific Islands, use a system of endorsement of extradition warrants which reduces the amount of time needed to execute.[107] Once again, there is no doubt that mutual recognition and respect have played an important part in this. In addition, Article 16(14) provides that:

> Nothing in this Convention shall be interpreted as imposing an obligation to extradite if the requested State Party has substantial grounds for believing that the request has been made for the purpose of prosecuting or punishing a person on account of that person's sex, race, religion, nationality, ethnic origin or political opinions or that compliance with the request would cause prejudice to that person's position for any one of these reasons.

101 Consolidated Information Received from States, *supra* n 60, para 62.

102 Gilbert, *supra* n 97, ch 6.

103 Security Council Resolution 1373 (2001); European Convention on the Suppression of Terrorism 1977, art 1, ETS No. 90; International Convention for the Suppression of Terrorist Bombing 1997, art 11, 2149 UNTS 284; and International Convention for the Suppression of Financing of Terrorism 1999, art 14, 39 ILM 270.

104 Gilbert, *supra* n 97, 106–107.

105 They include: Algeria, Angola, Austria, Azerbaijan, Belarus, Belgium, Benin, Bosnia and Herzegovina, Brazil, Bulgaria, Burkina Faso, Burundi, Cambodia, Cameroon, Cape Verde, Central African Republic, Chad, China (mainland), Comoros, Congo, Costa Rica, Côte d'Ivoire, Croatia, Cyprus, Djibouti, Egypt, France, Gabon, Germany, Greece, Honduras, Kazakhstan, Kuwait, Madagascar, Mali, Moldova, Morocco, Myanmar, Niger, Poland, the Russian Federation, Sao Tome and Principe, Switzerland, Tajikistan, the former Yugoslav Republic of Macedonia, Togo, Tunisia, Turkey, Ukraine and Uzbekistan. Consolidated Information Received from States, *supra* n 60, para 65.

106 Art 16(8).

107 Asian Development Bank (ABD) and Organisation for Economic Co-operation and Development (OECD), *Mutual Legal Assistance, Extradition and Recovery of Proceeds of Corruption in Asia and the Pacific* (ADB/OECD 2007), 73.

This so-called 'discrimination clause' is crucial from a human rights perspective and is explicitly provided for in domestic legislation of some countries, such as Brunei,[108] Fiji[109] and Malaysia.[110] Whilst the inclusion of the imposition of the death penalty and trial *in absentia* as additional grounds for refusal was debated during the drafting stage, it was later concluded that the sentence 'extradition shall be subject to the conditions provided for by domestic law' would be sufficient to cover other grounds.[111]

1.2.6.2 Mutual legal assistance in criminal matters

Another important provision relates to mutual legal assistance in criminal matters. This is also facilitated bilaterally[112] or multilaterally,[113] with the UNTOC being the latest instrument to deal with this. The most important provision is Article 18 which encourages State Parties to facilitate the following measures:

- (a) Taking of evidence or statements from other persons:
- (b) Effecting service of judicial documents;
- (c) Executing searches and seizures, and freezing;
- (d) Examining objects and sites;
- (e) Providing information, evidentiary items and expert evaluations;
- (f) Providing originals or certified copies of relevant documents and records, including government, bank, financial, corporate or business records;
- (g) Identifying or tracing proceeds of crime, property, instrumentalities or other things for evidentiary purposes;
- (h) Facilitating the voluntary appearance of persons in the requesting State Party; and
- (i) Any other type of assistance that is not contrary to the domestic law of the requested State Party.

Therefore, the ambit of mutual legal assistance is broad and depends on the domestic law of each State Party.

108 Extradition Order 2006.
109 Extradition Act 2003.
110 Extradition Act 1992.
111 *Travaux Préparatoires*, *supra* n 7, 152 and 155.
112 See, for instance, Mutual Legal Assistance in Criminal Matters (Australia) Order 1999 (Hong Kong); and Mutual Assistance in Criminal Matters (Malaysia) Regulations 2006 (Australia).
113 European Convention on Mutual Assistance in Criminal Matters 1959, ETS No. 30; Inter-American Convention on Mutual Assistance in Criminal Matters 1992, OASTS No. 75; Southern African Development Community Protocol on Mutual Assistance in Criminal Matters 2002, <www.sadc.int/documents-publications/protocols>; and ASEAN Treaty on Mutual Legal Assistance in Criminal Matters 2004, <http://cil.nus.edu.sg/category/all>. See David McClean, *International Co-operation in Civil and Criminal Matters* (Oxford University Press 2002), ch 6.

There are other important points to highlight in this provision. Paragraph 8 provides that States cannot refuse mutual legal assistance on the basis of bank secrecy. This makes action against money laundering much easier. Another interesting part is paragraph 9 on double criminality. The draft paragraph stated that States 'may not decline' mutual legal assistance in the absence of double criminality. However, the actual wording of paragraph 9 was changed to 'may decline'. Some delegations during the drafting stage emphasised the importance of double criminality in mutual assistance[114] and it is evident that their view prevailed. However, as a compromise, the same paragraph leaves open the possibility of providing assistance on a discretionary basis even in the absence of double criminality. The principle of mutual recognition is therefore evident here. In addition, although the draft Article stated that offences covered in the UNTOC should not be regarded as political in nature,[115] the final version does not contain this sentence. Organised crime can therefore be designated as a political offence for the purpose of mutual legal assistance. Indeed, the interpretative note stipulates the possibility of the political offence exception.[116] This should also be contrasted with Article 16 where it is clearly stated that offences under the UNTOC should be deemed extraditable; hence, the political offence exception does not apply. Finally, the international community missed an important opportunity to include a discrimination clause as an additional ground for refusal of mutual legal assistance which was included in Article 16 on extradition. The US proposed a clause allowing refusal if a request has been made for the purpose of prosecution or punishment on the grounds of gender, race, religion, nationality or political opinion.[117] However, some delegates took the view that refusal on the ground of 'other essential interest' would cover this[118] and so the clause was eventually dropped. Worryingly, these inconsistencies can send conflicting messages to State Parties and promote fragmented, rather than integrated, responses to transnational organised crime.

An examination of State practice reveals that mutual legal assistance measures have been widely adopted by States. A number of States, such as Fiji[119] and South Africa,[120] have enacted legislation for mutual legal assistance which covers a variety of measures such as mutual provision of evidence, execution of sentences and orders and confiscation/transfer of criminal proceeds. Some[121] have gone further to include the use of special investigative techniques. Legislation in Trinidad and Tobago[122] applies only to cooperation between Commonwealth States, whilst this

114 *Travaux Préparatoires*, *supra* n 7, 177.
115 Ibid., 170.
116 Ibid., 199.
117 Ibid., 185.
118 Ibid.
119 Mutual Assistance in Criminal Matters Act 1997 as amended.
120 International Co-Operation in Criminal Matters Act 1996 as amended.
121 Argentina under the Law on International Co-operation in Criminal Matters 1996, s 68; and Australia under the Mutual Assistance in Criminal Matters Act 1987.
122 Mutual Legal Assistance in Criminal Matters Act 1997 as amended.

is not the case for Jamaica.[123] In addition, the legislation of Ghana,[124] Kenya[125] and Malaysia[126] contains detailed grounds for refusal, including the imposition of the death penalty[127] whilst the scope of refusal is limited in others.[128] These examples suggest that, although many States have legislative and other measures to facilitate mutual assistance in criminal matters, discrepancies are also recognised, once again demonstrating the strong force of State sovereignty.

There are a few more provisions aside from Article 18 which are relevant to mutual assistance in criminal matters. The first is Article 19 on joint investigations which encourages States to establish joint investigatory bodies through agreement or on a case-by-case basis. During the drafting stage, it was considered whether this regime should be included as part of general mutual legal assistance but it was decided that a separate provision should be created.[129] In addition to the EU example that will be given in Chapter 2, the Central American Network of Prosecutors against Organized Crime (REFCO), which was established in 2001, has been coordinating joint investigations against organised crime.[130] The second provision is Article 13 on international cooperation in the confiscation of criminal proceeds whereby States are to identify, trace and confiscate proceeds; issue confiscation orders upon request by other States; or facilitate the execution of foreign confiscation orders. An example of good practice here includes the establishment by the UNODC of the Asset Recovery Inter-Agency Network in Asia-Pacific.[131] Finally, the transfer of criminal proceedings (Article 21) and direct law enforcement cooperation (Article 27) are also encouraged. The latter is important as it can reduce political interference as well as the time needed to facilitate cooperation. It is worth noting in this regard that similar arrangements to those made by REFCO in Central America have been initiated in other regions such as Central Asia, South Caucasus and West Africa.[132] These examples demonstrate the increasing willingness of States to facilitate mutual assistance in criminal matters by gradually developing mutual trust and recognition. Further, it seems reasonable to argue that the UNTOC provides a broad framework to encourage State Parties in this regard.

123 Mutual Assistance in Criminal Matters Act 1997.

124 Mutual Legal Assistance Act 2010, s 15.

125 Mutual Legal Assistance Act 2011, s 11.

126 Mutual Assistance in Criminal Matters Act 2002, s 20.

127 New Zealand under the Mutual Assistance in Criminal Matters Act 1992; and Vanuatu under the Mutual Assistance in Criminal Matters Act 2002.

128 In Togo and Thailand, for instance, there are no human rights grounds under the Mutual Assistance in Criminal Matters Act 2000 and the Mutual Assistance in Criminal Matters Act 2002 respectively.

129 *Travaux Préparatoires, supra* n 7, 202.

130 *Activities of the United Nations Office on Drugs and Crime to Promote the Implementation of the Provisions on International Cooperation in the United Nations Convention against Transnational Organized Crime: Report of the Secretariat*, CTOC/COP/2014/10, para 22.

131 Ibid., para 34.

132 Ibid., para 21.

1.2.7 Protection and promotion of human rights

The protection and promotion of the human rights of victims, witnesses as well as perpetrators of transnational organised crime, should be an important part of the overall action against this kind of crime. With regard to victims, some forms of organised crime, such as human trafficking, sexual and labour exploitation as well as child sex tourism, clearly violate their human rights; their protection must therefore be regarded as a priority by States. From a practical point of view, sufficient protection will naturally encourage victims to trust the authorities and become more willing to cooperate with them in criminal investigations and proceedings against perpetrators. Unfortunately, international law on transnational organised crime as represented by the UNTOC is weak in this regard. It is important to acknowledge that Article 25 does touch upon victim protection and assistance. It also encourages States to provide appropriate measures, including compensation, and to acknowledge victims' views during criminal proceedings. Nevertheless, its language is not strong as can be seen from phrases such as 'within its means' and 'subject to its domestic law', leaving open the possibility of States not providing sufficient protection. Whilst the Trafficking Protocol attached to the UNTOC provides for the protection of privacy; assistance during criminal proceedings; protection of physical and mental well-being of victims; and temporary/permanent residence permits for trafficked victims,[133] the relevant provisions suffer from the same problem as Article 25 and the instrument's scope is inevitably limited to victims of human trafficking.

This means that the UNTOC must be supplemented by international human rights law. The benefit of using this branch of international law is that it covers all victims of organised crime with a human rights dimension. The ICCPR, for instance, places a duty on States to 'ensure that any person whose rights or freedoms as herein recognized are violated shall have an effective remedy, notwithstanding that the violation has been committed by persons acting in an official capacity'.[134] In relation to human trafficking, the United Nations Human Rights Council explicitly acknowledged that this provision applied to the victims of this crime.[135] As such, it seems reasonable to assume that the same is true for other forms of organised crime with a human rights dimension. There are other human rights treaties, such as the Forced Labour Convention 1930; the Convention on the Elimination of All Forms of Discrimination against Women 1979;[136] the Convention on the Rights of the Child 1989[137] and its Optional Protocol on Sale of Children 2000, which have in place relevant obligations to protect the affected victims.

133 Arts 6 and 7.

134 Art 2.

135 *Resolution 20/1: Trafficking in Persons, Especially Women and Children: Access to Effective Remedies for Trafficked Persons and Their Right to an Effective Remedy for Human Rights Violations*, A/HRC/20/L1 (2012).

136 1249 UNTS 13.

137 1577 UNTS 3.

A wide variety of measures should be taken to protect the victims of organised crime. First and foremost, their life and physical/mental well-being must be protected and restored. It is well established that State responsibility remains even when these violations of human rights have been committed by non-State actors;[138] this should apply equally to perpetrators of organised crime. If these victims are to participate in criminal investigations and proceedings, then their identity and safety must be guaranteed through effective witness protection schemes and other relevant assistance, such as interpretation/translation, legal assistance, safe accommodation as well as temporary residence permits for victims who are foreign nationals. Moreover, as victims of crime, access to compensation must be guaranteed. These are some of the measures which could be enhanced by the relevant human rights norms and principles.[139]

In addition, the protection of witnesses who may or may not necessarily be victims is also important. Article 24 of the UNTOC obliges States to take measures to provide protection from retaliation and intimidation of witnesses as well as their relatives and others close to them. This is closely interlinked to the obligation to prohibit obstruction of justice (Article 23 of the UNTOC) explained earlier. Paragraph 2 lists non-exhaustive measures such as physical protection through relocation and non-disclosure of the identity of a witness. The use of communications technologies such as video-link should also be provided. As the potential victims of human rights violations, it seems reasonable to argue that some of the measures noted above could and should also be provided to witnesses of organised crime. It will be shown later in this book that the human rights of witnesses are regarded as an equally important issue by the law enforcement authorities in Northern Ireland and the Republic of Ireland.

Further, the UNTOC does not contain specific provisions on the rights of defendants. It must, therefore, be supplemented by international human rights law. In addition to widely debated and scrutinised human rights, such as the right to liberty and security and prohibition against torture, inhuman or degrading treatment,[140] an important issue in the context of law enforcement against transnational organised crime is the use of special investigative techniques and their impact on the right to privacy. Article 20 of the UNTOC does not mention any relevant human rights norms and principles at all which is of great concern. This shortcoming is mitigated by international human rights law. For instance, the UN Human Rights Committee, which monitors the implementation of the ICCPR, stated in the past that in order to justify interferences with the right to privacy, States must specify in detail the circumstances under which such interferences may

138 See, for instance, the landmark case of *Velasquez Rodriquz v Honduras*, Inter-Am.Ct.H.R. (Ser. C) No. 4 (1988).

139 In relation to human trafficking, see Tom Obokata, *Trafficking of Human Beings from a Human Rights Perspective: Towards a Holistic Approach* (Martinus Nijhoff Publishers 2006).

140 The ICCPR, arts 7, 9, and 10.

be permitted in their national legislation.[141] In other words, these measures should have a clear legal basis. In addition, it has been established that any interference must be necessary and reasonable in that it must be proportionate to the legitimate aim pursued.[142] Whilst acknowledging that crime prevention is a legitimate aim, the UN High Commissioner for Human Rights has also endorsed the points raised by the Human Rights Committee.[143] In March 2015, in recognising the need to discuss and examine the right to privacy in the context of, among others, surveillance and its lawfulness, the UN Human Rights Council established the post of Special Rapporteur on the Right to Privacy.[144] Another important issue in relation to special investigative techniques is a person's right to a fair trial. It has been recognised, for instance, that undercover operations could amount to entrapment if a crime was instigated by the law enforcement agencies and that this would undermine the right to a fair trial.[145]

Similar to these special investigative techniques, confiscation of criminal proceeds also has a human rights dimension. The first question which should be asked is whether the criminals can retain criminal proceeds and related property under the rubric of 'right to property' which is recognised by the Universal Declaration of Human Rights 1948.[146] Whilst this right is not stipulated in legally binding universal instruments, such as the ICCPR or the International Covenant on Economic, Social and Cultural Rights 1966,[147] the right to property is recognised regionally in Africa,[148] the Americas[149] and Europe.[150] From the relevant provisions, it becomes apparent that a criminal cannot have the right to property if it has been obtained as a result of criminal activities. This right is recognised as a 'qualified right' in that it can be restricted in the public interest or as prescribed by law.[151] Consequently, criminal proceeds are not generally protected by human

141 General Comment No. 16 (Right to Privacy)(1988), HRI/GEN/1/Rev.1, para 8.

142 See, for instance, *Toonen v Australia*, Communication No. 488/1992, CCPR/C/WG/44/D/488/1992, para 8.3; and General Comment No. 31 (The Nature of the General Legal Obligation)(2004), CCPR/C/21/Rev.1/Add.13, para. 6.

143 *The Right to Privacy in the Digital Age*, A/HRC/27/37 (2014).

144 *Resolution 28: Human Rights, Democracy and the Rule of Law*, A/HRC/28/L.24 (2015).

145 See, for instance, *Teixeira de Castro v Portugal*, App no 25829/94 (1998); *Ludi v Switzerland*, App no 12433/86 (1992); and *Khudobin v Russia*, App no 59696/00 (2006).

146 G.A.Res. 217 A (III), art 17.

147 993 UNTS 3.

148 African Charter on Human and Peoples' Rights 1981 (African Charter), art 14, 1520 UNTS 217.

149 American Convention on Human Rights 1969 (ACHR), art 21, 1144 UNTS 143.

150 Protocol 1 to the European Convention on Human Rights 1952, art 1, ETS No. 9.

151 Art 1 of the Protocol 1 to the ECHR states 'No one shall be deprived of his possessions except in the public interest and subject to the conditions provided for by law and by the general principles of international law;" 2) The preceding provisions shall not, however, in any way impair the right of a State to enforce such laws as it deems necessary to control the use of property in accordance with the general interest or to secure the payment of taxes or other contributions or penalties.' Similar languages can be found in art 21 of the ACHR and art 14 of the African Charter.

rights law. It is also worth pointing out that temporary seizure of property, such as vehicles and aircraft used for criminal activities, would not be regarded as deprivation of such property.[152] However, as with the right to privacy, confiscation must be proportionate to the legitimate aim pursued.[153] This means that some of the principles noted above, such as the existence of a legal basis and its clarity, should be relevant to the right to property.[154]

In addition, non-conviction-based civil asset recovery has raised some human rights concerns although it has been argued that this is a good tool to combat organised crime.[155] Many States have concerns about this type of confiscation as a lower burden of proof is used and it is up to those affected to prove that the property was not obtained as a result of criminal activities.[156] In Europe, human rights complaints have been lodged against various States before the ECtHR. These have argued that in practice civil recovery is criminal in nature and, therefore, a presumption of innocence (as part of the right to a fair trial) should apply. Whilst this is a convincing argument, it has been held that the purpose of civil proceedings is to recover assets illegally possessed and not to determine a person's guilt.[157] Consequently, civil recovery is generally regarded as not breaching the relevant human rights norms and principles. At the same time, however, it has been made clear that sufficient procedural safeguards must be in place (public/open hearing, disclosure of the prosecution's case and an opportunity to rebut such an assumption on the balance of probabilities)[158] for civil recovery to be compatible with human rights principles.

In relation to international cooperation, one of the pertinent human rights norms applicable to perpetrators of organised crime is *non-refoulement*. In the landmark case of *Soering v United Kingdom*, the ECtHR held that the so-called 'death row phenomenon', which might entail, among other things, prolonged mental and physical abuse and suffering, could amount to inhuman and degrading treatment,[159] thus sparing the applicant from being extradited.[160] A related obligation is that those States which have abolished the death penalty should

152 *Air Canada v United Kingdom*, App no 18465/91 (1995).

153 *Phillips v United Kingdom*, App no 41087/98 (2001), para 51.

154 See, for instance, *Adzhigovich v Russia*, App no 23202/05 (2009), where the European Court of Human Rights (ECtHR) held that Russia violated the right to property as there was not a clear legal basis for confiscation.

155 Angela Leong, *The Disruption of International Organised Crime* (Ashgate 2007), 77; and Stefan Casella, 'The Case for Civil Forfeiture: Why In Rem Proceedings are an Essential Tool for Recovering the Proceeds of Crime' (2008) 11 *Journal of Money Laundering Control* 8.

156 Sambei, *supra* n 90, 9.

157 See, for example, *Engel v The Netherlands*, App nos 5100/71, 5101/71, 5102/71, 5354/72 and 5370/72 (1976); and *Walsh v United Kingdom*, App no 33744/96 (2000).

158 *Phillips v United Kingdom*, *supra* n 153, paras 43–47.

159 App no 14038/88 (1989).

160 See also *Maksudov and Rakhimov v Kyrgyzstan*, Communication Nos. 1461, 1462, 1476 & 1477/2006, CCPR/C/93/D/1461,1462,1476&1477/2006, para 12.6.

refrain from returning individuals to jurisdictions that still retain this punishment.[161] In addition to the death penalty, this principle is also pertinent to life imprisonment without parole or the possibility of review.[162] Aside from prohibition on torture, inhuman or degrading treatment, *non-refoulement* applies to other rights, such as the right to privacy[163] and the right to a fair trial.[164] It is worth highlighting that the *non-refoulement* obligation also arises from human rights violations committed by non-State actors. In *HLR v France*,[165] the applicant, a Colombian national who was convicted of drug offences, argued that he would face torture or inhuman treatment in the hands of drug traffickers if he were deported back to Colombia. The ECtHR, whilst not finding a breach of Article 3 in this particular case, recognised that Article 3 could apply to the conduct of non-State actors such as drug traffickers if the State in question did not provide sufficient protection.[166]

Although the principle of *non-refoulement* is very important from a human rights perspective, one practical implication is that it may make international law enforcement cooperation, such as extradition and mutual legal assistance, difficult. For instance, States such as Australia,[167] the Cook Islands,[168] Fiji,[169] Hong Kong[170] and Vanuatu[171] can refuse extradition or mutual legal assistance in criminal matters if the requesting States implement the death penalty. The UNTOC also allows refusal on human rights grounds as noted above. One way to mitigate this difficulty and defuse political tensions whilst simultaneously maintaining the spirit of human rights and international cooperation is to rely on the aforementioned principle of *aut dedere aut judicare*. This is a sensible alternative as it ensures that perpetrators of organised crime are punished one way or another. Another way is to fully observe and implement assurances that the person would not receive the death penalty. However, it must be acknowledged that giving assurances has been controversial as its effectiveness is not certain in many cases.[172] In order to avoid violations of human rights, it has been held, for example, that

161 *Judge v Canada*, Communication No. 829/1998, CCPR/C/78/D/829/1998, para 10.4; *G.T. v Australia*, Communication No. 706/1996, CCPR/C/61/D/706/1996, paras 8.2 and 8.3; and *Kwok Yin Fong v Australia*, Communication No. 1442/2005, CCPR/C/97/D/1442/2005, para 9.4.

162 *Harkins and Edwards v United Kingdom*, App nos 9146/07 and 32650/07 (2012).

163 *Mehemi v France*, App. No. 25017/94 (1997); and *Maslov v Austria*, App no 1638/03 (2008).

164 *Othman (Abu Qatada) v Others v United Kingdom*, App no 8139/09 (2012).

165 App no. 24573/94 (1997).

166 Ibid., para 40. See also *A v The Netherlands*, App no. 4900/06 (2010).

167 Extradition Act 1988, s 15B; and Mutual Assistance in Criminal Matters Act 1987, s 8(1A).

168 Extradition Act 2003, s 19.

169 Extradition Act 1977, s 11(4).

170 Mutual Assistance in Criminal Matters Ordinance 1997, s 5(3).

171 Extradition Act 2003, s 17(2)(e).

172 International Organisation for Migration, *Information Note on the Principle of Non-Refoulement* (International Organisation for Migration 2014), 8.

the reliability of assurances must be assessed and that there should be an effective mechanism to monitor and enforce these assurances.[173]

Another important area is the handling of evidence. It was noted above that the UNTOC actively encourages States to facilitate cooperation in evidential matters. However, a few human rights issues in relation to the right to a fair trial have emerged over the course of time. One example relates to the use of testimonies provided by witnesses residing abroad. To begin with, the right to a fair trial does not grant the defence an 'unlimited right to secure the appearance of a witness in court'.[174] Further, this right does not require that the defence must always be able to examine witnesses directly.[175] However, the defence should be afforded opportunities to cross-examine witnesses sufficiently.[176] The measures, such as hearings through video-links as stipulated in Article 18 of the UNTOC, will satisfy this but this can also be secured as long as the defence has an opportunity to put forward questions to witnesses.[177] Also, a violation may not necessarily be found if there is other evidence which the defendant can challenge and cross-examine.[178]

A related issue is evidence obtained through special investigative techniques such as the interception of communications. The use of such evidence is permitted in States such as France, Ireland, the Netherlands and Spain but not in others.[179] A question here is whether admitting such evidence obtained abroad would violate the right to a fair trial given that the authorisation processes for these measures vary between States. To begin with, the general principle that has developed, in the context of Europe at least, is that the admissibility of evidence is a matter of domestic law and the key question is whether the criminal proceedings as a whole are fair.[180] Thus, for example, the use of evidence obtained through special investigative techniques would not automatically lead to a violation of the right to a fair trial provided that it was not the sole evidence to be relied upon and the defendant had an opportunity to challenge the authenticity of such evidence.[181] Similar reasoning applies to improperly obtained evidence

173 *Maksudov and Rakhimov v Kyrgyzstan, supra* n 160, para 12; *Othman v the United Kingdom, supra* n 164, para 188–189; *Alzery v Sweden*, Communication No. 1416/2005, CCPR/C/88/D/1416/2005, para 11; and *Extension of Precautionary Measures (N. 259/02) regarding Detainees in Guantánamo Bay, Cuba* (2005) by the Inter-American Commission on Human Rights.

174 *P.V. v Germany*, App no 11853/85 (1987).

175 Ibid.

176 *A.M. v Italy*, App no 37019/97 (2000).

177 *P.V. v Germany, supra* n 174.

178 *A.M. v Italy, supra* n 176, para 25. See also *Haas v Germany*, App no 73047/01 (2005).

179 Privy Council, *Review of the Intercept as Evidence: Report to the Prime Minister and the Home Secretary* (2008), CM 7324, 31–35.

180 *Teixeira de Castro v Portugal, supra* n 145, para 34. The same principle should apply in the domestic law enforcement context.

181 *Schenk v Switzerland*, App no 10862/84 (1988), paras 46–48. See also *Khan v United Kingdom*, App no 35394/97 (2000).

(e.g. without legal basis).[182] These findings have been rightly criticised as they do not give sufficient weight to the manner in which the evidence was collected during the investigation stage.[183] Having said this, one notable exception is the use of evidence obtained as a result of torture as it is held to be a violation of the right to a fair trial.[184] This is not necessarily because such evidence is unreliable but because it undermines the fairness and legitimacy of criminal justice systems.[185] An added dimension is the principle of *non-refoulement* noted above. In the landmark case of *Othman v United Kingdom*, the ECtHR held that returning the applicant to Jordan would breach his right to a fair trial as there would be a risk of evidence obtained as a result of torture being used against him.[186] What becomes apparent in analysing the relevant jurisprudence is that the lack of sufficient human rights provisions in the UNTOC can be mitigated to some extent by the established human rights norms and principles. Many of these will be expanded upon further when exploring the State practice of Northern Ireland (UK) and the Republic of Ireland later.

1.3 Conclusion

International law on transnational organised crime as represented by the UNTOC is useful as it provides a broad framework for facilitating individual and collective action against transnational organised crime. It has been shown that it contains a number of important standards in this regard. However, as with other international treaties, strong emphasis is placed upon the protection of State sovereignty as evidenced by the weak language and the wide margin of appreciation afforded to States. This is also reflected in State practice where discrepancies in the implementation of international standards exist at the national level. In addition, it would appear that the UNTOC is not an effective instrument to deal with the protection of the human rights of victims and perpetrators of organised crime. Nevertheless, it has also been demonstrated that this branch of international law has been making some positive changes. A degree of harmonisation and mutual trust/recognition are emerging in certain areas and States are becoming more willing to use the UNTOC as a legal basis to facilitate international cooperation. Therefore, the value of international law to transnational organised crime should not be dismissed.

182 Ibid.

183 John Jackson and Sarah Summers, *The Internationalisation of Criminal Evidence: Beyond the Common Law and Civil Law Traditions* (Cambridge University Press 2012), 181.

184 *Jalloh v Germany*, App no 54810/00 (2006), para 99; *Harutyunyan v Armenia*, App no. 36549/03 (2007); and *Gäfgen v Germany*, App no 22978/05 (2010), para 165.

185 Jackson and Summers, *supra* n 183, 162.

186 *Supra* n 164.

2 Regional standards on action against transnational organised crime

2.1 Introduction

This chapter analyses the development of regional standards concerning organised crime with a particular focus on EU law. It begins with an analysis of the core principles of approximation of national criminal laws and procedures and mutual recognition of judicial decisions. It will be shown that the EU and its Member States have been instrumental in promoting these principles. The chapter continues with an analysis of core obligations established by the relevant legal instruments which mirrors the discussions on international standards in the previous chapter. Various international obligations and standards are implemented through EU law, thereby demonstrating a degree of synergy between the different levels of governance, although it is also evident that the measures adopted under EU law are more advanced and progressive than those under the UNTOC. Finally, the protection and promotion of human rights will be explored. Whilst the EU and its Member States have made some progress in this area, the ECHR continues to play a significant role in this regard.

2.2 Core principles

The first relevant principle is approximation of national criminal laws and procedures. Whilst its importance was recognised in the 1990s, it was the Treaty on European Union (TEU) as revised by the Treaty of Amsterdam which formally introduced this principle into the EU legal order.[1] It has also been recognised by the Treaty on the Functioning of the European Union (TFEU)[2] which has restructured the pre existing treaty arrangements. For instance, Article 82(2) states that judicial cooperation in criminal matters shall include approximation of

1 Treaty on European Union (Consolidated Version), arts 29 and 31, [1997] OJ C 340/145. On the historical development of approximation within the EU legal order, see Anne Weyembergh, 'The Functions of Approximation of Penal Legislation within the European Union' (2005) 12 *Maastricht Journal of European and Comparative Law* 149; and Francesco Calderoni, *Organized Crime Legislation in the European Union* (Springer 2010).

2 [2012] OJ C 326/47.

the laws and regulations of Member States in the following areas: a) mutual admissibility of evidence; b) the rights of individuals in criminal procedure; c) the rights of victims; d) any other specific aspects of criminal procedure which the Council has identified in advance by a decision. In addition, Article 83 provides for the establishment of minimum rules on the definitions and sanctions of serious offences with cross-border dimensions, such as the trafficking of human beings; sexual exploitation of women and children; illicit drug trafficking; illicit arms trafficking; money laundering; corruption; counterfeiting of means of payment; computer crime; and organised crime. With this, the competence of the EU to combat transnational organised crime has been reaffirmed.

In terms of legal instruments, so-called framework decisions have been adopted under the TEU. Many of these are still relevant today although some have been amended or repealed. While framework decisions are legally binding, they do not have direct effect.[3] This means that they cannot be directly enforceable by national courts and tribunals of Member States. Under the TFEU, directives are used to achieve approximation as stipulated in Articles 82 and 83. Article 288 provides that 'a directive shall be binding, as to the result to be achieved, upon each Member State to which it is addressed, but shall leave to the national authorities the choice of form and methods'. Member States therefore have some flexibility in implementing the principle of approximation. One noticeable difference between directives and framework decisions is that the former can have direct effect because Article 288 does not exclude this possibility unlike Article 34 of the TEU for framework decisions. In addition, infringement proceedings before the European Court of Justice (ECJ) can now be instituted against Member States which fail to implement directives.[4] The importance of these changes is that they will put additional pressure on Member States to take organised crime more seriously and strengthen their actions compared to the old regime. However, at the same time, Article 276 of the TFEU states that the ECJ does not have jurisdiction to review the validity or proportionality of operations carried out by the police and other law enforcement services. This unfortunately undermines the ability of the ECJ to provide independent oversight over some aspects of action against transnational organised crime within the EU territories.

The second important principle is the mutual recognition of judicial decisions in relation to criminal matters. This idea was first introduced by the UK during its Presidency in 1998 to promote judicial cooperation between Member States.[5] It was also recognised in the following year in the Tampere Conclusions where the principle was regarded as the cornerstone of criminal judicial cooperation.[6] In 2000 the European Commission consulted on the matter with the Council and

3 TEU, art 34.

4 TFEU, art 258.

5 Valsamis Mitsilegas, 'The Constitutional Implications of Mutual Recognition in Criminal Matters in the EU' (2006) 43 *Common Market Law Review* 1277, 1278.

6 Tampere Presidency Conclusions, para 33.

the European Parliament[7] and launched an initiative to promote this principle in the following year.[8] Then, the Hague Programme, which was established to strengthen the Area of Freedom, Security and Justice, reaffirmed the importance of this principle in preventing and suppressing serious crime.[9] Under the TFEU, mutual recognition is specifically mentioned in Article 82. The legal instruments are largely the same for mutual recognition (i.e. framework decisions and directives).

The principles of approximation of national criminal laws/procedures and mutual recognition are closely interlinked. To begin with, the main factor which encouraged the EU and Member States to promote the mutual recognition principle was the divergence between national legal systems as this undermined effective law enforcement cooperation.[10] Undoubtedly, mutual recognition becomes easier if a greater degree of approximation of national criminal laws and processes is achieved. In this sense, approximation can be regarded as a tool to promote mutual recognition.[11] However, the latter does not necessarily require the former. It has been noted in this regard that the aim of approximation is to eliminate differences whilst these differences are recognised under mutual recognition.[12] The ECJ also held that nothing in Title VI of the TEU makes the application of the principle of mutual recognition conditional upon the harmonisation of criminal laws of Member States.[13] For this reason, the principle of mutual recognition has been regarded as a good alternative to approximation of national laws and procedures as it does not require substantial alteration.[14] In any event, it is evident that the EU and its Member States have been more forthcoming in acknowledging the importance of two core principles when comparing State Parties to the UNTOC.

2.3 EU action against transnational organised crime

2.3.1 Prohibition of organised crime and criminal jurisdiction

Having explored the two key principles under EU law, it is now useful to analyse how they are reflected in and implemented through various measures. In relation to the prohibition of organised crime, an important instrument is the

7 Communication from the Commission to the Council and the European Parliament on Mutual Recognition of Final Decisions in Criminal Matters, COM (2000) 495 final.

8 Programme of Measures to Implement the Principle of Mutual Recognition of Decisions in Criminal Matters, [2001] OJ C 12/10.

9 [2005] OJ C53/1.

10 Mitsilegas, *supra* n 5, 1278.

11 Massimo Fichera, 'The European Arrest Warrant and the Sovereign State: A Marriage of Convenience?' (2009) 15 *European Law Journal* 70, 77.

12 Ibid., 74.

13 *Advocaten voor de Wereld v Leden van de Ministerraad*, [2007] ECR I-3633, C-303/05, para 59.

14 Mitsilegas, *supra* n 5, 1280.

Framework Decision on the Fight against Organised Crime[15] adopted in 2008. Under Article 1, a 'criminal organisation' is defined as:

> a structured association, established over a period of time, of more than two persons acting in concert with a view to committing offences which are punishable by deprivation of liberty or a detention order of a maximum of at least four years or a more serious penalty, to obtain, directly or indirectly, a financial or other material benefit;
>
> 'structured association' means an association that is not randomly formed for the immediate commission of an offence, nor does it need to have formally defined roles for its members, continuity of its membership, or a developed structure.

Whilst this definition is largely in line with the one under the UNTOC, one noticeable difference is the number of individuals (i.e. 2 persons as opposed to 3) needed to form a criminal organisation. The scope of this definition is therefore wider. The offences related to participation in a criminal organisation also mirror those under the UNTOC[16] as the Framework Decision allows Member States a degree of flexibility to choose between the conspiracy and participation models. This was an inevitable consequence as some EU Member States, particularly those within the civil law tradition, do not support conspiracy as a criminal offence.[17]

In relation to substantive crimes, there are other instruments which emphasise the obligation to prohibit.[18] An important point to note, however, is that there is

15 Council Framework Decision 2008/841/JHA of 24 October 2008 on the fight against organised crime, [2008] OJ L 300/42.

16 Arts 2 and 3.

17 See Calderoni, *supra* n 1.

18 See, for instance, Convention drawn up on the basis of Article K.3(2)(c) of the Treaty on European Union on the fight against corruption involving officials of the European Communities or officials of the Member States of the European Union, [1997] OJ C 195/2; Council Framework Decision 2003/568/JHA of 22 July 2003 on combating corruption in the private sector, [2003] OJ L 192/54; Framework Decision 2004/757/JHA of 25 October 2004 laying down minimum provisions on the constituent elements of criminal acts and penalties in the field of illicit drug trafficking, [2004] OJ L 335/8; Directive 2011/36/EU of the European Parliament and of the Council of 5 April 2011 on preventing and combating trafficking in human beings and protecting its victims, and replacing Council Framework Decision 2002/629/JHA, [2011] OJ L 101/1; Directive 2011/92/EU of the European Parliament and of the Council of 13 December 2011 on combating the sexual abuse and sexual exploitation of children and child pornography, and replacing Council Framework Decision 2004/68/JHA, [2011] OJ L 335/1; and Directive (EU) 2015/849 of the European Parliament and of the Council of 20 May 2015 on the prevention of the use of the financial system for the purposes of money laundering or terrorist financing, amending Regulation (EU) No 648/2012 of the European Parliament and of the Council, and repealing Directive 2005/60/EC of the European Parliament and of the Council and Commission Directive 2006/70/EC (Text with EEA relevance), [2015] OJ L 141/73.

currently no clear legal basis that obliges Member States to prohibit and punish fiscal or excise fraud such as tobacco smuggling or fuel laundering. In relation to tobacco products, it is important to mention that the EU has adopted two Directives in the past.[19] In addition, it has concluded several agreements with major tobacco companies, such as Philip Morris International, Japan Tobacco, British American Tobacco and Imperial Tobacco.[20] However, the first Directive did not contain any criminal law provisions and given that tobacco smuggling continues to exist within the EU territories, its effectiveness in suppressing this crime can be called into question. Similarly, whilst it is not yet possible to measure the effectiveness of the newest Directive, the same argument can be applied to it. As to agreements with tobacco companies, they will be penalised if they do not put enough effort into tackling tobacco smuggling.[21] Although encouraging cooperation from private corporations is a reasonable step to take, the current arrangements can be interpreted as shifting the responsibility of crime prevention to private entities. It has also been argued that these agreements have not been entirely effective in reducing the crime.[22] There is, therefore, scope for improvement in relation to these crimes.

Unlike the UNTOC, the EU instruments on substantive crimes go further by stipulating punishments that Member States can implement. For instance, participation offences under the Framework Decision on Organised Crime attract imprisonment of at least 2 to 5 years.[23] It also obliges States to designate the involvement of organised criminal groups as an aggravating factor in sentencing. This is important as the involvement of these groups naturally make their operations more dangerous and difficult to detect, and a heavier penalty might be justified for these reasons. Similarly, the Framework Decision on Drug Trafficking provides for imprisonment of at least 1 to 3 years for drug offences. Article 4 additionally lists aggravating circumstances with heavier penalties (maximum of at least 5 to 10 years' imprisonment), which include production/trafficking of large quantities of drugs or involvement of organised criminal groups. Moreover, human trafficking incurs the minimum imprisonment of at least 5 years (or 10 years under aggravating circumstances).[24] It is evident that these instruments, in contrast to the UNTOC, are designed to encourage States to find

19 Directive 2001/37/EC of the European Parliament and of the Council of 5 June 2001 on the approximation of the laws, regulations and administrative provisions of the Member States concerning the manufacture, presentation and sale of tobacco products, [2001] OJ L194/26; and Directive 2014/40/EU of the European Parliament and of the Council of 3 April 2014 on approximation of laws, regulations and administrative provisions of the Member States concerning the manufacture, presentation and sale of tobacco and related products repealing Directive 2001/37/EC, [2014] OJ L 127/1.

20 The European Anti-Fraud Office, <http://ec.europa.eu/anti_fraud/investigations/eu-revenue/cigarette_smuggling_en.htm>.

21 European Parliament, *Workshop on Cigarette Smuggling* (January 2014), 39.

22 Ibid., 40.

23 Art 3.

24 Art 4.

common ground and provide clearer guidance by promoting the approximation of substantive criminal law among Member States.

In terms of criminal jurisdiction, the rules stipulated in the EU instruments largely reflect the international standards as represented by the UNTOC. Under the Framework Decision on Organised Crime, the territorial principle is recognised as a mandatory ground for establishing jurisdiction.[25] The same provision also mentions the nationality principle (for both natural and legal persons) but this is regarded as an optional ground which allows Member States not to prosecute their own nationals. This is in line with the practice of some States as explained in Chapter 1. Interestingly, however, the Directives on Human Trafficking and Child Sexual Exploitation make the nationality principle mandatory. This is particularly useful in prosecuting and punishing nationals and habitual residents of the EU Member States who commit these crimes abroad.[26] Aside from the territorial and nationality principles, the passive personality and universality principle (i.e. the presence of perpetrators without territorial or nationality connections and *aut dedere aut judicare*) are also provided for. [27]

2.3.2 Intelligence-led law enforcement

There is no single comprehensive instrument that governs intelligence-led law enforcement through the use of special investigative techniques under EU law. However, Member States are encouraged to use them one way or another. The EU Human Trafficking Directive states in this regard that 'Member States shall take the necessary measures to ensure that effective investigative tools, such as those which are used in organised crime or other serious crime cases are available'.[28] This can be interpreted as including measures such as surveillance and interception of communications. These are also mentioned in the context of cross-border cooperation. The Convention on Mutual Legal Assistance in Criminal Matters between the EU Member States 2000[29] encourages measures such as controlled delivery (Article 12), covert investigations (Article 14) and interception of telecommunications (Title III). The Schengen *Acquis*,[30] which incorporated the Schengen Agreement 1985 and the Convention 1990 into the EU legal framework, also touches upon cross-border surveillance and hot pursuit.[31] In 2014

25 Art 7.

26 Proposal for a Directive of the European Parliament and of the Council on Combating Sexual Abuse, Sexual Exploitation of Children and Child Pornography, COM (2010) 94 final; and Proposal for a Directive of the European Parliament and of the Council on Preventing and Combating Trafficking in Human Beings and Protecting Victims, COM (2010) 95 final.

27 Similar provisions are included in the Framework Decision on Drug Trafficking (art 8).

28 Art 9(4).

29 [2000] OJ C 197/1.

30 TFEU, Protocol 19 Integrating the Schengen *Acquis* into the Framework of the European Union.

31 Arts 40 and 41.

the Commission and the European Parliament adopted the Directive on the European Investigation Order (EIO).[32] This builds upon previous instruments, most notably the Framework Decision on the European Evidence Warrant (EEW).[33] Under this regime, investigation measures such as covert investigations (Article 29) and interception of telecommunications (Chapter V) can be requested and implemented by Member States. In summary, it is apparent that the EU legal frameworks actively encourage Member States to facilitate intelligence-led law enforcement against serious cross-border crimes, including organised crime, and these are in conformity with the UNTOC.

2.3.3 *Confiscation of criminal proceeds/asset recovery*

Several instruments have been implemented in relation to confiscation of criminal proceeds. Under the TEU, 4 framework decisions were adopted,[34] but a number of issues have been raised to explain the ineffectiveness of these instruments. Chief among these are: the absence of a common approach to confiscation; conflicting legal traditions; and a lack of training on the part of law enforcement authorities. Consequently, the need for a new instrument was highlighted by the European Commission.[35] This has also been acknowledged in the Stockholm Programme which was designed to enhance the Area of Freedom, Security and Justice within the EU. This called for a more efficient system of asset recovery.[36] In response, Directive on the Freezing and Confiscation of Criminal Proceeds[37] was eventually adopted under the TFEU.

It is useful to compare the key features of this Directive with those of previous instruments. To begin with, its application is limited to serious crimes unlike previous instruments which covered crimes attracting imprisonment of 1 year.

32 Directive 2014/41/EU of the European Parliament and of the Council of 3 April 2014 regarding the European Investigation Order in criminal matters, [2014] OJ L 130/1.

33 Council Framework Decision 2008/978/JHA of 18 December 2008 on the European evidence warrant for the purpose of obtaining objects, documents and data for use in proceedings in criminal matters, [2008] OJ L 350/72.

34 Council Framework Decision 2001/500/JHA of 26 June 2001 on money laundering, the identification, tracing, freezing, seizing and confiscation of instrumentalities and the proceeds of crime, [2001] OJ L 182/1; Council Framework Decision 2003/577/JHA of 22 July 2003 on the execution in the European Union of orders freezing property or evidence, [2003] OJ L 196/45, Council Framework Decision 2005/212/JHA of 24 February 2005 on confiscation of crime-related proceeds, instrumentalities and property, [2005] OJ L 68/49; and Council Framework Decision 2006/783/JHA of 6 October 2006 on the application of the principle of mutual recognition to confiscation orders, [2006] OJ L 328/59.

35 Proposal for a Directive of the European Parliament and of the Council on the freezing and confiscation of proceeds of crimes in the European Union, COM (2012) 85 final, 7.

36 [2010] OJ C 115/1.

37 Directive 2014/42/EU of the European Parliament and of the Council of 3 April 2014 on the freezing and confiscation of instrumentalities and proceeds of crime in the European Union, [2014] OJ L 127/39.

In this regard, Article 3 provides a non-exhaustive list of crimes, including drug trafficking, human trafficking, counterfeiting, terrorism, corruption and participation in organised criminal groups. This Directive also allows for both conviction and non-conviction-based confiscation of proceeds.[38] Whilst Article 4(2) stipulates a suspect being ill or having absconded as instances where non-conviction-based confiscation can be instituted, this list is not exhaustive as the term 'at least' suggests. Having said this, whether the Directive will actually encourage Member States to allow expansive non-conviction-based confiscation is open to question as many of them have already opposed such a measure[39] although it is widely practised in the UK and the Republic of Ireland as will be explored later. In addition, the rights of defendants are also specifically recognised under the Directive.[40] Therefore, additional safeguards must be implemented by Member States. Another important aspect of this Directive is the use of confiscated proceeds. Article 10(3) encourages Member States to use the confiscated proceeds for public interest and social purposes. In addition to enhancing the capability of law enforcement agencies in combating transnational crime, these proceeds can be used to protect and compensate victims of organised crime, particularly human trafficking and slavery/forced labour where the physical and mental well-being of victims are greatly affected. It has also been suggested that these proceeds should be used to assist civil society organisations in educating the general public and conducting important activities for the prevention of crime.[41] The EU Directive therefore goes further than the UNTOC.

2.3.4 International cooperation

The EU and its Member States have been instrumental in facilitating international cooperation against transnational organised crime. There are a number of important treaties in this area. The first is the aforementioned Convention on Mutual Legal Assistance in Criminal Matters between the EU Member States through which requests for mutual assistance can be made directly by the judicial authorities of Member States (Article 6) although spontaneous information exchange related to criminal offences can be conducted without formal requests as long as that is permitted in their domestic legal frameworks (Article 7). This clarifies that the Convention aims to facilitate smoother cooperation on the ground through the promotion of mutual recognition. In relation to specific measures, the Convention also provides for mutual assistance in the temporary transfer of those in custody (Article 9); the hearing of testimonies by video/

38 Art 4.

39 See Michele Simonato, 'Directive 2014/42/EU and Non-Conviction Based Confiscation: A Step Forward on Asset Recovery?' (2015) 6 *New Journal of European Criminal Law* 213.

40 Art 8.

41 Stefano Montaldo, 'Directive 2014/42/EU and Social Reuse of Confiscated Assets in the EU: Advancing a Culture of Legality' (2015) 6 *New Journal of European Criminal Law* 195, 200.

telephone conferences (Articles 10 and 11); controlled delivery (Article 12); joint investigation teams (JITs) (Article 13); covert investigations (Article 14); and interception of telecommunications (Title III).

The second treaty regime is the Schengen *Acquis*. The relevant part is Title III on police and security. In addition to facilitating cooperation through judicial authorities, the Schengen *Acquis* allows direct police cooperation when this is permitted by the domestic legal frameworks of the EU Member States (Article 39). Of particular relevance in relation to organised crime is the possibility of cross-border surveillance under Article 40. Normally, this is done with the express permission of the concerned Member States. However, the same provision also allows surveillance of up to 5 hours without such permission in urgent cases. The offences for which such cross-border surveillance is permitted include human and drug trafficking. Article 41 additionally provides for 'hot pursuit'. Other mutual legal assistance measures are also listed in Part 2.

In addition, there is a treaty aimed at facilitating customs cooperation which is relevant for crimes such as fiscal/excise fraud. The Convention on Mutual Assistance and Cooperation between Customs Administrations 1997 (Naples II),[42] which was adopted under the TEU, builds upon the previous Convention on Mutual Assistance between Customs Administrations 1967. The main aim of this Convention is to facilitate cooperation for the purpose of preventing, detecting, prosecuting and punishing infringements of EU and national customs provisions.[43] The key measures stipulated under this instrument include the sharing of information (Article 10); cross-border surveillance (Article 21); hot pursuit (Article 20); controlled delivery (Article 22); covert investigations (Article 23); and JITs (Article 24). It is clear that these measures are similar to those in the EU Convention on Mutual Assistance in Criminal Matters and the Schengen *Acquis*. In any event, it is apparent that important international standards as represented in the UNTOC are reflected in these treaties.

There are other legal instruments designed to facilitate smoother international cooperation. A prominent example is the European Arrest Warrant (EAW).[44] This was the first measure adopted to promote the mutual recognition principle. Moreover, it has simplified extradition procedures between Member States, enabling them to bring criminals to justice sooner rather than later. The EAW regime therefore is a good example of an expedited procedure as envisaged by Article 16 of the UNTOC. There are a number of offences that have been included in the list of offences under which double criminality is relaxed, including participation in a criminal organisation; trafficking of human beings, drugs and weapons; corruption; and money laundering.[45] Since their adoption, EAWs have

42 [1998] OJ C 24/1.

43 Art 1.

44 Council Framework Decision 2002/584/JHA of 13 June 2002 on the European arrest warrant and the surrender procedures between Member States, [2002] OJ L 190/1.

45 Art 2.

regularly been relied upon by Member States. Between 2005 and 2013, a total of 99,841 EAWs were issued and the number has been steadily increasing.[46] The average surrender time for those who have consented to extradition is around 15 days; and for those who have not, it is approximately 48 days.[47] This clearly demonstrates that the EAW regime has been recognised by the EU Member States as an important tool to enhance the smoother administration of justice. The ECJ has also upheld the importance of respecting mutual recognition in executing EAWs.[48]

Another important arrangement is the establishment of JITs[49] as envisaged by Article 19 of the UNTOC. It follows from the aforementioned EU Convention on Mutual Assistance in Criminal Matters. However, the 9/11 attacks in the US and some delay in ratification of the Convention prompted the EU to adopt a separate framework decision.[50] These JITs aim to facilitate more proactive cross-border investigations into serious crimes, including organised crime, by seeking a degree of harmonisation on rules governing their operation among Member States.[51] They are to be set up for specific aims and for limited periods only;[52] prosecutors and judges as well as EU institutions such as Europol and Eurojust can participate in them, not just national police officers.[53] The available statistical information reveals that JITs have increasingly been facilitated by Member States and EU institutions. According to Eurojust, there were 122 JITs in 2014, with 45 for crimes such as participation in organised criminal groups; money laundering;

46 European Parliament, *At a Glance: European Arrest Warrant* (European Parliament 2014), 1. It is important to remember that not all of these relate to organised crime as EAWs are used for other serious offences such as theft, grievous bodily harm and murder.

47 European Commission, *Report on the Implementation since 2007 of the Council Framework Decision of 13 June 2002 on the European arrest warrant and the surrender procedures between Member States*, SEC (2011) 430 final, 3.

48 See. for instance, *Ministerul Public – Parchetul de pe lângă Curtea de Apel Constanţa v Ciprian Vasile Radu* [2013] ECLI-39, C-396/11; and *Stefano Melloni v Ministerio Fiscal* [2013] ECLI-107, C-399/11.

49 Council Framework Decision 2002/465/JHA of 13 June 2002 on joint investigation teams, [2002] OJ L 162/1.

50 Ludo Block, 'Combating Organised Crime in Europe: Practicalities of Police Cooperation' (2008) 2 *Policing: A Journal of Policy and Practice* 74, 79. This Framework Decision will cease to exist as soon as the Convention on Mutual Legal Assistance is ratified by all Member States.

51 Tom Schalken and Maarten Pronk, 'On Joint Investigation Teams, Europol and Supervision of Their Joint Actions' (2002) 10 *European Journal of Crime, Criminal Law and Criminal Justice* 78.

52 Art 1.

53 Art 1(12). See also TEU, art 30 and TFEU, art 88; Council Act drawing up a Protocol amending the Convention on the Establishment of a European Police Office (Europol Convention) and the Protocol on the Privileges and Immunities of Europol, the Member of Its Organs, the Deputy Directors and Employees of Europol, [2002] OJ C 312/1; and Council Decision 2002/187/JHA of 28 February 2002 setting up Eurojust with a view to reinforcing the fight against serious crime, [2002] OJ L 61/1.

and human and drug trafficking being formed during that year.[54] This may be compared with 10 new JITs being set up in 2009[55] and 30 in 2011.[56]

Moreover, EIOs are also designed to facilitate more effective mutual assistance in criminal matters. To begin with, the Directive on EIO was adopted as the scope of the pre-existing instruments, most notably the Framework Decision on EEW,[57] is limited as it applies to evidence which already existed and is available in the form of objects, data and documents. This means that EEWs cannot be issued for the purpose of interviewing suspects/witnesses or for obtaining evidence in real time (e.g. through the use of special investigative techniques such as interception of communications).[58] The Directive aims to ameliorate some of these shortcomings. To begin with, the relevant authority in one Member State can issue an order authorising specific investigation measures to be facilitated in another Member State for the purpose of obtaining evidence. With the exception of the gathering of evidence within the framework of JITs,[59] investigation measures under EIOs may include, but are not limited to, the temporary transfer of suspects (Articles 22 and 23) and the use of telephone or video-links (Articles 24 and 25) in addition to the special investigative techniques mentioned above. The Directive also incorporates some safeguards against misuse, such as the tests of necessity and proportionality.[60] Member States must also respect the rights of suspects and defendants. All in all, it is evident that many of the international standards on international cooperation are reflected at the EU level.

2.3.5 Protection and promotion of human rights

The EU and its Member States have made some progress in relation to the protection and promotion of human rights. To begin with, the Charter of Fundamental Rights of the European Union[61] is now legally binding on all Member States by virtue of the entry into force of the Lisbon Treaty in 2009. The Charter is applicable when the EU institutions or Member States are implementing EU law.[62] The relevant rights include a prohibition on torture, inhuman or degrading treatment (Article 4); the right to liberty and security (Article 6); and the right to a fair trial (Article 47), presumption of innocence (Article 48), legality and

54 Eurojust, *Annual Report 2014*, 21.

55 Eurojust, *Annual Report 2009*, 34.

56 Eurojust, *Annual Report 2011*, 11.

57 *Supra* n 33. Another important instrument is the Framework Decision on execution of orders freezing property or evidence.

58 European Commission, *Green Paper on Obtaining Evidence in Criminal Matters from One Member State to Another and Securing Its Admissibility*, COM (2009) 624 final, 4. It should also be noted that the Framework Decision on the EEW was implemented by only 2 States (Denmark and Finland), making this instrument ineffective.

59 Art 3.

60 Art 6.

61 [2010] OJ 83/389.

62 Art 51.

proportionality of criminal offences and punishments (Article 49); and the application of the *ne bis in idem* principle (Article 50). Whilst these are mostly relevant to the perpetrators, Article 47 provides for access to a remedy for those whose rights have been violated. It seems reasonable to assume that this Article applies also to the victims of transnational organised crime which has a human rights dimension, such as human trafficking and exploitation.

Aside from the Charter, Article 82(2) of the TFEU specifically authorises the Council and the European Parliament to establish minimum rules on the rights of individuals in criminal proceedings as well as victims of crime. This is an important change as protection of their rights was not sufficiently provided for under the previous treaty regime. In relation to protection of victims, there were two key instruments under the TEU: the Framework Decision on the Standing of Victims in Criminal Proceedings[63] and the Directive on Compensation for Crime Victims.[64] It has, however, been acknowledged that implementation of these instruments at the national level was far from satisfactory[65] and there were calls for a new instrument under the TFEU.[66] In response, the European Parliament and the Council adopted the Directive Establishing Minimum Standards on the Rights, Support and Protection of Victims of Crime in 2012.[67] This Directive represents an improvement as protection and assistance are to be provided outside of criminal proceedings. To begin with, Article 1 makes it clear that the 'Directive shall apply to victims in a non-discriminatory manner, including with respect to their residence status'. This is significant as many victims of organised crime are non-EU nationals. Measures stipulated under the Directive include, but are not limited to, provision of relevant information; interpretation/translation; access to confidential support services free of charge; legal aid; protection of privacy; and compensation. It is also noteworthy that it obliges Member States to pay particular attention to vulnerabilities surrounding the victims of organised crime.[68] This instrument is further supplemented by

63 Council Framework Decision 2001/220/JHA of 15 March 2001 on the standing of victims in criminal proceedings, [2001] OJ L 82/1.

64 Directive 2004/80/EC of 29 April 2004 relating to compensation to crime victims, [2004] OJ L 261/15.

65 European Commission, *Report Pursuant to Article 18 of the Council Framework Decision of 15 March 2001 on the Standing of Victims in Criminal Proceedings*, COM (2009) 166 final; Portuguese Association for Victim Support, *Victims in Europe: Implementation of the EU Framework Decision on the Standing of Victims in Criminal Proceedings in the Member States of the European Union* (2009); Proposal for a Directive Establishing Minimum Standards on the Rights, Support and Protection of Victims of Crime, COM (2011) 275 final, 2; and the Stockholm Programme, *supra* n 36.

66 Resolution of the Council on a Roadmap for Strengthening the Rights and Protection of Victims, in particular in Criminal Proceedings, [2011] OJ C 187/1.

67 Directive 2012/29/EU of the European Parliament and of the Council of 25 October 2012 establishing minimum standards on the rights, support and protection of victims of crime, and replacing Council Framework Decision 2001/220/JHA, [2012] OJ L 315/58.

68 Art 22(3).

subject-specific instruments such as the Directives on Human Trafficking and Child Sexual Exploitation which contain provisions on the protection of victims of these crimes.

In relation to the rights of defendants, a similar development can be recognised. It was not possible to adopt an instrument on this due to opposition by some Member States such as the Czech Republic, the Republic of Ireland and the UK.[69] In recognition of the need to strengthen their rights during criminal proceedings, the Council published a roadmap for enhancing procedural rights during criminal proceedings in 2009. This mentioned the following priority areas: translation and interpretation; information on rights/charges; legal advice/aid; communication with relatives, employers and consular authorities; special safeguards for vulnerable individuals; and pre-trial detention.[70] Some of these measures have been formalised under the TFEU. The relevant instruments are the Directive on the Right to Interpretation and Translation during Criminal Proceedings,[71] the Directive on the Right to Information during Criminal Proceedings,[72] and the Directive on the Right of Access to a Lawyer in Criminal and EAW Proceedings and to Communicate with Third Persons and Consular Authorities.[73] Proposals in relation to presumption of innocence,[74] legal aid[75] and safeguards for children suspected of crime[76] are being considered and negotiated at the time of writing. Finally, the rights of defendants are further strengthened by the ECHR to which all EU Member States are Parties and to which the EU recently acceded. Many of the human rights principles mentioned earlier have indeed been developed by the ECHR, and therefore the Council of Europe system provides an additional layer of human rights protection. A detailed analysis of relevant human rights norms and principles will be provided throughout this book.

69 Ed Cape and Jacqueline Hodgson, 'The Right to Access to a Lawyer at Police Stations: Making the European Union Directive Work in Practice' (2014) 5 *New Journal of European Criminal Law* 450, 451.

70 [2009] OJ C 295/1.

71 Directive 2010/64/EU of the European Parliament and of the Council of 20 October 2010 on the right to interpretation and translation in criminal proceedings, [2010] OJ L 280/1.

72 Directive 2012/13/EU of the European Parliament and of the Council of 22 May 2012 on the right to information in criminal proceedings, [2012] OJ L 142/1.

73 Directive 2013/48/EU of the European Parliament and of the Council of 22 October 2013 on the right of access to a lawyer in criminal proceedings and in European arrest warrant proceedings, and on the right to have a third party informed upon deprivation of liberty and to communicate with third persons and with consular authorities while deprived of liberty, [2013] OJ L 294/1.

74 Proposal for a Directive of the European Parliament and of the Council on the strengthening of certain aspects of the presumption of innocence and of the right to be present at trial in criminal proceedings, COM (2013) 821 final.

75 Proposal for a Directive of the European Parliament and of the Council on provisional legal aid for suspects or accused persons deprived of liberty and legal aid in European arrest warrant proceedings, COM (2013) 824 final.

76 Proposal for a Directive of the European Parliament and of the Council on procedural safeguards for children suspected or accused in criminal proceedings, COM (2013) 822 final.

2.4 Critical appraisal of the EU action against transnational organised crime

There is no doubt that the EU and its Member States have been more proactive in implementing measures against transnational organised crime individually and collectively compared to other regions of the world, and that the two core principles, approximation of national criminal laws and procedures and mutual recognition of judicial decisions, have gradually found their place in the Area of Freedom, Security and Justice. Further, the relevant instruments related to action against organised crime amply reflect the obligations imposed by the UNTOC. Nevertheless, a closer look at actual implementation of a variety of EU legal instruments reveals a number of issues, shortcomings and concerns. To begin with, approximation of national laws and criminal procedures has not been consistently realised. For instance, the definitions of 'criminal organisation' or 'criminal group' vary between Member States. There is no mention of a 'structured group' under the Austrian,[77] German,[78] Hungarian[79] and Slovenian[80] legislation whilst the Estonian[81] and Spanish[82] Criminal Codes speak of a 'permanent organisation'. The benefit element is not mentioned in most statutes, and the Danish and Swedish legislation do not contain a definition of a criminal group or organisation that is in line with either the Framework Decision or the UNTOC.[83] In terms of offences related to criminal organisations, mere membership (or belonging) is criminalised in Estonia[84] and Greece[85] whilst leading and/or forming a criminal organisation are punished in Bulgaria,[86] Germany,[87] Romania[88] and Slovenia.[89] These discrepancies do not necessarily demonstrate that Member States have been reluctant to abide by the relevant European standards but they certainly highlight the point expressed elsewhere that criminal offences are defined according to a State's own social, political, legal and cultural underpinnings.

In relation to the punishments, an important question to be asked is whether the minimum rules stipulated in the relevant instruments reflect the serious nature of the various forms of organised crime. In other words, are punishments

77 *Supra* ch 1 n 78, s 278.
78 Criminal Code 1971 as amended, s 129.
79 Criminal Code 2012, s 459.
80 Criminal Code 2006, art 294.
81 Criminal Code 2001 as amended, s 255.
82 Criminal Code 1995, art 570 *bis*.
83 European Commission, *Study on Paving the Way for Future Policy Initiatives in the Field of Fight against Organised Crime: The Effectiveness of Specific Criminal Law Measures Targeting Organised Crime* (February 2015), 31, 42 and 43.
84 *Supra* n 81, s 255.
85 Criminal Code 1950 as amended, art 187.
86 Criminal Code 1968 as amended, art 321.
87 *Supra* n 78, s 129.
88 Criminal Code 2009, s 367.
89 *Supra* n 80, art 294.

proportionate to the offences committed? Drug offences are not regarded as seriously in Europe as they are in other regions such as Asia where many States still impose the death penalty. Consequently, 1 to 3 years' imprisonment stipulated in the Framework Decision on Drug Trafficking may be regarded as reasonable by the EU Member States. However, an argument may be made that other crimes such as human trafficking and exploitation should attract heavier penalties as these are widely regarded as gross violations of human rights. Whilst States impose heavier penalties in practice,[90] the Directive on Human Trafficking could have set a higher threshold than 5 years' imprisonment. The same argument can be raised for child sex offences.[91] A related question is whether these punishments are sufficient to deter perpetrators from committing organised crime in the future. The national courts do not normally impose maximum penalties, particularly when perpetrators are first time offenders or minor players. Other factors, such as mitigating circumstances and cooperation with law enforcement authorities, can also affect sentencing. Even with the imposition of custodial sentences, prisoners are often released early on parole. Given the amount of profit criminals can make, spending some time in prison may not ultimately serve as an effective deterrent.

State practice on punishment also reveals a great degree of divergence. Money laundering in Finland attracts a maximum of 2 years' imprisonment[92] whereas the same offence carries up to 5 years' and 18 years' imprisonment in Croatia[93] and Malta[94] respectively. The punishment for drug trafficking in France is imprisonment for 10 years,[95] in Hungary 2 to 8 years[96] and in Spain 3 to 6 years.[97] Further, under the Estonian Criminal Code, human trafficking is punished with imprisonment between 1 and 7 years,[98] and the same offence carries 4 to 10 years in Slovakia.[99] What these examples show is that the minimum rules/thresholds for substantive organised crime offences as envisaged by the TEU and the TFEU have not always been accepted by Member States and that approximation of substantive criminal laws has been difficult to achieve in practice. The principle of State sovereignty therefore remains strong in this area.

It has also not been easy to implement the principle of mutual recognition on the ground. In relation to EAWs, for instance, of the 99,841 EAWs issued between 2005 and 2013, only 26,120 resulted in actual surrender of suspects or

90 See ch 3 on the legislative frameworks on substantive crimes in the United Kingdom (including Northern Ireland) and the Republic of Ireland.
91 Under the Directive on Child Exploitation, coercing a child, who has reached the age of sexual consent, into prostitution attracts only 5 years' imprisonment.
92 Criminal Code 1889 as amended, ch 32, s 6.
93 Criminal Code 1997 as amended, art 279.
94 Prevention of Money Laundering Act 1994, s 3.
95 *Supra* ch 1 n 64, arts 222–236.
96 *Supra* n 79, s 176.
97 *Supra* n 82, art 368.
98 *Supra*, n 81, s 133.
99 Criminal Code 1961 as amended, s 179.

defendants.[100] It has also been pointed out that, whilst Member States must recognise EAWs issued by others, a decision not to execute it is not always respected as EAWs themselves can continue to be valid.[101] In addition, proportionality has been raised as an ongoing problem with EAWs because some States are known to issue them even for very minor offences,[102] such as possession of small quantities of drugs,[103] whilst others do not.

In addition to the difficulty in implementing the two core principles, the scope of some instruments also raises concerns. The EIO regime is a case in point. Its scope is very wide as it can be issued and executed for 'any investigative measure',[104] and it has been rightly argued that this can undermine the principle of legality.[105] Although validation of EIOs by a 'judicial authority' may ensure impartial oversight, it has been pointed out that a public prosecutor can also be regarded as a judicial authority.[106] The same argument has also been raised in relation to the definition of an 'executing authority' which may not require judicial scrutiny or intervention.[107] Further, due to a lack of consistent standards, a wide margin of appreciation is given to a judicial authority in determining the necessity and proportionality of investigative measures to be conducted.[108] Finally, the execution of EIOs can be refused on various grounds, including national security, classified information related to intelligence activities and human rights grounds (Article 11). This opens up the possibility that the mutual recognition principle will not be respected in the same way as other instruments such as EAWs.

In terms of State practice, the implementation of various obligations established under relevant instruments has not been consistent in some areas. For instance, whilst the available evidence suggests that Member States are increasingly reliant on JITs to conduct investigations against organised crime, a number of important issues have been highlighted. Some Member States avoid participation by referring to grounds for refusal such as sovereignty and internal security.[109] The double

100 European Parliament, *supra* n 46, 1.
101 Fair Trial International, *The European Arrest Warrant Seven Years On – The Case for Reform* (Fair Trial International 2011), 6–7.
102 European Parliament, *Report with Recommendations to the Commission on the Review of the European Arrest Warrant*, A7-0039/2014, 13.
103 Dan Helenius, 'Mutual Recognition in Criminal Matters and the Principle of Proportionality: Effective Proportionality or Proportionate Effectiveness?' (2014) 5 *New Journal of European Criminal Law* 349, 361.
104 Art 2.
105 Annalisa Mangiaracina, 'A New and Controversial Scenario in the Gathering of Evidence at the European Level: The Proposal for a Directive on the European Investigation Order' (2014) 10 *Utrecht Law Review* 113, 120.
106 Ines Armada, 'The European Investigation Order and the Lack of European Standards for Gathering Evidence: Is a Fundamental Rights-Based Refusal the Solution?' (2015) 6 *New Journal of European Criminal Law* 8, 12.
107 Ibid., 13.
108 Ibid., 15.
109 European Commission, *supra* n 83, 326.

legal basis (both the Framework Decision on JITs and the Convention on Mutual Legal Assistance) also created some confusion among the law enforcement and judicial authorities in implementing relevant obligations. For instance, the UK incorporated the Framework Decision into its domestic law whilst the Netherlands uses the Convention as the legal basis for JITs.[110] Because of this, the UK was regarded as an ineligible partner on JITs in the past.[111] In addition, the diverse criminal procedures among Member States, including the rules related to disclosure of evidence and retention of personal data as well as the reluctance on the part of the law enforcement authorities to share sensitive intelligence, were said to have made it difficult to set up JITs.[112] This suggests that, in reality, it is not always easy to build mutual trust among frontline law enforcement agencies.

Finally, the protection and promotion of the human rights of victims and perpetrators of transnational organised crime should be carefully assessed. In relation to victim protection, some uncertainty remains for victims of organised crime who are non-EU nationals. Although the principle of non-discrimination stipulated in Article 1 of the Directive on Victims of Crime is to be welcomed, if Member States decide to repatriate or return foreign victims by enforcing immigration laws and regulations, then the support and assistance stipulated in the Directive become meaningless to them. A clear example of this is access to compensation. It is extremely difficult for non-EU victims to seek compensation once they are returned to their States of origin but both the Directives on Victims of Crime and on Compensation are silent as to how non-EU victims can receive appropriate compensation. These instruments should have created additional obligations to allow these victims to remain in the Member States whilst they received relevant assistance and support. This lack of clear obligations can be interpreted as shifting the burden of victimisation to their States of origin. This is not fair, particularly when the victimisation occurs within the EU territories.

As for the rights of perpetrators of transnational organised crime, various issues have also been highlighted. For instance, the European Parliament has expressed concern over the lack of fundamental rights safeguarded within the Framework Decision on EAW.[113] In particular, human rights protection has not been included as part of the mandatory refusal to execute EAWs under Article 3, thus leaving Member States with a wide margin of appreciation.[114] It has also been noted that the absence of minimum standards related to judicial oversight over EAWs has led to inconsistent State practice with regard to protection of fundamental

110 Ibid., 332.

111 Ibid.

112 Ibid., 333–334. See also Toine Spapens, 'Joint Investigation Teams in the European Union: Article 13 JITs and the Alternatives' (2011) 19 *European Journal of Crime, Criminal Law and Criminal Justice* 239.

113 European Parliament, *supra* n 46, 4; and European Commission, *supra* n 47, 7.

114 In *Radu*, *supra* n 48, the European Court of Justice ruled (para 39) that the judicial authorities are not required to refuse to execute EAWs even when fundamental rights have been breached.

rights[115] in areas such as pre-trial detention and access to legal representation during surrender proceedings.[116] Ironically, the protection of human rights has been said to create a degree of tension as the domestic courts may be forced to examine the human rights situations of other Member States in deciding whether to refuse surrender.[117] Despite these concerns, the ECJ has ruled that the principle of mutual recognition can take precedence over the protection of human rights.[118] Such decisions have rightly been criticised.[119]

Similarly, there are several issues with the Directive on Access to a Lawyer. According to Article 2, the Directive is applied from the moment the suspects or accused persons are informed by the competent authorities that they are suspected or accused of having committed a criminal offence. Article 3 further provides that suspects or accused persons shall have access to a lawyer before they are questioned by the police, or another law enforcement or judicial authority. This suggests that the Directive is applicable to the criminal investigation stage. However, it has been pointed out that it does not guarantee the presence of a lawyer during police interrogations.[120] Indeed, Article 3(3)(b) states that this should happen 'in accordance with the procedures under national law', thus giving a margin of appreciation to Member States to decide how the lawyer's participation is to be secured during questioning.[121] It has also been argued that the wording of Article 2 can be manipulated by the authorities to delay access to a lawyer by not informing the suspects or accused persons promptly.[122] Further, when investigations take place in another Member State, the right of access to a lawyer is not always guaranteed.[123] This also applies to EAW proceedings as access to a lawyer is relevant only in the executing and not the issuing State.[124] These loopholes mean that the current EU instruments do not sufficiently protect the rights of suspects and accused persons, and must be supplemented by the ECHR.[125] In summary,

115 European Parliament, *supra* n 46, 5.

116 European Commission, *supra* n 47, 6.

117 On this, see Luisa Marin, 'The European Arrest Warrant and Domestic Legal Orders: Tension between Mutual Recognition and Fundamental Rights: The Italian Case' (2008) 15 *Maastricht Journal of European and Comparative Law* 473.

118 See the cases of *Radu* and *Melloni*, *supra* n 48.

119 Ermioni Xanthopoulou, 'The Quest for Proportionality for the European Arrest Warrant: Fundamental Rights Protection in a Mutual Recognition Environment' (2015) 6 *New Journal of European Criminal Law* 32.

120 Cape and Hodgson, *supra* n 69, 467.

121 Lorena B Winter, 'The EU Directive on the Right to Access to a Lawyer: A Critical Assessment' in Stefano Ruggerri (ed.), *Human Rights in European Criminal Law: New Developments in EU Legislation and Case Law After the Lisbon Treaty* (Springer 2015), 121.

122 Ibid., 118.

123 Ibid., 128.

124 The Directive provides only for the obligation to inform the suspects of the possibility of appointing a lawyer in issuing States but actual appointment is not guaranteed.

125 See, for instance, *Salduz v Turkey*, App no 36391/02 (2008), in which the ECtHR held that access to a lawyer should be provided as from the first interrogation of a suspect by the police (para 55). In addition, in *Cadder v Her Majesty's Advocate* [2010] UKSC 43, the

implementation of the European standards on organised crime, including promotion and protection of human rights, has not always been an easy task.

2.5 Conclusion

This chapter explored the core regional standards on transnational organised crime in EU law. It is important to acknowledge that the EU and its Member States have been making good progress in promoting and implementing individual and collective responses. Similar institutional and legal developments cannot be seen in other regions of the world, such as Africa, the Americas, Asia and the Middle East. In addition, approximation (harmonisation) and mutual recognition principles have clearly been recognised and implemented more proactively by the EU Member States. However, at the same time, the examination of State practice reveals that national implementation is not always consistent as the relevant instruments allow a wide margin of appreciation for Member States. Moreover, there is much to be done in terms of protecting and promoting the human rights of victims and perpetrators of organised crime. Therefore, the role of human rights law is also important within the EU territories.

UK Supreme Court held that the right to a fair trial was breached if the prosecution relies on evidence of the accused's interview by police when a solicitor was not present. Finally, in *Stojkovic v France and Belgium*, App no 25303/08 (2011), the ECtHR held that France was in breach of the right to a fair trial, because the applicant, who was wanted by the French authorities for his involvement in robbery there, did not have access to a lawyer in Belgium where he was detained and interviewed, despite the fact that the letter rogatory designated him as a 'legally assisted witness' entitling him to consult a lawyer.

3 Legislative frameworks on substantive offences

3.1 Introduction

Having explored important international and regional standards on transnational organised crime in the previous two chapters, this chapter will now proceed to examine how they are incorporated and implemented in practice at the national level through the case studies of Northern Ireland (UK) and the Republic of Ireland. It provides an overview of the key legislative frameworks on organised crime offences with a particular focus on participation in organised criminal groups; human trafficking; drug offences; and fiscal/excise fraud, such as fuel and tobacco smuggling, which have been identified as priority areas in both jurisdictions. It begins with an analysis of the definitions of organised crime/criminal groups that are stipulated in the respective legislations. It then explores the legislative frameworks for the aforementioned offences in both jurisdictions, including their punishment provisions. It will be shown that the legislative frameworks in both jurisdictions are largely in conformity with the international and regional standards explored in the previous chapters. Given that both the UK and the Republic of Ireland are based on the common law tradition and have a shared history, many similarities can be perceived in the legislative frameworks. However, some differences also exist, which demonstrates the importance of State sovereignty in action against transnational organised crime. In addition, whilst the identified crimes in Northern Ireland are mainly regulated through Westminster Acts of Parliament as they are regarded as reserved matters, the devolution of policing and criminal justice in this jurisdiction is gradually making some differences in terms of policy development and law enforcement.

3.2 Definitions of organised crime/criminal group

In the UK, despite the fact that it ratified the UNTOC in 2006, there was no legal definition of an 'organised criminal group' until 2015. Prior to that, the law enforcement agencies in the UK, including Northern Ireland, had used working definitions. For instance, the Serious Organised Crime Agency (SOCA), the predecessor to the NCA, provided the following definition:

> The definition of organised crime is individuals, normally working with others, with the capacity and capability to commit serious crime on a continuing basis, which includes elements of planning, control and coordination, and benefits those involved.[1]

This was much broader than the one presented in the UNTOC and the EU Framework Decision on Organised Crime as it did not specify the number of individuals that needed to be involved and therefore could be applied to criminals who worked alone. Northern Ireland used a similar definition with some variations:

> An organised crime gang consists of individuals, normally working with others, with the capacity and capability to commit serious crime on a continuing basis.[2]

One noticeable difference between the SOCA definition and that of the OCTF is the absence of a 'benefit' element in the latter. This left open the possibility of it being applied to a variety of criminal groups and activities. In any event, it is evident from these definitions that the UK has not been following the UNTOC or the EU Framework Decision rigorously. It has also been discovered that frontline officers have paid little attention to the international/European definitions.[3]

In practice, however, the absence of a legal definition has not had a negative impact on law enforcement against organised crime in Northern Ireland. The law enforcement officers have been able to distinguish organised crime from ordinary crime by using a mechanism known as CRIMNET which provides detailed information on organised crime and criminal groups.[4] Consequently, they seem to have developed a good understanding of organised crime without the need to focus too much on the definitions. Interestingly, judges in Northern Ireland have also stated that it is not really necessary to have a definition of organised crime or organised criminal group as crimes are punished sufficiently under relevant legislation.[5] Another important aspect is international cooperation. It may be argued that different perceptions of organised crime can make it difficult to achieve this. However, it has been discovered that the absence of a legal definition in Northern Ireland has not, for instance, undermined cross-border cooperation with the Republic of Ireland.[6] Stakeholders from both jurisdictions believed that variations

1 Home Office, *Local to Global: Reducing the Risk from Organised Crime: Home Office Organised Crime Strategy* (2011), 8.
2 OCTF, *The Northern Ireland Organised Crime Strategy 2012–2014*, 4.
3 Interviews with PSNI officers on 26 October and 17 November 2012.
4 Ibid.
5 Interviews with the Recorder of Belfast, a High Court judge and a Crown Court judge on 25 June, 26 July and 18 September 2013 respectively.
6 Interviews with PSNI officers, *supra* n 3; and Interviews with HMRC officers on 14 November 2012 and 24 June 2013.

were cosmetic and did not cause a problem in working together to tackle organised crime.[7] All of this points to the conclusion that the definitions have not dictated the types of responses to be implemented on the ground. An important consideration for the frontline officers seems to have been having a broad and shared understanding of organised crime/criminal groups.

This situation changed when Westminster enacted the Serious Crime Act 2015. Section 45 now provides a legal definition of 'organised criminal group':

> 'organised criminal group' means a group that
>
> a) has as its purpose, or one of its purposes, the carrying on of criminal activities, and
> b) consists of three or more persons who act, or agree to act, together to further that purpose.

'Criminal activities' within this Act are those carried out 'with a view to obtaining (directly or indirectly) any gain or benefit' and carry a term of imprisonment of 7 years or more. The Explanatory Notes to this legislation mention the UNTOC,[8] and therefore it is clear that this provision was included to comply with this instrument. Having said this, as explained in chapter 1, the threshold for the notion of 'serious crime' is higher under the Serious Crime Act 2015 compared to the UNTOC. This means that some offences such as possession of some types of illegal drugs may not be covered. Further, the UK definition does not specify the type of structure that such a group should have. It is evident therefore that the Serious Crime Act 2015 is not entirely in conformity with the UNTOC which highlights the importance of State sovereignty in implementing action against transnational organised crime.

The adoption of this definition is beneficial in that it can enhance the principle of legality. However, it does not apply to Northern Ireland or Scotland as of this writing due to the devolution of policing and criminal justice. Given the experience of law enforcement agencies noted above, it is not clear whether incorporation of the same definition will make any difference in terms of actual law enforcement. Nevertheless, these jurisdictions are not yet able to prosecute and punish offences related to participation in organised criminal groups. This leaves a legislative gap which may have ramifications such as the concentration of criminal activities in Northern Ireland and Scotland. It is therefore desirable to have a common definition for all jurisdictions in the UK in order to maintain consistency in investigation, prosecution and punishment of crimes committed by organised criminal groups.

Similar to the UK, there is a legal definition of 'criminal organisation' in the Republic of Ireland. Under Part 7 of the Criminal Justice Act 2006, it is defined as:

7 Ibid.; and interviews with Garda officers on 8 and 9 May 2013.
8 Para 140.

a structured group, however organised, that—

(a) is composed of 3 or more persons acting in concert,
(b) is established over a period of time,
(c) has as its main purpose or main activity the commission or facilitation of one or more serious offences in order to obtain, directly or indirectly, a financial or other material benefit.

Moreover, 'a structured group' is a group which:

(a) is not randomly formed for the immediate commission of a single offence, and
(b) does not need to have formally defined roles for its members, continuity of its membership or a developed structure.

Finally, a 'serious offence' carries a minimum of 4 years' imprisonment. Compared to the Serious Crime Act 2015, therefore, the Irish definition is more in line with the UNTOC. Indeed, in explaining his decision to amend the 2006 Bill to include 'Part 7 Organised Crime', the then Minister for Justice, Equality and Defence Michael McDowell stated that the amendments were necessary in order to comply with this instrument.[9] Although the term 'organised' is not included in this definition, the willingness to abide by the international standards is also evident in the Republic of Ireland.

However, the above definition was subsequently amended by the Criminal Justice (Amendment) Act 2009:

'criminal organisation' means a structured group, however organised, that has as its main purpose or activity the commission or facilitation of a serious offence;

'Structured group' means a group of 3 or more persons, which is not randomly formed for the immediate commission of a single offence, and the involvement in which by 2 or more of those persons is with a view to their acting in concert;

for the avoidance of doubt, a structured group may exist notwithstanding the absence of all or any of the following:

(a) formal rules or formal membership, or any formal roles for those involved in the group;
(b) any hierarchical or leadership structure;
(c) continuity of involvement by persons in the group.

9 Select Committee on Justice, Equality, Defence and Women's Rights Debate, 'Criminal Justice Bill 2004' (10 May 2006). The Republic of Ireland ratified the UNTOC in June 2010.

The most notable aspect of the amended definition is the removal of the phrase 'a financial or other material benefit'. This makes the current Irish definition wide in scope compared to the Serious Crime Act 2015. In the Irish context, the legislation also allows the following special measures to be taken once a crime is committed by a criminal organisation:

1) The use of the Special Criminal Court.[10]
2) Higher sentences for organised crime offences.[11]
3) Ability of the court to draw inferences from failure to answer questions, failure to account for movements, actions or associations.[12]
4) Admissibility of opinion evidence on the existence and operations of criminal gangs by Garda officers.[13]

These raise a number of issues from a human rights perspective. The Irish Council for Civil Liberties (ICCL) made the important point that the definition could institutionalise a popular notion of organised crime and also be used to justify quite draconian crime control.[14] A similar view was expressed by the Irish Human Rights Commission prior to the enactment of the 2009 Act.[15] The law enforcement community in the Republic of Ireland disagreed with this, stating that, in general, they were able to distinguish organised crime from ordinary crime and apply the definition appropriately.[16] This was also confirmed by a High Court judge in the Republic who noted that the law enforcement agencies had not abused the definition.[17] In any event, the definitions also do not seem to be significant when it comes to law enforcement in the Republic of Ireland as the key agencies have a shared understanding of what organised crime or a criminal group is.

It is useful at this stage to see whether the above definitions can be used to prosecute and punish criminal groups in both jurisdictions. According to the NCA, approximately 5,800 criminal groups are currently operating in the UK.[18] The majority of these groups are said to be based on the network model explained in Chapter 1 although there are also structured groups that are mainly based on familial ties.[19] The PSNI has estimated that there are between 160 and 180

10 S 8.
11 Ss 6 and 12.
12 S 9.
13 S 7.
14 Interview with an ICCL representative on 23 October 2013. See also ICCL, *Combating Organised Crime and Respecting the Rule of Law: Human Rights Based Alternatives to the Criminal Justice (Amendment) Bill 2009*, 10–11.
15 Irish Human Rights Commission, *Observations on the Criminal Justice (Amendment) Bill 2009*, 12.
16 Interviews with Garda officers, *supra* n 7; and interviews with public prosecutors on 23 July 2013.
17 Interview with a High Court judge on 23 June 2013.
18 NCA, *supra* intro n 23.
19 Ibid.

organised crime groups operating in their jurisdiction.[20] It has become evident that these groups are mainly home-grown, small groups[21] as opposed to being structured or hierarchical organisations. A similar picture emerges in the Republic of Ireland[22] although the number of criminal groups there is much less at around 25 groups according to the Commissioner of An Garda Síochána.[23] However, the presence of foreign criminal groups has also been recognised. For instance, Chinese criminal groups are involved in cannabis cultivation in Northern Ireland whereas the involvement of Vietnamese nationals has been recognised for the same crime in the Republic.[24] Many of the home-based criminals in both jurisdictions are said to have forged alliances with these and other criminals located in States such as Cambodia, Malaysia, the Netherlands and Spain in order to facilitate drug trafficking and tobacco smuggling.[25] In summary, it is evident that there is no single way to describe organised criminal groups in Northern Ireland and the Republic of Ireland as different types of groups are carrying out criminal activities. Having said this, the legal definitions stipulated in the respective legislation are broad enough to cover these groups, provided that they are applied appropriately.

3.3 Participation in an organised criminal group

The UNTOC and the EU Framework Decision on Organised Crime oblige States to criminalise participation in organised criminal groups. For its part, the Serious Crime Act 2015 has created the new offence of 'participating in the activities of an organised criminal group' which carries a maximum of 5 years' imprisonment:

> (1) A person who participates in the criminal activities of an organised crime group commits an offence.
> (2) For this purpose, a person participates in the criminal activities of an organised crime group if the person takes part in any activities that the person knows or reasonably suspects—
>
> (a) are criminal activities of an organised crime group, or
> (b) will help an organised crime group to carry on criminal activities.
>
> . . .
>
> (4) Activities are within this subsection if—
>
> . . .
>
> (b) they constitute an offence in England and Wales punishable on conviction on indictment with imprisonment for a term of 7 years or more.[26]

20 Ibid.
21 OCTF, *supra* intro n 9; and interviews with PSNI officers, *supra* n 3.
22 See, for instance, PSNI and An Garda Síochána, *supra* intro n 12.
23 *Independent*, 'Garda Commissioner Says 25 Criminal Gangs at Centre of Ireland's Underworld' 21 November 2014.
24 PSNI and An Garda Síochána, *Cross-Border Organised Crime Assessment 2012*, 8.
25 Ibid., 5 and 22.
26 S 45.

This provision has incorporated the second option available under the UNTOC. In effect, this can be used to prosecute and punish the bosses of criminal groups who 'instruct others to act on their behalf but who do not themselves carry out criminal acts'.[27] This reduces the need to enact more legislation proscribing mere membership in criminal organisations, such as the US did under the Racketeer Influenced and Corrupt Organizations Act 1970.[28] In addition, the offence of conspiracy can be prosecuted under the Criminal Law Act 1977 which means that both participation offences can be punished in the UK. Finally, the punishment of 5 years' imprisonment conforms to the EU Framework Decision on Organised Crime.

However, this participation offence under Section 45 does not apply to Northern Ireland. This represents a clear legislative gap and increases the possibility of forum shopping by criminals. This problem is mitigated to some extent by the Criminal Attempts and Conspiracy (Northern Ireland) Order 1983 which has, in essence, incorporated the Criminal Law Act 1977 of England and Wales by recognising the offence of conspiracy in the same way as they do.[29] This can certainly apply if one agrees to commit various forms of organised crime but is not necessarily suited to targeting others who do not directly commit crimes. In order to maintain consistency throughout the UK and prevent organised crime more effectively, Northern Ireland should establish offences related to participation in an organised criminal group in addition to the offence of conspiracy.

In the Republic of Ireland, the Criminal Justice Act 2006 as amended by the Criminal Justice (Amendment) Act 2009 is pertinent to this. Section 72 provides that:

> 1) A person is guilty of an offence if, with knowledge of the existence of the organisation referred to in this subsection, the person participates in or contributes to any activity (whether constituting an offence or not)—
>
> (*a*) intending either to—
>
> (i) enhance the ability of a criminal organisation or any of its members to commit, or
>
> (ii) facilitate the commission by a criminal organisation or any of its members of, a serious offence

27 Home Office, *Serious Crime Act 2015 Fact Sheet: Offence of Participating in Activities of Organised Criminal Group* (March 2015), 1.

28 There have been some discussions on whether to criminalise membership of a criminal organisation since the mid-1990s, but this never materialised. See Home Affairs Committee, *Third Report on Organised Crime: Minutes of Evidence and Memoranda* (1994), 115; and Home Office, *One Step Ahead: A 21st Century Strategy to Defeat Organised Crime* (Home Office 2004), 40.

29 For Scotland, see *Maxwell v H.M. Advocate* 1980 JC 40.

It is evident that the Irish legislation criminalises the second option under the UNTOC. In addition, conspiracy is a common law offence[30] in the Republic of Ireland and is punished in a similar way to how it is in the UK. Having said this, Section 71 of the 2006 Act also provides for an offence of conspiracy for serious crimes,[31] and it has been noted that the 2009 Act has developed the 2006 Act to make conspiracy more relevant to organised crime.[32]

There are, however, noticeable differences between the UK and Irish versions. For instance, the punishment is different as the Irish legislation provides for a maximum of 15 years' imprisonment, a term that is 3 times longer than in the UK legislation. This certainly sends a clear message that the Irish government takes organised crime seriously as well as having a stronger deterrent effect. In addition, whilst full knowledge in relation to the existence of a criminal organisation is required under the Irish legislation, it is also possible to be prosecuted for having 'reasonable suspicion' in line with the UK's Serious Crime Act 2015. Here, although the UK legislation may increase the rate of prosecution in relation to participation offences, it may also lead to inconsistency in law enforcement depending on how 'reasonable suspicion' is interpreted. It is therefore important for clear guidance to be provided in due course. Further, in addition to participation in a criminal organisation, the Irish legislation created a new offence of 'directing' such an organisation,[33] which includes supervising/controlling criminal activities or giving orders. Interestingly, the punishment for this offence is heavier as it attracts a maximum sentence of life imprisonment. It is clear that Section 71A is designed to target bosses of criminal organisations or others who do not directly commit various forms of organised crime. From the point of view of legality, this provision is much better than the UK version as the wording of the latter ('any activity') is vague and excessively wide in scope.

An important issue was raised by the Deputy Director of Public Prosecutions in relation to the Irish legislation. In practice, it seems difficult to prove a connection between the existence of a criminal organisation, which can be established by the opinion evidence of a member of An Garda Síochána,[34] and the proof that the accused participated in the activities of the organisation.[35] For this reason, there seems to be a preference to prosecute for substantive offences such as drug trafficking as this enhances the chance of successful prosecutions.[36] A defence lawyer in this jurisdiction also pointed out that there was never any immediate need for organised crime legislation as criminal gangs are mostly arrested for

30 See, for instance, *R v Jones* [1832] 110 ER 485, 487.

31 The legislation does not replace the common law offence, however.

32 Law Reform Commission, *Report on Inchoate Offences* (2010), 72.

33 S 71A.

34 Criminal Justice Act 2006, s 71B, as inserted by Criminal Justice (Amendment) Act 2009, s 7.

35 Interview with the Deputy Director of Public Prosecution on 23 July 2013.

36 Ibid.

stand-alone crimes.[37] The recent research into the legislative frameworks to address organised crime within the EU territories also seems to confirm this.[38] Nevertheless, participation offences and offences related to directing a criminal organisation or giving orders can be useful as these have the potential to curtail activities which contribute to the actual commission of organised crime. This is the reason why these offences are provided for in international and European standards. However, it is essential that sufficient procedural safeguards are afforded to the suspects or defendants of transnational organised crime and that both jurisdictions provide clear guidance on the interpretation of various terms in their respective legislation.

3.4 Human trafficking

With respect to national approaches to human trafficking, there are some differences between Northern Ireland and the rest of the UK. The most recent legislation that is applicable to England and Wales on this subject is the Modern Slavery Act 2015. This legislation consolidated the previous statutes that were applicable to human trafficking and exploitation: the Sexual Offences Act 2003 (trafficking for sexual exploitation); the Asylum and Immigration (Treatment of Claimants, etc.) Act 2004 (trafficking for labour exploitation); and the Coroners and Justice Act 2009 (slavery and forced labour). Section 2 of the 2015 Act stipulates the following definition of human trafficking:

> (1) A person commits an offence if the person arranges or facilitates the travel of another person ("V") with a view to V being exploited.
> (2) It is irrelevant whether V consents to the travel (whether V is an adult or a child).
> (3) A person may in particular arrange or facilitate V's travel by recruiting V, transporting or transferring V, harbouring or receiving V, or transferring or exchanging control over V.
> (4) A person arranges or facilitates V's travel with a view to V being exploited only if—
>
> (a) the person intends to exploit V (in any part of the world) during or after the travel, or
> (b) the person knows or ought to know that another person is likely to exploit V (in any part of the world) during or after the travel.

According to Section 3, 'exploitation' includes slavery, servitude, forced labour, sexual exploitation, removal of organs and securing services by force/threat or from children and vulnerable persons. Taken together, the trafficking definition under the 2015 Act is similar to the ones provided by the Trafficking Protocol

37 Interview with a defence lawyer on 23 June 2013.
38 European Commission, *supra* ch 2 n 83, 206.

attached to the UNTOC and the EU Human Trafficking Directive. This once again demonstrates the willingness of the UK government to abide by the relevant standards. One noticeable difference from these instruments is the lack of the element of coercion and/or deception, making the definition under the 2015 Act somewhat wider. Another important area is the increase in the punishment from 14 years to life imprisonment. This is a welcome change as it sends a message to criminals that they will face severe consequences for engaging in this crime. Finally, in terms of criminal jurisdiction, the nationality principle is recognised in addition to the territorial principle.[39]

The Modern Slavery Act 2015 does not extend to Northern Ireland. In this jurisdiction, the Northern Ireland Assembly recently passed the Human Trafficking and Exploitation (Criminal Justice and Support for Victims) Act (Northern Ireland) 2015 which has created identical offences of human trafficking, slavery, servitude and forced labour, with the same levels of punishment for them, thereby maintaining consistency throughout the UK.[40] Having said this, there are a few important differences between Northern Ireland and England and Wales in terms of their legislative frameworks. For instance, the Northern Irish legislation clearly stipulates so-called 'aggravating circumstances'[41] whereas the Modern Slavery Act 2015 does not. A practical difference here is that the courts in Northern Ireland must take these into consideration and reflect them in sentencing whereas a degree of discretion is afforded to the courts in England and Wales. In this regard, the relevant Sentencing Guidelines[42] do not contain all circumstances that are stipulated by the Northern Irish legislation, such as offences committed by public officials, and this creates the possibility of convicted traffickers not receiving appropriate sentences there. In addition, the Northern Irish legislation provides for a minimum sentence of 2 years' imprisonment for trafficking and exploitation offences.[43] This is an important difference as the Sentencing Guidelines for sex trafficking in England and Wales provide for a starting point of 18 months for trafficking which is done without coercion or deception.[44] Moreover, although human trafficking is regarded as an indictable offence in Northern Ireland (it can be tried only before the Crown Court), it is a hybrid offence in England and Wales (triable by either the Magistrates' Court or the Crown Court), attracting summary convictions of up to 12 months' imprisonment. Therefore, the impact of devolution is evident in Northern Ireland.

39 S 2(6).

40 In Scotland, the Human Trafficking and Exploitation (Scotland) Act 2015 has been enacted. It contains a definition similar to the ones provided by the Modern Slavery Act 2015 and the Human Trafficking and Exploitation (Criminal Justice and Support for Victims) Act (Northern Ireland) 2015.

41 S 6.

42 Sentencing Council, *Sexual Offences: Definitive Guideline* (2014).

43 S 7.

44 Sentencing Council, *supra* n 42, 101.

In addition to these criminal justice aspects, discrepancies can be recognised with regard to the protection of victims of human trafficking. The Northern Irish legislation has included provisions on this, and this is significant as it enhances the accountability of the Northern Ireland government if it does not provide necessary protection. Section 18(4) now specifies a period of 45 days during which the so-called Competent Authorities[45] make a decision as to the status of the victims (known as 'a reflection period') and also make it clear that provision of assistance and support must not be conditional upon victims participating in criminal investigation or proceedings.[46] In addition, those in a position to provide assistance must pay particular attention to the vulnerabilities of victims, such as their gender, age and physical/mental illness, including disabilities.[47] Finally, the Act stipulates a non-exhaustive list of assistance measures which include, but are not limited to, safe accommodation, financial/material assistance, medical and psychological assistance and legal representation. In looking at these, it is evident that the Northern Irish legislation on human trafficking is far more advanced than the Modern Slavery Act 2015 in terms of victim protection and is more in line with the EU Trafficking Directive.

Finally, the legislative frameworks designed to address the demand for trafficked people should be analysed. In relation to sexual exploitation, the Policing and Crime Act 2009 imposes a fine of up to £1,000 upon those who purchase sexual services from trafficked victims.[48] This applies even where clients have no knowledge that those providing sexual services are trafficked victims. The offences of this type are commonly known as strict liability offences as they do not require criminal intent. Whilst this may raise an issue of fairness, offences of this type[49] have existed in this jurisdiction to address issues of social concern and it has been held that strict liability offences do not necessarily infringe presumption of innocence under the ECHR.[50] It is also important to mention that the Northern Irish legislation has amended the Sexual Offences (Northern Ireland) Order 2008 in order to prohibit purchase of sexual services generally.[51] Lord Morrow, who originally proposed this new offence, believed that this would reduce the demand for prostitution as well as sex trafficking.[52] He based his argument on the perceived success of Sweden which has also criminalised prostitution generally. However,

45 They are the UK Human Trafficking Centre and the Home Office Immigration and Visas.

46 S 18(5).

47 Ibid.

48 Ss 14 (England and Wales) and 15 (Northern Ireland).

49 These also include road traffic offences and possession of prohibited items such as weapons and drugs.

50 *R v Lambert* [2001] UKHL 37; and *R v G* [2008] UKHL 37.

51 S 15.

52 *Proposed Changes in the Law to Tackle Human Trafficking: Consultation Paper* (August 2012), 11–12.

it has been argued that the Swedish model has actually driven prostitution indoors and online,[53] and therefore has not reduced the demand for prostitution or human trafficking.[54] Whether this new offence in Northern Ireland will produce the desired result remains to be seen.

As for labour exploitation, the prohibition of slavery and forced labour under the Modern Slavery Act 2015 could discourage employers in various sectors from enslaving trafficked victims. This is complemented by the Immigration, Nationality and Asylum Act 2006 which addresses the hiring of illegal migrants with a civil penalty of up to £20,000 per migrant and/or imprisonment of up to 2 years.[55] There are a couple of shortcomings to this legislation: first, it mainly applies to third country nationals and excludes trafficked victims who are UK or EU nationals with the right to stay and work; secondly, imprisonment for 2 years may not be regarded as an effective punishment. It is important to mention here that the Immigration Bill 2015, currently under consideration before Parliament, will make some changes when enacted. For instance, in addition to the requirement of 'full knowledge' that someone is an illegal migrant, the phrase 'reasonable cause to believe' will be inserted into the relevant provision of the 2006 Act.[56] More importantly, the penalty will be increased from 2 to 5 years' imprisonment.[57] Further, illegal working closure notices and enforcement orders[58] can be imposed. Taken together, these have the potential to deter employers from employing and exploiting vulnerable migrants.

Similarly, the Republic of Ireland has a single statute to combat human trafficking: the Criminal Law (Human Trafficking) Act 2008. Under this legislation:

> "traffics" means, in relation to a person (including a child)—
>
> (a) procures, recruits, transports or harbours the person, or
>
> (i) transfers the person to,
> (ii) places the person in the custody, care or charge, or under the control, of, or
> (iii) otherwise delivers the person to,
>
> another person,
>
> (b) causes a person to enter or leave the State or to travel within the State,

53 Global Alliance against Traffic in Women, *Moving Beyond 'Supply and Demand' Catchphrases: Assessing the Uses and Limitations of Demand Based Approaches in Anti Trafficking* (GAATW 2011), 29–30.
54 The Trafficking Research Project, *Submission to Lord Morrow's Private Bill* (October 2012), 4.
55 Ss 15 and 21.
56 Cl 9.
57 Ibid.
58 Cl 12 and Sch 3.

(c) takes custody of a person or takes a person—
    (i) into one's care or charge, or
    (ii) under one's control,

or

(d) provides the person with accommodation or employment.[59]

In terms of the *actus reus* of this offence, this definition is similar to the UK/Northern Ireland one as there is no element of deception and/or coercion stipulated in the Trafficking Protocol and the EU Human Trafficking Directive. One noticeable difference is the inclusion of a provision of accommodation or employment. This allows landlords as well as those who provide jobs to be covered by this legislation. In relation to exploitation, the definition of exploitation under the 2008 Act has been problematic. Whilst it mentions labour/sexual exploitation and removal of organs, it has not covered new and emerging forms, such as begging and exploitation in criminal activities. This has been addressed by the Criminal Law (Human Trafficking) (Amendment) Act 2013 which has extended the scope of exploitation to include these missed issues. In addition, similar to the Modern Slavery Act 2015, the punishment for human trafficking is also life imprisonment.

A major shortcoming in the Irish legislation is that it does not contain provisions on protection of victims of trafficking although a certain amount of assistance, such as a reflection period, medical/psychological assistance and subsistence, is provided outside the legislative framework.[60] As argued above, the absence of a legal basis can be problematic from the point of view of accountability and the importance of having legislation on protection was stressed by the Group of Experts on Action against Trafficking in Human Beings (GRETA) established by the European Convention on Action against Trafficking in Human Beings 2005.[61] In 2010 the Irish government proposed legislation in the form of the Immigration, Residence and Protection Bill which would introduce rules on the identification of victims, a reflection period and residence permits. Whilst this is a positive development, the fact that this has not yet been enacted casts some doubt on the commitment of the Irish government to protect the victims of human trafficking.

In relation to the demand for trafficked people, the 2008 Act prohibits soliciting or importuning for the purpose of prostitution of trafficked victims.[62] The

59 S 1.

60 Administrative Immigration Arrangements for the Protection of Victims of Human Trafficking, <www.inis.gov.ie/en/INIS/Pages/PB08000021>.

61 ETS No. 197. See *Report Concerning the Implementation of the Council of Europe Convention on Action against Trafficking of Human Beings by Ireland* (September 2013), 63. A similar opinion was previously expressed in relation to the United Kingdom in *Report Concerning the Implementation of the Council of Europe Convention on Action against Trafficking of Human Beings by United Kingdom* (September 2012), 87.

62 S 5.

punishment regime is tougher in this jurisdiction as the Act provides for up to 5 years' imprisonment. Interestingly, these acts are not regarded as strict liability offences as the legislation provides for a defence of no knowledge or reasonable belief. This difference in turn is reflected in the severity of punishment. As for labour exploitation, although the 2008 Act provides definitions of slavery and forced labour, it does not explicitly prohibit these crimes. It has been argued that the definition of trafficking under this legislation, particularly 'providing employment and accommodation' could be used to prosecute and punish forced labour.[63] There is a risk associated with this reasoning as providing employment and exploiting or enslaving trafficked victims are not necessarily the same acts. It also seems difficult to establish a link between providing accommodation and forced labour. A lack of stand-alone offences of slavery and forced labour affects the principle of legality and enhances judicial discretion which may go beyond the original legislative intent. In order to avoid this, it is desirable to establish these offences in the Republic of Ireland. Having said this, the Employment Permits Act 2003 prohibits hiring migrants without proper employment permits similar to the UK's Immigration, Nationality and Asylum Act 2006. The punishments are substantially higher with a maximum fine of €250,000 and/or 10 years' imprisonment upon conviction on indictment.[64] Whilst these may have a stronger deterrent effect, various concerns were expressed by lawyers and NGOs that this legislation simultaneously denies the victims access to remedies because of the illegal nature of such employment.[65] There is, therefore, scope for further examination and improvement in the Republic of Ireland.

3.5 Drug offences

On paper, the UK legislative framework for prosecuting drug offences seems sufficient both in terms of the definition of offences and the penalties they attract. The primary legislation is the Misuse of Drugs Act 1971 which defines a series of offences, including unlawful supply, import or export (all these are collectively known as 'trafficking' offences); unlawful production; and possession. Each offence is rated against a classification system which is used to set an appropriate penalty. For instance, the maximum sentence for supplying, importing or exporting Class A drugs, such as cocaine, heroin and ecstasy, is life imprisonment; in relation to Classes B (e.g. cannabis and ketamine) and C drugs (e.g. anabolic steroids and GHB) it is 14 years' imprisonment. The maximum sentence for possession is 7 years' imprisonment for Class A drugs, reduced to 5 years for Class B drugs

63 See, for instance, an opinion of Ellis Barry presented in a seminar organised by the Migrant Rights Council and the Irish Congress of Trade Unions in June 2010; and Department of Justice and Equality, *Examination of the Adequacy of Current Irish Legislation in Relation to the Criminalisation of Forced Labour* (2011), 14.

64 S 2.

65 See *Hussein v The Labour Court & Anor* [2012] IEHC 364; and GRETA's Irish Report, *supra* n 61, 13.

and 2 years for Class C drugs. In addition, the Drugs Act 2005 stipulates aggravating circumstances for the supply of drugs, such as distribution near educational establishments and the use of minors as couriers. The legislative framework in Northern Ireland is the same due to the fact that the misuse of drugs is a reserved matter. Taken together, drug legislation in the UK is generally in conformity with the 1988 UN Narcotic Trafficking Convention and the EU Framework Decision on Drug Trafficking mentioned in previous chapters, and the law enforcement community in this jurisdiction has expressed the view that the current arrangements are good enough to tackle drug offences.[66] A High Court judge also stated that there was no major lacuna in the current drug legislation.[67]

In the Republic of Ireland, the primary legislation is the Misuse of Drugs Act 1977 as amended.[68] This is supplemented by the Criminal Justice (Psychoactive Substances) Act 2010 which covers substances which are not specifically proscribed under the 1977 Act. These statutes define the penalties for unlawful production, possession and supply of drugs. Unlike the UK, the Republic of Ireland does not have a similar classification system. For simple possession of drugs, the penalties range from a fine of €1,000 (or €1,250 on conviction on indictment) for cannabis to up to 7 years' imprisonment for other drugs.[69] In relation to other offences, the penalties are based on the values and quantities of the drugs. Under Section 15A of the 1977 Act, it is an offence to be in possession of controlled drugs with a market value of over €13,000 for sale or supply. The penalties for this offence have been amended by the Criminal Justice Act 1999 and the Criminal Justice Act 2007. Now, any person found guilty can face up to life imprisonment and a fine. Further, where the market value of the drugs is €13,000 or more, a person faces a mandatory minimum sentence of 10 years save in exceptional or special circumstances. Similar penalties apply to any person convicted of importing drugs with a value of €13,000 or more.[70]

Although the Irish legislative framework on drug offences is also generally in line with the relevant international and regional standards, various issues have been raised at the same time. Garda officers, prosecutors and defence lawyers all agreed that a classification system was desirable for clarity and coherence.[71] They pointed to the fact that a person found in possession of cannabis with a market value of €13,000 could attract the same custodial sentence as a person found in possession of €13,000 worth of heroin or cocaine. A question was also raised as

66 Interviews with PSNI officers, *supra* n 3.

67 *Supra* n 5.

68 See the Misuse of Drugs Act 1984, the Criminal Justice Act 1999, the Criminal Justice Act 2006, the Criminal Justice Act 2007 and the Misuse of Drugs (Amendment) Act 2015.

69 On conviction on indictment. The penalty is up to 12 months' imprisonment on summary conviction and/or €2,500 fine.

70 Misuse of Drugs Act 1977, ss 15B and 27, as amended by the Criminal Justice Act 2006.

71 Interviews with Garda officers *supra* n 7; interviews with defence lawyers on 16 December 2013; and interviews with public prosecutors, *supra* n 16.

to the reasonableness of applying a mandatory sentence of 10 years for possession of drugs with an estimated street value of over €13,000 because such a sentence disregards the need for individualisation of punishment (taking into account offenders' personal circumstances) and proportionality in sentencing.[72] The Court of Criminal Appeal even called it draconian in at least one case.[73] Defence lawyers and the ICCL additionally highlighted the undesirable consequence of overcrowded prisons because of the mandatory sentences.[74] Some of these concerns were shared by the Law Reform Commission in its report on mandatory sentences, including those related to drug offences, published in June 2013.[75] After a careful analysis of the legislation, jurisprudence, other State practices and scholarly publications, it observed that the existing arrangement was not effective as it did not serve as a strong deterrent.[76] It also recognised that the market value of €13,000 was prioritised at the expense of other relevant factors such as 'the role, motive and the state of mind of offenders'. This resulted in inconsistent and disproportionate punishments which affected the principle of justice.[77] Consequently, the Commission recommended that presumptive sentencing under the 1977 Act should be repealed.[78] The recent report also showed that in many cases such sentencing was not imposed by the Irish courts in practice.[79] This indeed enhances the call for its abolition.

In addition, an interesting constitutional issue has emerged recently in the Republic of Ireland. In the case of *Bederev v Ireland*,[80] the Court of Criminal Appeal held that the government's power to declare certain substances as 'controlled drugs' under Section 2(2) of the 1977 Act breached Article 15.2.1 of the Irish Constitution which provides that 'the sole and exclusive power of making laws for the State is hereby vested in the Oireachtas', thus effectively legalising some of the controlled drugs designated under the Act, such as ecstasy and ketamine. In response, the Oireachtas rushed through emergency legislation in the form of the Misuse of Drugs (Amendment) Act 2015 which added the controlled drugs designated by the Government Order to the Schedule of the 1977 Act, once again making them illegal.[81] This legislation also allows the Oireachtas to reconfirm statutory instruments adopted under the 1977 Act as valid and enforceable as if they were Acts of the Oireachtas.[82] In contrast, controlled drugs

72 Department of Justice and Equality, *White Paper on Crime, Third Discussion Document: Overview of Submissions Received* (April 2011), 39.
73 *DPP v D.L.* [2008] IECCA 133.
74 *Supra* n 14 and 71.
75 Law Reform Commission, *Mandatory Sentences* (June 2013).
76 Ibid., 175.
77 Ibid., 175–176, 178, 181.
78 See also Irish Penal Reform Trust, *Position Paper 3: Mandatory Sentencing* (August 2013).
79 Judicial Research Office, *Analysis of Sentencing for Possession or Importation of Drugs for Sale or Supply* (December 2013).
80 [2015] IECA 38.
81 Misuse of Drugs (Amendment) Bill 2015: Explanatory and Financial Memorandum.
82 Ibid.

are listed in a Schedule of the UK's Misuse of Drugs Act 1971, and the same question was never raised in that jurisdiction.

There are two more relevant issues that are pertinent to both jurisdictions. The first is the status of new psychoactive substances (NPS), commonly referred to as 'legal highs'. According to the OCTF, the emergence of NPS has been posing challenges for law enforcement authorities in Northern Ireland.[83] These substances are often purchased from 'head shops' and internet sites. If the internet servers are located abroad, this makes investigations more complicated. Classification of NPS for the purpose of criminalisation is not straightforward given the amount of time it takes to carefully analyse their contents and effects. According to the law enforcement community in Northern Ireland, they have indeed been experiencing some difficulties in detecting and preventing the use of such substances.[84] In the UK, including Northern Ireland, the Misuse of Drugs Act 1971 also regulates NPS. An important amendment was made to it through the Police Reform and Social Responsibility Act 2011 which allows the Home Secretary to issue Temporary Class Drug Orders for substances which were not appropriately classified previously after consulting with the Advisory Council on the Misuse of Drugs. The government then has up to 12 months to place these substances under permanent control through the 1971 Act.[85] Importation, exportation, production and supply of substances placed under these orders will attract the maximum penalties of 14 years' imprisonment and an unlimited fine on indictment. The UK government claims that this regime has been successful as it has been able to ban over 500 substances.[86]

There has been ongoing debate about the status of NPS in the UK. At the beginning of 2013, for instance, the UK All Party Parliamentary Group (APPG) for Drug Policy Reform published a report entitled *Towards a Safer Drug Policy: Challenges and Opportunities Arising from 'Legal Highs'*. After consulting a number of relevant experts and stakeholders, the APPG made some recommendations. First, it noted that the Temporary Class Drug Orders should last indefinitely to allow sufficient time to assess the risk of NPS.[87] It also noted with concern the ineffectiveness of the current classification system and recommended that the Advisory Council on the Misuse of Drugs should be an independent entity so that it can facilitate a risk-based assessment without political influences.[88] Finally, instead of simply banning NPS, the APPG urged the UK government to consider alternative approaches, such as regulation through trading standards

83 OCTF, *supra* intro n 9, 9.

84 Interviews with PSNI officers, *supra* n 3.

85 See Advisory Council on the Misuse of Drugs, *Temporary Class Drug Order on Benzofury and NBOMe Compounds – Letter to the Home Secretary* (June 2013).

86 Psychoactive Substances Bill Factsheet: Overview of the Misuse of Drugs Act 1971 (June 2015).

87 APPG, *Towards a Safer Drug Policy: Challenges and Opportunities Arising from 'Legal Highs'* (2013), 6.

88 Ibid., 7.

and/or consumer protection legislation as well as decriminalisation.[89] These alternative approaches were also supported by experts and scholars.[90] The ineffectiveness of the current drug laws in addressing NPS was also recognised by the Parliamentary Home Affairs Committee[91] as well as the Expert Panel on NPS.[92]

In January 2016, the Psychoactive Substances Act 2016 was enacted. The Expert Panel on NPS had previously endorsed the measures to tackle the supply of NPS and this legislation responds to this with the creation of new offences of producing, supplying and importing/exporting NPS with a term of 7 years' imprisonment.[93] In order to deter suppliers, such as head shops, from selling NPS, the Act also provides civil penalties through prohibition and premises notices/orders.[94] In addition, the law enforcement authorities are to be granted additional powers of entry, search and seizure.[95] Whilst the Act does not intend to criminalise the users of NPS, it is evident that the government is not willing to consider other approaches, such as those noted above, to regulate the supply side of the chain. Another important point to note is the definition of a 'psychoactive substance'. It is understood to mean 'any substance which is capable of producing psychoactive effect in a person'.[96] This is a vague and broad definition which may affect the principle of legality. Further, inconsistency in law enforcement could also result as the effect of NPS can be different for each individual.

In contrast, the legislation related to NPS, i.e. the Criminal Justice (Psychoactive Substances) Act 2010, has been in operation for some time in the Republic of Ireland. This demonstrates that the Irish government has been more willing to acknowledge the dangers of NPS and recognised the need to deal with them earlier than the UK. Indeed, this legislation has been used as a model for the aforementioned UK Act, which is the reason why many provisions appear more or less the same. For instance, the 2010 Act has introduced offences for selling, importing and exporting NPS,[97] and also provides for civil penalties of prohibition notices and orders as well as enhanced powers for entry, search and seizure.[98] However, there are some notable differences. The 2010 Act has created the offence of advertising NPS which does not appear in the UK Act. In addition, a

89 Ibid., 8.

90 Adam Winstock and Chris Wilkins, *'Legal Highs': The Challenges of New Psychoactive Substances* (Transnational Institute 2011); Toby Seddon, 'Drug Policy and Global Regulatory Capitalism: The Case of New Psychoactive Substances' (2014) 25 *International Journal of Drug Policy* 1019; and Peter Reuter, *Options for Regulating New Psychoactive Drugs: A Review of Recent Experiences* (UK Drug Policy Commission 2011).

91 Home Affairs Committee, *Drugs: New Psychoactive Substances and Prescription Drugs*, HC 819 (December 2013), 14.

92 *New Psychoactive Substances Review: Report of the Expert Panel* (September 2014).

93 Ss 4–10.

94 Ss 12–20.

95 Ss 36 to 47.

96 S 2.

97 S 3.

98 Ss 7, 8, 12, 13 and 14.

closure order which prohibits the convicted individuals from operating businesses related to NPS[99] has been incorporated into the Irish legislation. Another difference relates to individuals and entities authorised to issue prohibition notices. Whilst this is to be done by a senior Garda officer in the Republic of Ireland,[100] the UK Act envisages a role for local authorities in this. On the one hand, this appears reasonable as sharing the responsibility can save time and resources for the law enforcement authorities but, on the other, the question may be asked whether a local authority is an appropriate entity to perform such a function. Moreover, whilst the UK Act provides for aggravating circumstances, such as committing relevant offences on or in the vicinity of school premises or using under-age couriers,[101] a similar provision does not exist under the Irish legislation. Despite the fact that both jurisdictions are based on the common law tradition and share many attributes in relation to the operation of their criminal laws and justice systems, these examples clearly demonstrate the divergence in attitude towards drug use and misuse.

Although it was noted that the Irish legislation has been successful in shutting down head shops, the sale or distribution of NPS through the internet remains a problem[102] – a concern that has been repeated by the European Monitoring Centre for Drugs and Drug Addiction.[103] Users are purchasing them from their own personal or drug networks,[104] and it has also emerged that the ban on NPS has led some users to turn to hard drugs, such as cocaine and ecstasy.[105] It is worth highlighting that the use of NPS among young people between the ages of 16 and 24 has increased from 16 per cent in 2011 to 22 per cent in 2014.[106] This shows that a criminal justice response alone is not sufficient; this should be accompanied by measures to address the demand for NPS through education and awareness-raising in parallel with supply reduction measures.[107] Further, the Irish government might consider alternatives such as regulation instead of prohibition.

Finally, the debates on decriminalisation or legalisation of some of the drugs should be mentioned. Decriminalisation generally means that, although possession or use is still illegal, the law enforcement authorities choose not to enforce the law strictly and/or that the drug use is dealt with through the civil system

99 S 10.

100 S 7.

101 S 6.

102 National Advisory Committee on Drugs, *An Overview of New Psychoactive Substances and the Outlets Supplying Them* (2011), 14.

103 *Guardian*, 'Is Irish Ban on Legal Highs Driving Markets Underground?' 30 June 2015.

104 Marie-Claire Van Hout and Rebekah Brennan, 'Curiosity Killed M-Cat: Post Legislative Study on Mephedrone Use in Ireland,' (2012) 19 *Drugs: Education, Prevention and Policy* 156, 158.

105 Ibid.

106 European Commission, *Young People and Drugs: Report* (August 2014), 7–9.

107 HM Government, *Government Response to New Psychoactive Substances Review Expert Panel Report* (October 2014), 6–7.

instead of the criminal justice system.[108] It is well known that Portugal has followed this policy from the early 2000s. Instead of imposing criminal penalties against the user of drugs, the Portuguese government has established so-called 'Dissuasion Commissions' across the country to deal with those caught with small quantities of all types of drugs for personal use.[109] Their members consist of clinical psychologists, sociologists and jurists and are supported by others, such as social workers and doctors. Those caught in possession are required to appear before a Commission and, depending on the level of addiction, it may take further action, such as by issuing a warning or ordering rehabilitation treatment. For repeat offenders, it can impose sanctions, such as banning the person from certain places or overseas travel or issuing them with a fine. It has been noted that Portugal's emphasis on treatment instead of penalisation has dramatically reduced drug use domestically.[110] Decriminalisation is also practised in other States, such as Italy, the Netherlands, Spain and Switzerland.[111]

Whether decriminalisation will be considered and implemented by the UK and Irish governments is open to question. Whilst the majority of MPs in the UK have acknowledged that the current drug laws and policies are not entirely effective, they have simultaneously expressed an opinion that it would be difficult to have a thorough debate due to the controversial nature of drug laws and policies.[112] Having said this, the Parliamentary Home Affairs Committee has recommended that the government considers this option further. In contrast, the Irish government seems more forthcoming about the idea of decriminalisation. The Joint Committee on Justice, Defence and Equality of the House of Oireachtas has acknowledged the success of the Portuguese model,[113] and the Minister of State for National Drug Strategy Aodhán O'Ríordáin was quoted as saying in July 2015 that he would consider the matter further in a Cabinet meeting, starting with the decriminalisation of cannabis.[114] This may be a sensible step as public interest in this issue is very high.

In terms of legalisation, there is growing global support for allowing this, at least in relation to cannabis. It is well known that some states in the US, such as Alaska, Colorado, Oregon and Washington, have already legalised the possession of cannabis. The key benefits of legalisation would be that it would take the profits

108 Home Affairs Committee, *Drugs: Breaking the Cycle, Ninth Report of the 2012–2013 Session* (December 2012), 89.

109 Ibid., 92.

110 Ibid., 96; and Caitlin E. Hughes and Alex Stevens, 'What Can We Learn from the Portuguese Decriminalisation of Illicit Drugs?' (2010) 50 *British Journal of Criminology* 999.

111 J. Michael Blackwell, 'The Costs and Consequences of US Drug Prohibition for the People of Developing Nations' (2014) 24 *Indiana International and Comparative Law Review* 665, 671.

112 Home Affairs Committee, *supra* n 108, 99.

113 Joint Committee on Justice, Defence and Equality, *Report of Visit by a Committee Delegation to Examine the Impact of Portuguese Approach to the Possession of Certain Drugs* (June 2015).

114 *Irish Times*, 'Drugs Meeting Finds "Wide Consensus" on Decriminalisation' 29 July 2015.

away from criminals; force them out of the supply/demand chain; and put its production and sale under the regulation or control of public authorities.[115] Moreover, legalisation would allow the public authorities to create employment opportunities and raise tax revenue which could be channelled into a variety of important purposes.[116] In Colorado, for example, the taxes raised from the retail sale of cannabis have been used to improve education in schools, public safety and health.[117] In the UK, there has been increasing interest and support for the legalisation of cannabis as well. For instance, a petition submitted to Parliament gathered over 200,000 signatures which was enough to initiate a parliamentary debate on this issue.[118] However, the UK government's position remains that the use of cannabis must be prevented[119] and there are currently no plans to legalise it. The sentiment seems to be the same in the Republic of Ireland. When different types of drugs were legalised accidentally by the High Court decision noted above, the Irish government was very quick to introduce emergency legislation to reverse it. Moreover, the statement by the Minister for National Drug Strategy did not go as far as suggesting the legalisation of cannabis. Therefore, it seems reasonable to conclude that there is not enough appetite at this stage in Ireland either. Whilst it is important to acknowledge the potentially harmful effects of all drugs on human health, and the UK and Irish governments' rationale for maintaining the status quo is understandable, many stakeholders, including politicians, agree that the current drug laws and policies are not working properly. There is, therefore, some merit in discussing and analysing the effectiveness of alternative approaches such as decriminalisation and legalisation which are more based on solid scientific evidence as well as paying due regard to the voices of citizens.

3.6 Fiscal and excise fraud

Action against fiscal and excise fraud, such as tobacco smuggling and fuel laundering, is based on the system of customs and excise taxation on specific commodities in both jurisdictions in line with the EU standards mentioned in the previous chapter. In the UK (including Northern Ireland), Section 170 of the Customs and Excise Management Act 1979 criminalises fraudulent evasion of duty, and this generally applies to those who smuggle commodities without paying appropriate taxes. The penalty for this offence on summary conviction is a fine which is three times the value of the goods and/or imprisonment of 6 months.

115 Blackwell, *supra* n 111, 691.

116 Ibid.; and Jonathan P. Caulkins *et al.*, 'High Tax States: Options for Gleaning Revenue from Legal Cannabis' (2012–2013) 91 *Oregon Law Review* 1041.

117 David Blake and Jack Finlaw, 'Marijuana Legalization in Colorado: Lessons Learned' (2014) 8 *Harvard Law and Policy Review* 359, 372–373.

118 *Make the Production, Sale and Use of Cannabis Legal*, <https://petition.parliament.uk/petitions/104349>. This petition closed in January 2016.

119 Ibid.

Upon conviction on indictment, a penalty of any amount and/or 7 years' imprisonment may be imposed. The 1979 Act also provides for the offences of handling goods subjects to unpaid excise and taking preparatory steps for evasion of excise duty.[120] The Fraud Act 2006 supplements the 1979 Act by prohibiting a range of fraud offences with a maximum of 10 years' imprisonment.

There is other legislation which targets the supply side. In relation to tobacco smuggling, for example, the Tobacco Products Duty Act 1979 (as amended) places a duty on tobacco manufacturers not to supply their products to individuals who are likely to smuggle them[121] and a failure to do so can result in imposition of a fine of up to £5 million. It is worth highlighting that in 2014 British American Tobacco was fined £650,000 for oversupplying their products in Belgium.[122] Intermediaries such as hauliers and tobacco retailers can also face revocation of their licence, a fine of up to £5,000 and/or a ban on sales for up to 6 months.[123] An interesting development in relation to tobacco is the move towards plain packaging which would remove promotional aspects such as logos, graphics and colour schemes. Under Section 94 of the Children and Families Act 2014, the Secretary of State may make regulations related to retail packaging of tobacco products. Added to this, the Standardised Packaging of Tobacco Products Regulations 2015 was passed recently. Some have argued, particularly those in the tobacco industry, that this move would increase smuggling of cheap and counterfeit tobacco products.[124] However, there is no concrete evidence to support such a claim as yet[125] and HMRC has also taken the view that the risk of an increase in smuggling as a result of plain packaging would not be very high.[126] It remains to be seen whether the new regime will have an impact on this crime.

As for the consumers of these goods, the Excise Goods (Holding, Movement and Duty Point) Regulations 2010 provide for an imposition of a fine of up to 100 per cent of the value of the tax evaded. In addition to smugglers/traffickers, anyone in possession of smuggled products on which the relevant taxes have not been paid are included in this.[127] In relation to illegal fuels, those who take in or use laundered fuel are liable to a penalty of an amount equal to the evaded duty under the Hydrocarbon Oil Duties Act 1979[128] and the Finance Act 1994.[129] In

120 Ss 170A and 170B.

121 S 7A.

122 BBC News Online, 'HMRC Fines Cigarette Maker for Oversupplying Belgium,' <www.bbc.co.uk/news/business-30038328>.

123 Tobacco Products Duty Act 1979, s 8H; Home Affairs Committee, *Tobacco Smuggling: First Report of the Session 2014–2015*, 10; and HMRC, *Tackling Tobacco Smuggling – Building on Our Success* (April 2011), 11.

124 Luk Joossens, *Smuggling, the Tobacco Industry and Plain Packs* (Cancer Research UK 2012), 1.

125 Ibid.

126 Home Affairs Committee, *supra* n 123, 11–13.

127 HMRC, *supra* n 123, 11.

128 S 13.

129 S 9.

more serious cases, imprisonment of up to 7 years may be imposed.[130] These measures, if enforced rigorously, can send a strong message to the general public and contribute to the reduction of the demand for illegal fuels. It therefore seems reasonable to conclude that the legislative frameworks on fiscal/excise fraud are appropriate in the UK; certainly they go further than the relevant standards (or lack thereof) explored elsewhere.

The legislation pertaining to fiscal/excise fraud in the Republic of Ireland presents a similar range of prohibition. Section 102 of the Finance Act 1999, as amended, criminalises the improper selling or supplying of mineral oil with a fine of €5,000 or 12 months' imprisonment. These increase to €126,970 or 5 years respectively upon indictment under the Finance Act 2010. The Finance Act 2014 created additional powers to revoke oil traders' licences. Under Section 79 of the Finance Act 2003, as amended, attempting to supply or sell alcohol without paying appropriate tax or producing or supplying illegally produced alcohol carries (on summary conviction) a fine of €5,000 or up to 12 months' imprisonment. On indictment, the penalties are increased to a fine not exceeding €126,970 or 5 years' imprisonment. Similar arrangements exist for tobacco products fraud under Section 78 of the Finance Act 2005 as amended. In addition, the Finance Act 2013 has created an offence of illegal manufacturing of tobacco products with a similar punishment regime as other statutes.[131] Further, similar to the UK, the Republic of Ireland passed new legislation called the Public Health (Standardised Packaging of Tobacco) Act 2015. Manufacturing retail packaging in contravention of this Act and importing or selling tobacco products whose packaging does not conform to the Act are criminalised with 8 years' imprisonment on conviction on indictment.[132]

There are a few points to be raised in relation to the legislative frameworks in the Republic of Ireland. Whilst the imposition of large fines in Ireland may have a stronger deterrent effect compared to the UK, a custodial sentence of 5 years' imprisonment seems rather low. In this regard, an important point was raised by the officers of Revenue, Irish Tax and Customs that the amount of illegal profit made from fiscal and excise fraud is similar to that of drug trafficking and yet the punishment regimes are quite different.[133] In order to strengthen the deterrent effect, heavier penalties could be considered by the political community in the Republic. Also, provisions are lacking in relation to the purchase of illegal cigarettes, fuel and alcohol, and a question may be asked about whether some type of penalty should be imposed. A body called Retail against Smuggling was established to tackle cigarette smuggling in the Republic of Ireland, which has recommended an on-the-spot fine before the Joint Committee on Finance, Public Expenditure and Reform.[134] Although there is an argument to apply such a penalty

130 S 13(5).

131 S 56.

132 Ss 15 and 16.

133 Interviews with Revenue, Irish Tax and Customs on 20 December 2013.

134 Joint Committee on Finance, Public Expenditure and Reform, *Correspondence 2012/354* (October 2012).

to illegal fuel or alcohol, it is not clear whether this is an effective use of resources on the part of law enforcement agencies and the judiciary.[135] In addition, the impact of such a measure on demand is also not clear. A thorough debate and careful study are needed to address this problem.

A question that may be asked in relation to fiscal and excise fraud in both jurisdictions is whether lowering taxes for relevant commodities could represent a way forward in tackling smuggling. The key factor which encourages their smuggling is undoubtedly the high taxes and prices that are applied to these goods. For example, there is clear evidence for this in the US.[136] For commodities such as alcohol and tobacco, higher taxes may be justifiable on public health grounds. Nevertheless, they can also be counterproductive as higher taxes may encourage consumers to turn to counterfeit goods that are often of poor quality and have a negative impact upon their health. Counterfeit fuels can also damage vehicles and appliances. These considerations might justify the lowering of taxes for these goods. However, a recent study has shown that lowering relevant taxes (and commodity prices) does not always lead to less smuggling.[137] Therefore, this option may not ultimately attract wide support.

Alternatively, what could be considered at the European level is the approximation of prices of commodities, including taxes imposed upon them, which are the target for fraud. The average price for a pack of 20 cigarettes in the UK and the Republic of Ireland are £9.16 and £7.80 respectively whilst these are much lower in continental Europe, ranging from £5.46 in France to £3.78 in Spain.[138] This provides a strong incentive for those residing in States with higher commodity prices to purchase or even smuggle these products from the States with lower prices. If the prices of these commodities are similar, then consumers will perhaps not see a pressing need to opt for smuggled ones. However, securing sufficient political support from Member States may be difficult in reality. Even if there is strong appetite, such a measure should also be accompanied by more rigorous customs checks against commodities coming from non-EU States as well as better coordination and cooperation at an international level.

3.7 Conclusion

This chapter has presented an overview of the UK and Irish legislative frameworks related to core crimes: participation in organised criminal groups, human trafficking, drug offences and fiscal/excise fraud which have been identified as serious organised crimes in both jurisdictions. In general, these are in line with the

135 Interviews with HMRC officers, *supra* n 6.

136 Tax Foundation, Cigarette Taxes and Cigarette Smuggling by State (March 2014), <http://taxfoundation.org/article/cigarette-taxes-and-cigarette-smuggling-state>.

137 Luk Joossens *et al.*, *How Eliminating the Global Illicit Cigarette Trade Would Increase the Tax Revenue and Save Lives,* (International Union against Tuberculosis and Lung Disease, 2009), 17.

138 As of March 2015. Tobacco Manufacturers Association, EU Cigarettes Prices, <www.the-tma.org.uk/tma-publications-research/facts-figures/eu-cigarette-prices>.

international and regional standards as represented by the UNTOC and EU law. Their importance therefore has been acknowledged by both the UK and Irish governments. It has also been shown that strict adherence to a criminal justice approach may not always produce positive results, particularly for crimes such as possession of drugs and fiscal/excise fraud. There is of course no guarantee that the practices in other jurisdictions which have embraced wider approaches will work in the UK and the Republic of Ireland due to political, cultural, social and legal differences. However, it is clear that wider and more thorough debates that involve all governmental and non-governmental stakeholders, including the general public, are needed in order to develop and implement more effective responses to transnational organised crime in both jurisdictions.

In comparing the UK and the Republic of Ireland, it can be said that there is a great degree of similarity in terms of the definitions and the punishment regimes for some offences. In some instances, the Irish model has been transposed into the UK legislation. This has undoubtedly been a more straightforward process due to the shared history and the common law tradition. Whilst these similarities can also make cross-border cooperation between the two jurisdictions easier, it has been discovered that similarities in definitions of various forms of organised crime are not particularly significant when it comes to practical cooperation between the relevant authorities, such as the police, public prosecutors and customs agencies. The present analysis has also revealed that distinct differences exist between the UK and the Republic of Ireland in the formulation of legislation, thereby highlighting the importance of State sovereignty in action against transnational organised crime. It is therefore evident that harmonisation or approximation of national criminal laws and procedures is not an easy principle to implement.

Finally, it is evident that devolution of policing and criminal justice has had an impact upon the responses to some forms of organised crime in Northern Ireland. Despite the fact that crimes explored in this chapter are regarded as reserved matters, a degree of variation can also be perceived. It is important to recognise that devolution has led to positive developments in some areas such as human trafficking where the punishment regime and protection of victims have been enhanced compared to England, Wales and Scotland. Therefore, the practice in this jurisdiction should be used as a model for others. However, there is a degree of uncertainty and risk in relation to others, including participation offences. A lack of a clear legal basis not only goes against the principle of legality but can also make Northern Ireland more vulnerable to forum shopping and the concentration of criminal activities. In terms of prohibition of substantive organised crime offences, therefore, it may be desirable to have a uniform approach in all parts of the UK.

4 Criminal investigation and prosecution of transnational organised crime

4.1 Introduction

This chapter provides an analysis of criminal investigation and prosecution against transnational organised crime in Northern Ireland and the Republic of Ireland. It begins with a brief description of the relevant law enforcement authorities in both jurisdictions. It then examines criminal investigation with a focus on the use of special investigative techniques, such as surveillance, interception of communications and covert human intelligence sources. Particular attention is given to the ways in which law enforcement officers balance the need to adhere to human rights standards whilst conducting an effective investigation. The chapter moves on to consider relevant matters related to prosecution, such as legal guidance, the provision of immunity for assisting offenders and the intimidation of witnesses, victims and informants. Having explored national law enforcement practices, the chapter provides an analysis of cross-border cooperation. In addition to formal mechanisms established through respective legislation, informal arrangements, which are often facilitated by the law enforcement agencies, will be highlighted.

4.2 Key law enforcement agencies

The primary responsibility for crime prevention in Northern Ireland rests with the PSNI. Within this, the Organised Crime Branch takes a lead in the investigation of the various forms of organised crime. Previously, there were various units dealing with organised crime, such as the Drug Squad, Robbery Squad and the Economic Crime Bureau. They were merged into a single Organised Crime Branch in 2010 after a strategic decision was made that the PSNI should focus on the totality of organised crime rather than on individual criminalities related to illicit goods and services.[1] The PSNI is assisted by two national agencies. The first is HMRC. Two directorates within the Northern Ireland Department of HMRC are particularly pertinent to this research. The Criminal Investigation Directorate is tasked with investigating relevant organised crime offences such as fiscal and

1 Interview with the Head of the PSNI Organised Crime Branch on 13 September 2013.

excise fraud.[2] This Directorate is complemented by the Risk and Intelligence Service (Criminal Intelligence Group) which is responsible for profiling and criminal intelligence work.[3] The second agency is the NCA which was established by the Crime and Courts Act 2013. It builds on the work of its predecessor SOCA and has several commands that are relevant to organised crime: Child Exploitation and Online Protection Centre (CEOP), Organised Crime Command, Economic Crime Command, Intelligence and Operations Directorate, Specialist Capabilities (e.g. UK Human Trafficking Centre) and National Cyber Crime Unit.[4]

An important point to stress in relation to action against organised crime in Northern Ireland is the strong emphasis placed upon a multi-agency approach. For example, a clear line of communication/coordination is facilitated by CRIMNET (explained in Chapter 3) which allows all of those concerned to decide which agency is best placed to lead a particular investigation. Regular coordination meetings also take place in order to facilitate effective communication and minimise duplication of efforts, with each agency clearly understanding their role without causing unnecessary friction and competition. This multi-agency approach is greatly enhanced by the OCTF which was first established in Northern Ireland in 2000 and as from April 2010 came under the auspices of the Department of Justice.[5] The OCTF brings together the PSNI, HMRC and other law enforcement agencies, as well as the local business community. It is structured into a stakeholder group (chaired by the Minister of Justice), a strategy group (chaired by the Director of Policing and Community Safety) and 9 sub-groups. These sub-groups deal with major crimes, including armed robbery, cybercrime, intellectual property crime, criminal finance, drugs, immigration and human trafficking and fuel fraud, and most of them are chaired by senior law enforcement officers.[6] They meet several times a year or more where appropriate. The OCTF recently published the *Northern Ireland Organised Crime Strategy*[7] which sets out the main law enforcement objectives for tackling organised crime, such as making Northern Ireland a hostile environment for organised criminals, informing the public of crime trends and the work of the OCTF and supporting communities affected by organised crime.

The law enforcement community in Northern Ireland generally regards the OCTF as useful in building good working relationships that facilitate coordinated responses to transnational organised crime. Whilst it is not a decision-making or operational body, matters discussed are often fed into ongoing practical action

2 HMRC, *Code of Practice 9: HM Revenue & Customs Investigations Where We Suspect Fraud* (2014).
3 Interviews with HMRC officers, *supra* ch 3 n 6.
4 See <www.nationalcrimeagency.gov.uk> for further information.
5 For more information, see <www.octf.gov.uk>.
6 OCTF, *supra* intro n 9, 6.
7 The Northern Ireland Organised Crime Strategy 2012–2014, *supra* ch 3 n 2.

against organised crime.[8] This suggests that the OCTF and sub-groups are not merely talking shops, and this has been confirmed by the law enforcement stakeholders. To illustrate this with some examples, an in-depth examination of money service bureaus that have been involved in illegal activities came from discussions within the criminal finance sub-group.[9] This has enabled those concerned to establish good working relationships, leading to the identification of widespread fraud that had direct links to dissident Republicans. Another example is the creation of an NGO engagement group for the trafficking of human beings.[10] The active participation of the civil society sector is particularly important for this crime as it has been instrumental in providing assistance to victims and raising awareness. In summary, this multi-agency approach in Northern Ireland is an example of good practice.

In the Republic of Ireland, the key law enforcement agency is An Garda Síochána, the Irish national police force. Law enforcement against organised crime is primarily the responsibility of its National Bureau of Criminal Investigation which was established as an effective and active response to the proliferation of serious and organised crime. Formed in 1997 with the amalgamation of a number of national investigation units, including the Organised Crime Unit, the Bureau works in conjunction with other departments with responsibility for organised crime, including the Bureau of Fraud Investigation, the National Drugs Unit, the Criminal Assets Bureau (CAB) and the National Immigration Bureau (including the Human Trafficking Investigation and Co-Ordination Unit). Originally established in 2005 on a temporary basis, the Organised Crime Unit was made permanent in 2008.[11] However, it is not as large as the PSNI's Organised Crime Branch.

Another important agency is Revenue, Irish Tax and Customs which is equivalent to the UK's HMRC. It is an independent agency which was established by Government Order in 1923 and is tasked with collecting taxes and duties and implementing customs controls. In recent times, there has been an increased focus on certain fiscal and safety threats associated with the smuggling of drugs, tobacco and counterfeit products.[12] It investigates and prosecutes appropriate cases of serious tax and duty evasion and works with other countries and law enforcement partners in the fight against organised crime.

Unlike Northern Ireland, the Republic of Ireland does not have a formal structure akin to the OCTF. This is, of course, not to state that it does not consider a multi-agency approach important. For example, Section 36 of the Garda Síochána Act 2005 requires the establishment of joint policing committees to operate at local level and engage with local senior police officers on a monthly basis. Both An Garda Síochána and Revenue, Irish Tax and Customs have liaison officers attached to each other to facilitate effective communication and action, and the

8 Interview with the Head of the PSNI OC Branch, *supra* n 1.
9 Interviews with PSNI officers, *supra* ch 3 n 3.
10 For more information, see <www.octf.gov.uk/Human-Trafficking-Partners>.
11 For more information, see <www.garda.ie>.
12 Revenue, Irish Tax and Customs, *Annual Report 2014*.

level of cooperation seems to be very positive.[13] Having said this, it is certainly useful to have a structure akin to the OCTF as that can enhance proactive involvement of, and coordination with, other relevant agencies as well as the civil society sector. Strong political leadership in this regard can send a clear message that the Irish government takes organised crime seriously and can boost public confidence in law enforcement. It is worth pointing out that 95 per cent of the respondents in the crime survey conducted in the Republic of Ireland stated that the government should take a tougher stance on organised crime.[14] This demonstrates that public interest in organised crime is high and the establishment of a task force can be seen as a positive development.

4.3 Intelligence-led law enforcement

Given the complex and sophisticated nature of transnational organised crime, proactive intelligence-led law enforcement with the use of special investigative techniques is essential for successful detection, prevention and suppression. Both jurisdictions have legislative frameworks to facilitate this. In Northern Ireland, the key legislation is the Regulation of Investigatory Powers Act 2000 (RIPA).[15] RIPA contains provisions for interception of communications,[16] surveillance and use of Covert Human Intelligence Sources (CHIS).[17] These powers are used to detect crime generally, and therefore the legislation does not create special powers specifically for transnational organised crime. In relation to interception of communications, a warrant must generally be issued by the Home Secretary.[18] His/Her power is to be monitored by the Interception of Communications Commissioner who holds or must have held a high judicial office,[19] thereby providing some safeguards against the abuse of power. However, a High Court judge in Northern Ireland argued that there should be more active judicial involvement in decision-making.[20] An important step which can be taken in this regard is prior judicial authorisation of interception. This is already conducted in States such as Australia,[21] Canada,[22] Germany,[23] the Netherlands,[24] Poland,[25]

13 Interviews with Garda officers and Revenue, Irish Tax and Customs, *supra* ch 3 n 7 and 133.
14 Red C, *Crime Survey Opinion Poll 2010*, 3.
15 This applies to England and Wales also. For Scotland, the relevant legislation is the Regulation of Investigatory Powers (Scotland) Act 2000.
16 Pt 1, ch 1.
17 Pt 2, ss 29, 30 and 31 (Northern Ireland) which sets out that authorisation for conduct in Northern Ireland shall be exercisable by the Office of the First Minister and Deputy First Minister (concurrently with being exercisable by the Secretary of State).
18 Ss 6–8.
19 S 57.
20 Interview with a High Court judge, *supra* ch 3 n 5.
21 Telecommunications (Interception and Access) Act 1979 as amended.
22 Pt VI of the Criminal Code 1985 as amended.
23 Criminal Procedure Code 1950 as amended, s 100b.
24 Special Powers of Investigation Act 2000.
25 Criminal Procedure Code 1997 as amended, ch 26.

South Africa,[26] Spain,[27] Switzerland[28] and the US.[29] There have been some cases in recent times where interception of communications and related conduct (e.g. data retention) by agencies such as the Government Communications Headquarters (GCHQ) have been found to be in violation of Article 8 of the ECHR (right to privacy),[30] and some concerns have also been expressed by the United Nations Human Rights Committee.[31] Prior judicial authorisation would ensure compliance with the Human Rights Act 1998, including the relevant norms explored in Chapter 1, strengthen its justification and avoid complaints being made at a later stage. This in turn would boost public confidence in law enforcement.

In terms of surveillance, there are three types stipulated under RIPA: directed surveillance, intrusive surveillance and CHIS.[32] Directed surveillance largely involves surveillance that takes place in public places and is considered less serious.[33] Authorisation for this type of surveillance can be given by high-ranking officers in respective agencies. If surveillance is to take place in private premises (e.g. in a dwelling or private vehicle), then it is considered to be intrusive. In both cases, a test of proportionality and necessity must be employed before authorisation can be given.[34] In relation to intrusive surveillance, an independent Surveillance Commissioner determines whether or not to support it.[35] Finally, CHIS generally refers to informants or undercover officers[36] and the authorisation process is the same as directed surveillance.[37] All special investigative techniques stipulated in RIPA can be reviewed by the Investigatory Powers Tribunal.[38]

26 Regulation of Interception of Communications and Provision of Communication Related Information Act 2002.

27 Criminal Procedure Code 1882 as amended, ss 197–199.

28 Criminal Procedure Code 2007, art 272.

29 18 USC Chapter 19, §2518 (Procedure for Interception of Wire, Oral or Electronic Communications). It is important to mention, however, that the President of the United States can, under the Foreign Intelligence Surveillance Act 1978, authorise interception in relation to foreign nationals (or persons working on behalf of foreign governments) for intelligence purposes only.

30 *Belhadj and Others v Security Service, Secret Intelligence Service, Government Communications Headquarters, Secretary of State for Home Department and Secretary of State for Foreign and Commonwealth Office* [2015] UKIPTrib 13_132-H; and *Liberty and Others v Security Service, Secret Intelligence Service and Government Communications Headquarters* [2015] UKTrib 13_77H 2. See also Privacy International, *The Right to Privacy in the United Kingdom* (June 2015).

31 *Concluding Observation on the Seventh Periodic Report of the United Kingdom of Great Britain and Northern Ireland*, CCPR/C/GBR/CO/7 (2015), 10–11.

32 See pt II.

33 See Bethan Loftus and Benjamin Goold, 'Covert Policing and the Invisibilities of Policing' (2011) 12 *Criminology & Criminal Justice* 278.

34 Ss 28. and 32.

35 S 36.

36 S 26.

37 S 29.

38 Pt IV.

These measures are in line with Article 20 of the UNTOC, and the law enforcement community in Northern Ireland generally regards the current legal framework to be sufficient to tackle organised crime in terms of the powers granted to them.[39] Further, as the legislation applies equally to terrorism, it is capable of addressing its nexus with organised crime.

On the subject of RIPA authorisations for surveillance, it has been discovered that respective agencies have stringent authorisation processes in place. Any request for the use of these measures must be accompanied by clear justification, and the authorising officers must provide rigorous checks to ensure that requests are in line with RIPA (in terms of necessity and proportionality) and their own internal guidelines.[40] A lack of successful applications under the 'abuse of process' doctrine before the Northern Irish courts is one indication that the law enforcement community has been able to use special investigative techniques appropriately. A defence lawyer,[41] judges,[42] an independent human rights adviser within the PSNI[43] as well as the Interception of Communications Commissioner[44] have also concurred on this point.

RIPA was recently amended by the Protection of Freedoms Act 2012. Among others, Sections 37 and 38 now require judicial authorisation before the local authorities can obtain communication data, conduct directed surveillance or use CHIS. This change came in response to numerous instances of abuse of these powers by local authorities.[45] Another important aspect of this legislation is that it obliges the Home Secretary to issue a code of practice on the use of CCTV and appoint a Surveillance Camera Commissioner who monitors implementation of the code. In accordance with this, the Commissioner was appointed in September 2012 and the Surveillance Camera Code of Practice was published in June 2013. Similar to interception of communications, the use of CCTV cameras has been held to breach the right to privacy in the past,[46] and the new regime can prevent such violations of human rights. However, the amendment under the 2012 Act does not extend to requests made by the law enforcement agencies. On the one hand, there is a strong argument that the existence of stringent authorisation processes may not require judicial approval. On the other hand, judicial authorisation to all forms of special investigative techniques promotes consistency in law enforcement and enhances the legality of their use as well as human rights protection. All of these can have a positive impact upon public confidence in law enforcement against organised crime. Further, the implementation of judicial

39 Interviews with PSNI and HMRC officers, *supra* ch 3 n 3 and 6; and interviews with SOCA officers, 28 November 2012.

40 Ibid.

41 Interview with a defence lawyer on 22 November 2013.

42 *Supra* ch 3 n 5.

43 Interview with a PSNI human rights adviser 17 September 2013.

44 Interception of Communications Commissioner, *Annual Report 2015*, 42.

45 Home Office, *RIPA and Local Authorities: Impact Assessment* (2010).

46 *X v Local Authority* IPT/03/50/CH (2008); and *N v The Police* IPT/07/02/CH (2009).

authorisation could lead to a relaxation of the existing internal authorisation procedures. This could reduce internal frustration/friction and prevent authorising officers from reaching different decisions on the same or similar facts.

Another point to note is on the urgent authorisation procedure. RIPA provides for oral authorisation in urgent cases to be given for up to 72 hours when it is not possible to obtain a written authorisation.[47] It is to be acknowledged here that the law enforcement agencies sometimes must act quickly to prevent organised crime and ensure the safety of those concerned, and that good procedures are in place for this oral authorisation (e.g. recording of such authorisation).[48] It is also understandable that authorising officers may not be immediately available to process written applications. However, a question can simultaneously be raised as to whether these law enforcement agencies really require 72 hours. A shorter period seems to be a reasonable option as that could facilitate closer monitoring and encourage officers to utilise less intrusive means of investigation as much as possible. By way of comparison, in Australia[49] and Hong Kong[50] the initial period for urgent authorisation is limited to 48 hours; in Canada, a judge can give oral authorisation for up to 36 hours;[51] and law enforcement agencies in the Republic of Korea must obtain judicial approval within 36 hours.[52] These represent a better model.

In the Republic of Ireland, the use of surveillance by law enforcement agencies is regulated by the Criminal Justice (Surveillance) Act 2009. Surveillance under this Act means 'monitoring, observing, listening to or making a recording of a particular person or group of persons or their movements, activities and communications' or 'monitoring or making a recording of places or things'. Similar to Northern Ireland, this Act applies to arrestable offences generally and therefore does not create special powers for organised crime *per se*. However, it is important to acknowledge that, unlike in Northern Ireland, surveillance is to be approved by a judge.[53] He/She must be satisfied that surveillance is proportionate and that its duration is reasonable in achieving its objectives. Before applying to a judge, a superior officer (e.g. a rank above superintendent for An Garda Síochána and a rank above principal officer for Revenue, Irish Tax and Customs) will also have to consider proportionality and necessity.[54] This is undoubtedly a better model than that of the UK, including Northern Ireland. A High Court judge in the Republic of Ireland, who was designated to review the surveillance powers under this

47 Ss 34, 36 and 43.

48 Interviews with PSNI and HMRC officers, *supra* ch 3 n 3 and 6.

49 *Supra* n 21, s 10; and Surveillance Devices Act 2007, s 33.

50 Interception of Communications and Surveillance Ordinance 2006, s 22.

51 *Supra* n 22, s 184.3.

52 UNODC, *Current Practices in Electronic Surveillance in the Investigation of Serious and Organised Crime* (2009), 27.

53 Ss 4–5.

54 Ibid.

Act, noted that generally the law enforcement authorities used surveillance appropriately.[55]

However, there are some issues in relation to the current regime. For instance, a human rights organisation ICCL takes a view that judicial oversight should be enhanced through more rigorous scrutiny of relevant agencies and the publication of detailed annual reports.[56] Similar to the UK, urgent authorisation for surveillance can also be granted for up to 72 hours, and the Republic of Ireland therefore should review this aspect of the 2009 Act for the reasons stated above. Further, the scope of the 2009 Act is limited to surveillance with the use of devices; other measures, such as covert following and observation without surveillance devices, are not covered. It is desirable that legislative provision is made for all forms of surveillance for clarity, consistency and accountability. The need for a clear legal basis has also been stressed by the ECtHR on numerous occasions.[57]

Another relevant law in the Republic of Ireland is the Interception of Postal Packets and Telecommunications Messages (Regulation) Act 1993 which allows the relevant agencies to undertake interceptions for the investigation of serious crimes. Unlike surveillance noted above, the authorisation is given by the Minister for Justice and Equality. Similar to the UK, there is a designated High Court judge who monitors the operation of interception.[58] However, an argument may also be made for *prior* judicial authorisation similar to surveillance measures.[59] In the light of the recent case of *DPP v Damache*,[60] there seems to be increasing recognition that authorisation for intrusive measures should be given by an independent person, and a judge can certainly fulfil this role.

In relation to CHIS, there is currently no legislative framework governing this unlike the UK. Rather, it is regulated by An Garda Síochána's CHIS Management Policy (code of practice). This document is available to all officers and provides for the professional standards to maintain the confidence of the public and the courts.[61] Part 1 sets out the case for the proper management and use of CHIS. Part 2 reflects on the ethical and human rights standards to which An Garda Síochána subscribes. Finally, Parts 3 and 4 set out the standards for the collection, storage and use of information gathered by CHIS as well as the auditing of standards and systems in place. When asked whether a lack of legislation covering the

55 Interview with a High Court judge, *supra* ch 3 n 17.

56 Interview with an ICCL representative, *supra* ch 3 n 14.

57 See *Malone v United Kingdom*, App no 8691/79 (1984); *Kruslin v France*, App no 11801/85 (1990); *Taylor-Sabori v United Kingdom*, App no 47114/99 (2002); *Rotaru v Romania*, App no 28341/95(2000); and *Liberty and Others v United Kingdom*, App no 58243/00 (2008).

58 S 8.

59 Campbell, *supra* intro n 33, 84–85.

60 [2011] IESC 11.

61 Public Statement by the Commissioner of An Garda Síochána on the Management and Use of Covert Human Intelligence Sources (date of publication unknown), <www.garda.ie/Documents/User/Management and use of Covert Human Intelligence Sources.pdf>.

use of CHIS may pose an issue in terms of legality and accountability, the responses provided by the Garda officers varied. Some of them expressed the view that the existing code of practice for the use of CHIS provided adequate procedures for oversight and accountability.[62] Further, a retired judge, known as the CHIS Oversight Authority, monitors the CHIS regime and regularly reports to the Minister for Justice and Equality.[63] However, it is desirable to enact specific legislation on CHIS as it would strengthen the legality, accountability and protection of the CHIS and Garda officers. This view was also expressed by a judge of the High Court and the Special Criminal Court (SCC).[64] In summary, it is evident that there is scope for improvement in intelligence-led law enforcement in both Northern Ireland and the Republic of Ireland, particularly in terms of enhancing legality and accountability.

4.4 Practical issues in law enforcement

Although the legislative frameworks on special investigative techniques may be regarded as sufficient and generally in line with the relevant international and regional standards, a number of practical issues exist which are hampering their effective enforcement. For instance, intelligence-led law enforcement is not always easy, even for small jurisdictions like Northern Ireland and the Republic of Ireland. In this regard, the law enforcement communities there highlighted the practical difficulty in identifying criminal groups. Many of these are quite small in size and are network-based rather than large entities as explained in Chapter 3. Moreover, their relationships with each other can change from day to day as it is framed by both cooperation and competition.[65] This is exacerbated by the increasing presence of foreign criminals in both jurisdictions. Human trafficking and tobacco smuggling are examples of crimes where many of the criminals as well as their victims are from foreign States.[66] One human rights organisation in Northern Ireland further noted that local ethnic-minority groups work with the paramilitaries to commit crimes.[67] Infiltrating these groups is difficult due to the cultural and language barriers. They also have extensive criminal networks outside the island of Ireland, making it more vulnerable to organised crime.[68] In order to overcome some of these difficulties, the Head of the PSNI Organised Crime Branch recognised the need to put more resources into the use of interpreters,

62 Interviews with Garda officers, *supra* ch 3 n 7.

63 In the most recent Report of the Independent Oversight Authority for Covert Human Intelligence Sources (2014), for instance, T.C. Smyth, S.C. (Retired Judge of the High Court) was satisfied that there had been substantial compliance with An Garda Síochána's code of practice for the use of CHIS.

64 Interview with a judge of the High Court and the Special Criminal Court on 31 July 2013.

65 Interviews with PSNI and Garda officers, *supra* ch 3 n 3 and 7.

66 OCTF, *supra* intro n 9, 9 and 20.

67 Interview with the Northern Ireland Council on Ethnic Minorities on 5 November 2013.

68 OCTF, *supra* intro n 9, 9, 13 and 16.

the training of frontline officers and the use of CHIS who are foreign nationals.[69] Proactive recruitment of law enforcement officials from ethnic-minority communities would also be beneficial as they would be able to create a good rapport and working relationship with these communities.[70]

The sophisticated nature of organised crime is also hampering effective law enforcement. Criminals use advanced technologies and techniques, such as the internet, to carry out their illegal activities. They are also highly mobile and flexible, being able to adapt to changing circumstances.[71] In addition to the use of special investigative techniques noted above, it was stressed by the law enforcement communities in both jurisdictions that the powers stipulated under the proceeds of crime legislation are also useful. The Proceeds of Crime Act 2002 (POCA) of the UK allows the relevant authorities to closely monitor financial transactions of suspected offenders and piece together their criminal lifestyle. It also facilitates cooperation from financial institutions, particularly in relation to reporting suspicious activities. However, it has been discovered that this legislation is regarded as a specialism and is not well understood by the frontline officers.[72] Having said this, one example of good practice by the PSNI Organised Crime Branch has gone some way to negate this issue. Prior to 2010, financial investigations were not systematically carried out alongside criminal investigations into organised crime. Since a restructuring process, however, every team has been assigned a financial investigator.[73] In contrast, financial investigation has played, and continues to play, an important part in action against organised crime in the Republic of Ireland. It was discovered that the CAB and the Bureau of Fraud Investigation work closely with other units concerned with organised crime to facilitate parallel financial investigations.[74]

Some issues have also been raised in relation to the use of special investigative techniques. Many frontline officers felt that the legislation was sometimes being interpreted too strictly by authorising officers, making criminal investigations unnecessarily difficult, and that the authorisation process involved a great deal of bureaucracy which wasted valuable resources that could be better spent on investigations.[75] HMRC officers, however, highlighted the benefits of the authorisation process by arguing that it encourages professionalism in law enforcement and enhances the legitimacy of intelligence to be used in criminal investigations

69 *Supra* n 1.

70 It should be highlighted here that the Home Secretary recently expressed her concern over a lack of police officers from ethnic minority communities across the United Kingdom. *Guardian*, 'Police Forces are Too White' (22 October 2015).

71 Criminal Justice Inspectorate Northern Ireland, *Serious and Organised Crime: An Inspection on How the Criminal Justice System Deals with Serious and Organised Crime in Northern Ireland* (November 2014), 12.

72 Interviews with PSNI officers, *supra* ch 3 n 3.

73 *Supra* n 1; and Criminal Justice Inspectorate Northern Ireland, *supra* n 71, 41.

74 Interviews with Garda officers, *supra* ch 3 n 7.

75 Interviews with PSNI officers, *supra* ch 3 n 3.

and prosecutions.[76] This is indeed an important point as special investigative techniques entail a number of human rights issues which must be carefully considered and balanced as explained throughout this book. Alternatively, prior judicial authorisation should be seriously considered.

In addition, the human rights community in Northern Ireland has raised concerns about a lack of transparency in procedures, particularly for CHIS. These included a lack of public awareness as to the extent and nature of criminal conduct that might be committed by CHIS.[77] It is clear that this is a difficult issue as the disclosure of information on covert law enforcement operations can compromise the effective investigation of organised crime. However, there are a number of safeguards in place to prevent the abuse of CHIS. The PSNI has an internal human rights adviser and, in addition, the conduct of the PSNI is scrutinised by an independent human rights adviser of the Northern Ireland Policing Board.[78] Moreover, the Surveillance Commissioner regularly reviews the existing arrangements that are in place, and individuals can lodge complaints before the Investigatory Powers Tribunal as noted above. These should mitigate some of the uncertainties surrounding the use of CHIS in organised crime investigations.

The operation of CHIS has also met with some criticism in the Republic of Ireland. It was stated by the Garda Ombudsman Commission that guidance on CHIS was restricted to high-ranking officers and there was insufficient training for all officers.[79] The management of documents related to registration/recruitment of CHIS was also regarded as inadequate.[80] It was acknowledged that these led to unnecessary risks in the handling and management of CHIS. There does not seem to be a robust mechanism to address the failure to abide by the guidelines and procedures and this, therefore, leaves the question of accountability unclear. Moreover, a report by the Garda Ombudsman in 2013 highlighted problems with informant handling procedures, management and governance.[81] All of these strengthen the point raised above that legislation that sets out clear guidance and accountability is desirable in this jurisdiction.

A lack of adequate financial, human and technical resources to combat organised crime was another common concern expressed by the law enforcement communities in both jurisdictions. For example, the PSNI Organised Crime Branch had a budget of approximately £11 million in 2013 which was said to be a very small portion of the entire PSNI budget.[82] This has often forced the Branch to prioritise important cases with the result that some crimes or criminal groups

76 Interviews with HMRC officers, *supra* ch 3 n 6.

77 Interview with the Committee on the Administration of Justice (CAJ) on 20 August 2013.

78 Interviews with the Northern Ireland Policing Board on 18 September and 21 November 2013, and on 27 January 2014.

79 Garda Ombudsman Commission, *Special Report to the Minister of Justice and Equality* (May 2013), 4.

80 Ibid., 6.

81 Ibid., 1–12.

82 *Supra* n 1.

might not have received sufficient attention.[83] This also casts some doubt over whether organised crime is regarded as a priority within the PSNI. One way to alleviate this problem is to use criminal proceeds more effectively. Since 2011, the full value of assets confiscated from the 'criminal recovery process' (i.e. conviction-based confiscation) is returned to Northern Ireland.[84] One half of the pot is used to fund community projects through the Asset Recovery Community Scheme (ARCS) and the other half is returned to the law enforcement authorities under the Assets Recovery Incentivisation Scheme (ARIS). During 2014 and 2015, the total amount returned to Northern Ireland was £3.2 million, with £1,594,719 distributed to partner agencies including £282,698 to the PSNI, £223,507 to HMRC and £717,623 to the Public Prosecution Service (PPS).[85] In terms of its usage for law enforcement, in the past the ARIS money funded financial investigators and intelligence officers;[86] this demonstrates a good use of criminal proceeds to tackle organised crime. However, a separate arrangement exists under the 'civil recovery process' under which 50 per cent of the criminal proceeds confiscated are returned to Northern Ireland as part of ARIS but the other half is retained by the Home Office.[87] It would be desirable for the criminal proceeds confiscated through civil recovery to be returned to Northern Ireland so that relevant agencies could enhance their law enforcement capacity.

In contrast, a similar scheme does not exist in the Republic of Ireland as all criminal assets are sent directly to the Exchequer. A senior Garda officer reflected that there were arguments for and against this approach.[88] On the one hand, it is safer and more transparent for all the money recovered to be immediately transferred to the Exchequer. This view was also expressed by officers of Revenue, Irish Tax and Customs.[89] On the other hand, those funds might be used more effectively if fed into worthy projects designed to remedy the damage caused by organised criminals. They could also be used to enhance the capacity of the law enforcement community in this jurisdiction and send a clear message that criminals are not able to benefit from their activities. Therefore, the Irish government should consider establishing a similar system.

Further, the law enforcement communities could improve the relationship with local businesses which are at risk of involvement in organised crime. It has been discovered that obtaining cooperation in money laundering investigations from financial institutions, including accountants and money service bureaus, is still difficult even though significant progress has been made. The reasons for this include a lack of sufficient training, expertise and experience to detect and report financial crimes; a culture of fear which prevents them from reporting suspicious activities; and active collusion with criminals.[90] Other industries, such as agriculture,

83 Ibid.
84 OCTF, *supra* intro n 9, 32.
85 Ibid., 33.
86 Ibid.
87 Home Office, *The Proceeds of Crime Act 2002* (March 2014), 3.
88 Interview with a senior Garda officer on 23 September 2013.
89 Interviews with Revenue, Irish Tax and Customs, *supra* ch 3 n 133.

construction, catering and shellfish, are also known to exploit trafficked victims,[91] and there is an acute need to educate and prevent them from engaging in slavery and forced labour. All of these require the authorities concerned to facilitate more targeted community outreach initiatives, training and awareness raising.

Finally, the impact of devolution of criminal justice and policing in Northern Ireland should be mentioned. Most law enforcement stakeholders in the island of Ireland stated that devolution has made little difference in terms of day-to-day law enforcement activities against organised crime. However, some stated that devolution is making things easier to an extent. For example, direct communication with the Justice Minister and the Department of Justice can now be facilitated whereas in the past decisions were made in London, taking a longer time for action to materialise.[92] It was also noted that the Department of Justice and the Justice Minister have been very supportive of the work of the PSNI Organised Crime Branch. In addition, the law enforcement community has had more contact with politicians in the Assembly in recent times. The relevant agencies often provide briefings for the Members of the Legislative Assembly, and it seems that there is a strong interest within the Assembly in organised crime and law enforcement.[93] These are undoubtedly positive changes which can strengthen action against transnational organised crime in this jurisdiction.

Having said this, there has been a controversial issue in Northern Ireland. The advent of the NCA has reopened the political debate on the accountability of national agencies such as the NCA and HMRC in Northern Ireland. A question here is the extent to which devolution has an impact upon how they operate and are held accountable. The representatives of SOCA, before the NCA came into existence, stated that certain political parties continued to have issues with the organisation due to the lack of sufficient local accountability.[94] One example of this may be seen in the rejection by the Assembly of a consent motion tabled by the Ulster Unionist Party in February 2013 for the purpose of legislating for the NCA. Such a political sentiment has further practical implications. The establishment of the NCA on 7 October 2013 led to the removal of powers previously entrusted to SOCA in Northern Ireland, such as the powers of a constable. There has also been considerable confusion about the potential impact on civil asset recovery. Despite this, it was felt that the position of the NCA would be secure because a UK-wide response is necessary for organised crime;[95] the most recent development will confirm this as will be shown in Chapter 5. The NCA also has

90 Interviews with PSNI Officers, *supra* ch 3 n 3.

91 Department of Justice, *Northern Ireland Human Trafficking and Exploitation Strategy 2015/16*, 7.

92 Interviews with representatives of the Department of Justice on 19 April 2013 and 29 May 2013.

93 Interviews with PSNI and HMRC officers, *supra* ch 3 n 3 and 6.

94 Interviews with SOCA officers, *supra* n 39.

95 Ibid.

extensive networks abroad that could be utilised by the law enforcement community in Northern Ireland where appropriate. In summary, whilst there are examples of good practice in criminal investigation into organised crime both in terms of legislative frameworks and their enforcement in Northern Ireland and the Republic of Ireland, it is also evident that there is much scope for improvement in various areas.

4.5 Protection and promotion of human rights

In addition to these practical matters, there are several key human rights issues that should be highlighted in relation to criminal investigation into transnational organised crime. It is important to acknowledge from the outset that all agencies interviewed regard the protection and promotion of human rights to be an integral part of their work. In Northern Ireland, the PSNI has in-house human rights training which all officers must undergo upon recruitment.[96] The training itself consists of workshops and online modules which individual officers can take at their own pace. There is also a specific human rights legal adviser who can be contacted by officers to seek clarification on human rights issues in law enforcement. An independent human rights adviser within the Policing Board also closely scrutinises the compliance of the PSNI. These are examples of good practice and clearly demonstrate that the law enforcement community in Northern Ireland takes human rights seriously. One point to note, however, is that there is no compulsory human rights training for new officers after the initial training; the onus is left on each individual officer to undergo additional training, although regular updates on new/emerging human rights issues as well as national and European case law appear to be circulated widely.[97] The extent to which they serve as 'training' is not clear, and it is important that more formal human rights training be provided on a regular basis. This also applies to other agencies. Moreover, human rights training is not generally conducted by external human rights organisations, and there is scope to make use of their expertise more proactively in the future. This could also enhance mutual trust with the civil society sector and boost public confidence in law enforcement.

In the Republic of Ireland, Garda officers reported that they are aware of human rights considerations in their day-to-day work but rarely refer to the common ECHR provisions such as Articles 2 (Right to Life), 6 (Right to a Fair Trial) and 8 (Right to Private and Family Life).[98] This is mainly because of the Irish Constitution which appears to contain many of the same safeguards. However, there is no doubt that the constitutional protection is complemented by the European Convention on Human Rights Act 2003 which is similar to the Human Rights Act 1998 in the UK. In terms of training, there is a human rights

96 Interviews with PSNI officers, *supra* ch 3 n 3.

97 Interview with a human rights adviser, *supra* n 43.

98 Interviews with Garda officers, *supra* ch 3 n 7.

element in most police training the majority of which is provided at the time of recruitment, as in Northern Ireland, and such training is also conducted when officers are promoted to a higher rank.[99] This suggests that lower-ranking officers may only have basic human rights training. More crucially, An Garda Síochána does not have an in-house human rights adviser. Although Garda officers can contact a department in Garda Headquarters that advises on such issues or simply contact a senior officer, the appointment of a dedicated human rights legal adviser would be beneficial, particularly as the Republic lacks clear legislation on certain areas, such as the use of special investigative techniques as explained above. Once again, this could have a positive impact on public confidence in law enforcement.

The principal human rights considerations encountered by law enforcement officers from both jurisdictions during investigations include Articles 2 (Right to Life), 6 (Right to a Fair Trial) and 8 (Right to Privacy) of the ECHR. Article 2 is particularly relevant to the protection of witnesses, CHIS and victims. In relation to human trafficking, for instance, protection of trafficked victims takes precedence even when this could affect their investigations.[100] The same applies to the protection of witnesses and jurors from intimidation and violence. In this regard, a need to ensure that information used during the proceedings cannot be traced back to the source has been highlighted.[101] In addition to observing the relevant obligations under the ECHR, proper implementation of the instruments such as the EU Directive on Victims of Crime explored in Chapter 2 is equally important. In this regard, the UK transposed this instrument in the autumn of 2015 through the adoption of the (revised) Code of Practice for Victims of Crime.[102] This Code was also given statutory footing in Northern Ireland through the Victim Charter (Justice (Northern Ireland) Act 2015) Order (Northern Ireland) 2015. In the Republic, the Directive will be formally transposed when the Criminal Justice (Victims of Crime) Bill, currently under scrutiny by the Oireachtas, is enacted in the near future. These undoubtedly represent a positive development.

The right to privacy under Article 8 of the ECHR is another right which can be affected, particularly by the use of special investigative techniques. This right is qualified in that it can be curtailed in the interests of national security, public safety and prevention of crime.[103] However, as set out in *Kennedy v United Kingdom*[104] and other jurisprudence noted elsewhere, the use of these measures must meet three conditions: 1) existence of a legal basis (in accordance with the law); 2) legitimate aim; and 3) proportionality (necessary in a democratic society). In the present case, the ECtHR held that RIPA had sufficient safeguards to protect the human rights of those affected in relation to the interception of

99 Ibid.
100 Interviews with PSNI officers, *supra* ch 3 n 3.
101 Interview with a SOCA officer, *supra* n 39.
102 Ministry of Justice, *Code of Practice for Victims of Crime* (October 2015).
103 Art 8(2).
104 App no 26839/05 (2010).

communications (including the decision of the independent Interception of Communications Commissioner) and did not violate the ECHR. The Criminal Justice (Surveillance) Act 2009 in the Republic of Ireland conforms to these principles to an extent. although the government could potentially be held liable in the future for the lack of a legal basis in relation to CHIS.

In addition, the treatment of suspects during investigations has human rights implications. In the Republic of Ireland, a period of pre-trial detention can be quite long. For drug trafficking, an initial maximum period of 48 hours may be extended by a further 120 hours upon application to a Circuit Court judge or a District Court judge.[105] It was argued by a defence lawyer that an extension for this initial period is routine in this jurisdiction.[106] Whilst judicial intervention adds a certain degree of safeguarding, some doubts were expressed by the human rights community in the Republic of Ireland as to the necessity of such a long period.[107] Pre-charge detention in the UK also raises concerns, particularly when organised crime has a nexus with terrorism. Whilst the previous period of 28 days under the Terrorism Act 2000 was reduced to 14 days with the Protection of Freedoms Act 2012, this is still a long period to be detained without charge. This is one area of law enforcement where extra powers in relation to terrorism can be used for organised crime if there is a clear nexus.

Another issue raised in the Republic of Ireland is access to a lawyer. In the UK, a suspect has a right to consult a duty solicitor at the police station upon arrest. In contrast, access to a lawyer is limited in the Republic of Ireland as they are not entitled to be present during a police interview. Defence lawyers and a human rights group have expressed concerns about this.[108] The Department of Justice and Equality recently commissioned a Working Group to Advise on a System Providing for the Presence of a Legal Representative During Garda Interviews. This was in response to the EU Directive on the Right of Access to a Lawyer mentioned in Chapter 2. When reporting their findings in July 2013, the Working Group acknowledged that the current policy of preventing a solicitor from being present at a Garda interview would come under increased pressure from the ECHR even if the Republic of Ireland decided not to opt into the EU Directive.[109] Given the complex nature of organised crime and a possibility of heavier penalties as well as the additional powers given to the law enforcement authorities, the presence of a lawyer during interviews is a reasonable step to take to respect and

105 Criminal Justice (Drug Trafficking) Act 1996, s 2. The Criminal Justice Act 2007, s 50, also allows detention of up to 7 days in relation to firearm offences.

106 Interview with a defence lawyer, *supra* ch 3 n 71.

107 Interview with an ICCL representative, *supra* ch 3 n 14. See also *Concluding Observations of the Human Rights Committee on Ireland's Second Periodic Report*, A/55/40 (2000) para 17; and Irish Human Rights Commission, *Submission to the Human Rights Committee on the Examination of Ireland's Third Periodic Report* (March 2008), 22.

108 Interviews with defence lawyers, *supra* ch 3 n 71; and interview with an ICCL representative, *supra* ch 3 n 14.

109 Report of the Working Group, 22.

protect the rights of suspects. The Republic of Ireland therefore should opt into the EU Directive and implement it through legislation.

4.6 Prosecution

The PPS in Northern Ireland was established by the Justice (Northern Ireland) Act 2002 and formally came into being in 2005 as the successor to the Department of the Director of Public Prosecutions. It is divided into four regions, each headed by a Regional Prosecutor (Assistant Director) who has overall responsibility for decisions over prosecutions with the exception of those cases which are considered by prosecutors in the Headquarters.[110] In general, organised crime offences come under the auspices of the Central Casework Unit which deals with cases of a serious or sensitive nature (e.g. terrorism offences or cases that involve the use of an informant or surveillance techniques). There are also a number of other sections within the PPS, each headed by an Assistant Director. These include Fraud and Departmental Prosecutions, Policy and Information and High Court and International Matters.[111]

In England and Wales, the Crown Prosecution Service (CPS) utilises so-called 'Legal Guidance' which describes up-to-date legal issues and charging standards in detail. Many of these are relevant to organised crime as they provide guidance related to drug offences, fraud, human trafficking and money laundering.[112] These are important not only for prosecution of organised crime but also for the facilitation of consistency in decision-making which can help boost public confidence in law enforcement. In contrast, the PPS in Northern Ireland does not produce Legal Guidance regularly. It recently adopted a policy on human trafficking[113] due to a growing interest in this crime but there are no guidelines for other forms of organised crime. This may be understandable as various statutes related to organised crime apply to England, Wales and Northern Ireland simultaneously, and therefore the PPS takes account of the existing CPS guidance. Indeed, the PPS prosecutors stated that they refer to the guidance where appropriate although they are not bound by it.[114]

However, the devolution of criminal justice and policing in Northern Ireland may require the PPS to create its own guidance in the future. When asked about this, prosecutors stated that the 'Code for Prosecutors',[115] which is applicable to all crime, provides detailed guidance on issues such as evidential/public interest tests, disclosure and unduly lenient sentences.[116] It is worth noting that public

110 PPS, *Annual Report and Resource Accounts 2014/15*, 13.
111 Ibid.
112 CPS, *Legal Guidance* <www.cps.gov.uk/legal>.
113 PPS, *Public Prosecution Service Policy for Prosecuting Cases of Human Trafficking* (September 2013).
114 Interviews with the PPS on 16 November 2012 and 30 January 2013.
115 *Code for Prosecutors* (revised 2008).
116 Interviews with the PPS, *supra* n 114.

interest considerations include offences carried out in pursuit of organised crime.[117] In addition, the PPS does produce internal guidance for prosecutors on law and practice that are relevant to organised crime, including the one on Ancillary Orders (e.g. Financial Reporting and Forfeiture) and on appropriate venues for drug-related offences.[118] 'Legislation Notes' are also pertinent as they ensure that the PPS prosecutors are kept up to date with relevant legislation and any subsequent changes. However, given its complex nature, the PPS could benefit from having specific guidelines/policies on organised crime to facilitate consistency in decision-making. In particular, there is a need for clearer guidelines on fuel and tobacco smuggling which are regarded as very serious offences in this jurisdiction.

Under the Justice (Northern Ireland) Act 2002, the PPS can provide prosecutorial advice to the PSNI where crimes are particularly serious. The PSNI can also seek advice from the PPS at any stage of the investigation. It would appear that one key difference between the PPS and the CPS in England and Wales is that a CPS prosecutor is assigned to each case from the very beginning of the investigation. In contrast, this is not normally the case in Northern Ireland, even though in some complex cases and in others that are dealt with by the Central Casework Unit, the PPS prosecutors are often assigned at an early stage of police investigations.[119] Whilst it is to be appreciated that this has some resource implications for a small jurisdiction like Northern Ireland, the CPS model could be adopted specifically for all cases that involve organised crime to facilitate more regular communications and exchanges of evidence and intelligence.

Another important aspect in relation to prosecution is immunity granted to assisting offenders. Sections 71 to 74 of the Serious Organised Crime and Police Act 2005 allow the PPS to enter into agreements with offenders to provide assistance in criminal investigations, including giving evidence. In return, the PPS may agree to provide immunity from prosecution and an undertaking on the use of evidence (that it will not be used against the assisting offenders) or to provide an account of assistance rendered to the court in support of a reduced sentence.[120] These measures are in line with Article 26 of the UNTOC and Article 4 of the EU Framework Decision on Organised Crime which oblige States to encourage cooperation from offenders; the PPS prosecutors acknowledge that this has the potential to dismantle criminal groups and catch crime bosses who are particularly difficult to prosecute due to lack of evidence. However, some concerns were also expressed as to the credibility/authenticity of information provided by such offenders; the protection of those assisting offenders also poses some challenges.[121]

117 Code for Prosecutors, *supra* n 115, 12.
118 Interviews with the PPS, *supra* n 114.
119 Ibid.
120 Ibid.
121 Ibid.

In addition, the intimidation of victims, witnesses and informants has been identified as an area of concern at the prosecution stage. For instance, it has been reported that intimidation of witnesses is a problem for crimes such as fuel laundering in Northern Ireland where there is strong link with terrorism.[122] The intimidation and harming of witnesses are prohibited under Article 47 of the Criminal Justice (Northern Ireland) Order 1996.[123] Although this is in line with Article 23 of the UNTOC which obliges States to criminalise obstruction of justice, these offences only attract up to 5 years' imprisonment. The reality then is that many receive reduced or suspended sentences which begs the question whether this serves as an effective deterrent. A strong argument can therefore be made for strengthening the punishment regime in order to send a clear message to criminals and enhance public confidence in law enforcement against organised crime.

Needless to say, criminalisation of witness intimidation must be accompanied by an effective witness protection programme. This now has statutory footing in the UK through the Serious Organised Crime and Police Act 2005.[124] The designated protection providers are the police forces (including the PSNI), the NCA and HMRC.[125] These providers can also seek assistance from other public bodies such as a court/tribunal and Parliament.[126] The legislation does not list particular measures to be taken and allows protection providers to adopt any arrangement that they consider appropriate. Whilst these look good on paper, it has been discovered that intimidation of witnesses still happens[127] which casts some doubt on the efficacy of the existing system. Related to this, it has been discovered that, although witnesses are willing to assist the PSNI, they are not willing to provide formal statements due to the fear of reprisal.[128] This culture of fear appears to be a pressing issue for a small community like Northern Ireland where everyone seems to know each other. It is worth highlighting in this regard that 68 per cent of respondents who took part in the recent organised crime survey believe that organised crime could lead to fear in the community.[129] Therefore, there is scope for improvement in relation to the current witness protection scheme and also to gaining the trust of witnesses in order to enhance prosecution against organised crime.

In the Republic of Ireland, the Office of the Director of Public Prosecutions (DPP) was established in 1974; all indictable offences are prosecuted by this office

122 Northern Ireland Affairs Committee, *supra* intro n 10, 110 and 118 (Ev 74 and 82).

123 This is equivalent to the Criminal Justice and Public Order Act 1994, s 51 in England and Wales. Ss 39 and 40 are applicable to witnesses who are victims of crime under the Criminal Justice and Police Act 2001.

124 Ch 4.

125 S 82.

126 S 85.

127 Interviews with PSNI officers, *supra* ch 3 n 3.

128 Ibid.; and interviews with the PPS, *supra* n 114.

129 Department of Justice, *Views on Organised Crime: Findings from the January 2013 Northern Ireland Omnibus Survey* (January 2013), 4.

in accordance with the Constitution. Like the PPS in Northern Ireland, the DPP in this jurisdiction is also an independent agency. It has three divisions. First, there is a directing division which makes decisions on serious cases (22 prosecutors). Within this, there are sub-divisions, some of which deal specifically with organised crime, such as human trafficking and corruption. Then, there is a solicitors' division which implements the direction to prosecute and deals with court work. Finally, there is an administrative division. In addition, there are 32 State solicitors operating outside Dublin who are private solicitors on contract.[130] Unlike the PPS in Northern Ireland where prosecutors are involved and make a decision in every case, prosecutors in the Republic have delegated some of these tasks to An Garda Síochána with the result that they make decisions in most summary or lesser offences. With respect to serious cases of organised crime, however, An Garda Síochána cannot charge a suspect without referring them to the Office of the DPP. This is in line with Section 8 of the Garda Síochána Act 2005. The Office of the DPP has a system in place to ensure that An Garda Síochána receive direction as quickly as possible. Prosecutors are placed on a mobile phone roster a week at a time so that Garda officers can receive direction outside hours if necessary.[131] An Garda Síochána also contact prosecutors regularly for their views and/or advice or to discuss a strategy in advance of taking any action.[132]

Unlike the CPS in England and Wales, the Office of the DPP does not have prosecution guidance/guidelines on organised crime, and given that organised crime cases are not as widespread as in the UK, there does not appear to be an acute need to create one. When asked whether prosecutors should have their own guidelines, one prosecutor answered that this would facilitate consistency in decision-making.[133] Other prosecutors felt this was not necessary as the relatively small size of the directing division (22 persons) ensures that there is good interaction between prosecutors which, in turn, promotes uniformity in decision-making. However, for the reasons stated above, publication of such guidance is beneficial in many respects, and therefore should be considered further.

In terms of immunity from prosecution, this could be facilitated by the DPP in order to elicit useful evidence and cooperation in prosecuting and punishing organised crime. Aside from the area of cartel immunity under the Competition Act 2002, there is no statute which provides detailed guidance on immunity and other measures like the Serious Organised Crime and Police Act 2005 in the UK, although there is an internal guideline on the matter. On this issue, the Deputy Director of Public Prosecutions stated that the current system works well and therefore there is no pressing need to legislate.[134] Another prosecutor noted that the granting of immunity and other measures is used sparingly in practice because

130 For more information, see the website of the Office of DPP at <www.dppireland.ie>.

131 Interviews with public prosecutors, *supra* ch 3 n 16.

132 Ibid.

133 Ibid.

134 Ibid.

evidence emanating from such sources is treated with much more caution by a judge or jury.[135] However, similar to the use of special investigative techniques, a lack of legislation raises issues in terms of transparency and legality, and therefore it is desirable that this is rectified.

Finally, obstruction of justice was also highlighted as a problem in the Republic of Ireland.[136] Intimidation of witnesses attracts 15 years' imprisonment under Section 41 of the Criminal Justice Act 1999 as amended by the Criminal Justice (Amendment) Act 2009. This may have a stronger deterrent effect and is an example of good practice as Ireland clearly recognises the significance of punishing this offence. The Irish legislation is also in conformity with international and regional standards. However, similar to Northern Ireland, securing a conviction for this offence does not appear to be common. It has been reported in this regard that between 2003 and 2013, 72 convictions were secured out of 315 cases that involved witness and jury intimidation.[137]

Witness protection programmes are provided by An Garda Síochána and there is no underpinning legislation in the Republic.[138] This raises an issue of clarity and accountability, and it has been argued that the Irish practice breaches the Council of Europe Recommendation on Protection of Witnesses (2005) which has emphasised the need for an adequate legal framework on witness protection.[139] In terms of the measures available under witness protection, an inadequacy has been identified by the Supreme Court;[140] it has been pointed out that the existing system does not adequately address issues such as the causes of intimidation and the effects of measures such as relocation.[141] This latter point was also identified as a problem by An Garda Síochána. Many witnesses do not want to be involved in the witness protection programmes in practice because, for instance, they do not want to be away from their family.[142] One practical consequence of this is that, although these witnesses are willing to assist criminal investigations, they become reluctant to provide evidence to be used in court. An additional difficulty is that witnesses in small towns or communities do not come forward for fear of being targeted by criminals.[143] This highlights the complex nature of the culture of fear in this jurisdiction also.

Finally, available statistical information sheds some light on the prosecution practice in relation to organised crime. In Northern Ireland, of 176 cases related

135 Ibid.

136 Interviews with Garda officers, *supra* ch 3 n 7.

137 *Irish Examiner*, 'Fewer than 25% Witness Intimidation Convictions' 30 July 2013.

138 Campbell, *supra* intro n 33, 150.

139 Ibid.

140 *DPP v Gilligan* [2005] IESC 78.

141 Campbell, *supra* intro n 33, 150; and Paddy Hillyard, 'The Normalisation of Special Powers from Northern Ireland to Britain', in Phil Scraton (ed.), *Law, Order and the Authoritarian State: Readings in Critical Criminology* (Open University Press 1987), 300.

142 Interviews with Garda officers, *supra* ch 3 n 7.

143 Ibid. See further John Connolly, *National Drug Intervention, What Works* (Health Research Board 2011).

to money laundering referred in 2014, the PPS decided to prosecute 128.[144] Whilst this demonstrates a high rate of prosecution, the same is not true for other crimes. For instance, of 88 cases on fiscal and excise fraud referred by HMRC in the same year, only 37 of them were prosecuted.[145] As for the Republic of Ireland, although relevant statistical information is not available, it has been noted that prosecution for human trafficking is still low.[146] It is premature to draw a definitive conclusion on the efficacy of prosecution in the island of Ireland from these statistics alone as there may be a number of factors which are beyond the control of the PPS and the Office of the DPP. However, the low rate of prosecution can encourage criminals to operate in the island of Ireland more proactively and also affects public confidence.

4.7 Cross-border cooperation in criminal investigation and prosecution

4.7.1 Key measures

An important measure that facilitates cross-border cooperation is extradition. In the UK, including Northern Ireland, the Extradition Act 2003 incorporates the regime of EAWs explored in Chapter 2. In return for streamlining extradition within EU Member States, the legislation contains several safeguards to protect the rights of suspects/defendants. For example, it provides for a number of grounds for refusal, including double jeopardy, extraneous consideration (where there is the likelihood of persecution or no guarantee of a fair trial), passage of time, age and speciality.[147] Another notable aspect is the inclusion of human rights considerations as an additional ground for refusal. Section 21 provides that a judge must decide whether extradition would be compatible with the UK's obligations under the ECHR. This goes further than what is set out in the Framework Decision on EAW as it does not recognise human rights protection as a mandatory ground for non-execution. According to the Recorder of Belfast, issues are occasionally raised in relation to Article 3 (where defendants could face inhuman treatment in their home States)[148] or Article 8 (where they have strong family ties in Northern Ireland).[149] In practice, most of these cases are generally unsuccessful as they lack merit.[150] This seems to be in line with ECHR jurisprudence which states that it is only in exceptional cases where protection of human

144 OCTF, *supra* intro n 9, 30.

145 Ibid.

146 GRETA Report on Ireland, *supra* ch 3 n 61.

147 Ss 12–17.

148 See, for example, *Lithuania v Campbell* [2013] NIQB 19, where extradition was refused by the Northern Ireland Court as the defendant would likely be held in conditions in breach of art 3 of the ECHR.

149 Interview with the Recorder of Belfast, *supra* ch 3 n 5.

150 Ibid.

rights outweighs the legitimate aim of preventing serious crime, including organised crime.[151] In any event, judges in Northern Ireland agree that these safeguards are rigorously examined and applied where appropriate.[152]

The use of EAWs attracted widespread support from the law enforcement community in Northern Ireland and EAWs are frequently issued and received in this jurisdiction. The vast majority of EAWs originate from Eastern Europe, including Lithuania, Poland and Slovakia, with the Republic of Ireland being described as the next highest user.[153] The PSNI receives a higher number of EAWs than they transmit, and in numerical terms there could be about 40 to 50 that they are working on at any one time.[154] The Northern Ireland Branch of SOCA relied upon the EAWs much less, perhaps only once or twice a year.[155] All of this appears to indicate that extradition related to organised crime is not as frequent as in the rest of the UK[156] and that in most cases criminals are prosecuted and punished in the appropriate jurisdictions.

A common opinion expressed by the law enforcement agencies is that scrapping EAWs would be problematic if there was no suitable alternative. A High Court judge also agreed that they are a very important instrument as they facilitate good cross-border cooperation.[157] Moreover, the Ministers of Justice for Northern Ireland and the Republic of Ireland also affirmed their value in tackling serious cross-border crimes.[158] The key principle behind the implementation of EAWs is mutual recognition of judicial decisions as explained in Chapter 2, and the judges in both jurisdictions stated that mutual recognition has been established between the two jurisdictions without any problems, which is partly due to/a result of similarities in historical foundations and culture as well as their shared common law tradition.[159] This is an example of good practice where the EU principle is successfully implemented at the national level. However, mutual recognition and trust are said to be difficult to achieve with civil law jurisdictions in continental Europe as the criminal procedures are different.[160]

There are a few more legislative frameworks that are relevant to cross-border law enforcement cooperation. Perhaps the most important is the Crime (International Co-operation) Act 2003. The key measures under this Act include, but are not limited to, mutual service of process and provision of evidence;

151 See, for instance, *King v United Kingdom*, App no 9742/07 (2010).
152 *Supra* ch 3 n 5.
153 Interviews with PSNI officers, *supra* ch 3 n 3.
154 Ibid.
155 Interviews with SOCA officers, *supra* n 39.
156 In 2014, for instance, a total of 138 EAWs were issued in the UK as a whole. See NCA, *Wanted by the UK: European Arrest Warrant Statistics 2009–2015.*
157 Interview with a High Court judge, *supra* ch 3 n 5.
158 Joanna Dawson and Sally Lipscomb, *The European Arrest Warrant* (House of Commons Briefing Paper) (June 2015), 24.
159 Interviews with judges in Northern Ireland, *supra* ch 3 n 5; and interviews with judges in the Republic, *supra* n 64 and ch 3 n 17.
160 Interviews with Garda officers, *supra* ch 3 n 7.

hearing of evidence via video-links; execution of asset freezing orders; and transfer of prisoners.[161] Another important aspect is that, together with the Police Reform Act 2002, the 2003 Act has incorporated the EU Framework Decision on JITs and also permits foreign surveillance operations to be conducted in the UK. In addition, under Articles 17 to 20 of the EU Convention on Mutual Legal Assistance in Criminal Matters 2000 and RIPA, international requests for interceptions of communication may be executed.[162] Finally, the Naples II Convention on customs cooperation has been implemented through the existing legislative provisions, namely the European Communities Act 1972 and Section 9 of the Customs and Excise Management Act 1979. It is apparent that the arrangements for wider criminal justice cooperation are broadly in line with the international and regional standards as represented by the UNTOC and EU law.

In relation to prosecution of cross-border offences, a starting point is deciding whether or not to exercise criminal jurisdiction over them. The rule is laid out in the legislation on substantive offences. For instance, the Modern Slavery Act 2015 allows exercise of jurisdiction over human trafficking based upon territorial, flag and nationality principles.[163] The UK can also exercise jurisdiction over predicate offences committed abroad in connection with money laundering which takes place in the UK.[164] In addition, universal jurisdiction over ships trafficking drugs abroad is also a possibility under the Criminal Justice (International Co-operation) Act 1990. The legislative frameworks on organised crime therefore recognise various forms of criminal jurisdictions as explored in Chapter 1.

The CPS has published guidance on how to deal with jurisdictional conflicts.[165] The document draws upon the *Eurojust Guidelines* on the matter,[166] which sets out the preliminary presumption that, if possible, a prosecution should take place in the jurisdiction where the majority of the criminality occurred. This reaffirms the primacy of the territoriality principle. Other factors that may arise include the location of the accused, the existing extradition/surrender arrangements with other States as well as the interests of victims and witnesses. It cautions, however, that the sentencing powers of courts must not be a primary factor in deciding in which jurisdiction a case should be prosecuted. By way of illustration, in the case of *R v Matyas Pis*,[167] the defendant trafficked two women from Hungary

161 See also the pre-existing legislation, the Criminal Justice (International Co-operation) Act 1990 for transfer of prisoners and the Criminal Justice and Data Protection (Protocol No. 36) Regulations 2014, which transposed the EU Framework Decisions on Orders Freezing Property and Evidence 2003 and on Confiscation Orders 2006.

162 Home Office, *Request for Mutual Assistance in Criminal Matters: Guidelines for Authorities Outside of the United Kingdom* (March 2015), 30.

163 Ss 2 and 35.

164 POCA, pt 7.

165 CPS, *Jurisdiction*, <www.cps.gov.uk/legal/h_to_k/jurisdiction/#an12>.

166 *Eurojust Guidelines: Making the Decision – Which Jurisdiction Should Prosecute?* (2003). This is to be revised in 2016. See *Eurojust News* (Issue 14, January 2016), 5.

167 [2012] NICC 14.

via Dublin airport to Belfast for the purpose of sexual exploitation. It was evident that the substantive offences of sexual exploitation and trafficking occurred in Northern Ireland, and therefore a decision was taken to prosecute him in this jurisdiction.[168] It was confirmed by prosecutors in both jurisdictions that generally no problem arises in making this type of decision as they are able to communicate with each other closely and effectively to avoid jurisdictional conflicts.

Another important piece of legislation is the Criminal Jurisdiction Act 1975. Under the Act, a range of offences committed within the Republic of Ireland can be tried in Northern Ireland. Reciprocal arrangements are contained in the Criminal Law (Jurisdiction) Act 1976 in Ireland.[169] These include murder, manslaughter, kidnapping or false imprisonment and some criminal damage offences and offences against the person. Schedule 1 of the 1975 Act also includes hijacking, explosive substances offences and firearms offences. The main thrust behind these statutes was the need to address terrorism more effectively. However, in a session of the Parliamentary Northern Ireland Affairs Committee that was dedicated to cross-border cooperation, the PSNI raised the important question as to whether the list of offences should be updated beyond terrorism-related crimes. In particular, Deputy Chief Constable Gillespie suggested that organised crimes such as human trafficking, e-crime, money laundering and fraud should be included.[170] The law enforcement officials, judges and defence lawyers in both jurisdictions also commented that the time was right to update this legislation. Having said this, the ICCL expressed the important point that discrepancies related to the treatment of defendants in both jurisdictions can lead to fragmented approaches in protecting their human rights.[171] If this legislative change is to happen, both governments must ensure fair treatment of defendants, bearing in mind the relevant EU and ECHR standards highlighted earlier.

The Republic of Ireland also seems to have good legislative frameworks to facilitate international cooperation. The European Arrest Warrant Act 2003 is one such example.[172] Incoming requests are passed to the Department of Justice and Equality (Central Authority) and then to the Office of Chief State Solicitor which seeks the endorsement of the High Court.[173] Outgoing requests are forwarded by the Office of the DPP to the Department of Justice and Equality which in turn

168 Interviews with the PPS, *supra* n 114.

169 S 14.

170 Northern Ireland Affairs Committee, *Second Report, Cross-Border Co-operation between the Governments of the United Kingdom and the Republic of Ireland* (2009).

171 Interview with an ICCL representative, *supra* ch 3 n 14.

172 Other legislation include the Extradition Act 1965, the Extradition (European Convention on the Suppression of Terrorism) Act 1987, the Extradition (Amendment) Act 1987, the Extradition (Amendment) Act 1994, the Extradition (European Union Conventions) Act 2001 and the European Arrest Warrant (Application to Third Countries and Amendment) and Extradition (Amendment) Act 2012.

173 Department of Justice and Equality, *The European Arrest Warrant, a Guide to Irish Procedures* (January 2006), 7–10.

transmits them to the requested States.[174] Similar to the Extradition Act 2003 of the UK, the Irish legislation also contains a number of safeguards, including compatibility with the ECHR.[175] The Irish government recently published its Annual Report for 2014 on the operation of the 2003 Act. According to this, it received 183 EAWs from Member States, with 37 of these coming from the UK, including 8 from Northern Ireland.[176] It also issued 78 EAWs to other Member States in the same year with the majority of these (49) being transmitted to the UK.[177] Similar to the law enforcement community in Northern Ireland, the representatives from An Garda Síochána and the Office of the DPP, as well as a High Court judge, confirmed that EAWs are an effective resource and are normally carried out relatively quickly. This once again highlights their importance in tackling transnational organised crime.

In terms of other cross-border cooperation, several other statutes should be mentioned. First, the Criminal Justice (Joint Investigation Teams) Act 2004 incorporates the aforementioned EU Framework Decision on JITs in the same way as the UK legislation. In addition, the Irish government has enacted another piece of legislation, the Criminal Justice (Mutual Assistance) Act 2008, which has transposed important international and European standards.[178] It includes provisions on, among other things, taking evidence in connection with criminal investigations or proceedings in another country;[179] search for and seizure of materials on behalf of another country;[180] and confiscation and forfeiture orders made in another country.[181] It also provides for international cooperation in the interception of communications[182] and controlled delivery.[183] Unlike the UK legislation, however, the 2008 Act does not explicitly touch upon foreign surveillance operations that are to be conducted in the Republic. Another noticeable difference is that the 2008 Act explicitly provides for grounds for refusing mutual legal assistance, which include prosecution and punishment on grounds of various distinctions such as gender, race and religion, infliction of torture or breaches of the ECHR.[184] Whilst the UK can refuse mutual assistance on these grounds,[185] the Irish legislation represents a better model for the purpose of clarity and accountability. Moreover, in relation to customs cooperation, the Customs and Excise (Mutual Assistance) Act 2001 incorporates the Naples II Convention.

174 Ibid.
175 Pt 3.
176 Department of Justice and Equality, *Report on the Operations of the European Arrest Warrant Act 2003* (2014), 14.
177 Ibid., 17.
178 The UNTOC as well as EU instruments are mentioned in Schedules of this Act.
179 Ss 62–75. This includes the use of video/telephone links.
180 Ss 31–48.
181 Ss 49–57.
182 Ss 22–30.
183 Ss 88–92.
184 S 3.
185 Home Office, *supra* n 162, 15.

Finally, similar to the UK, the Irish legislation also provides for various forms of criminal jurisdictions. Under the Criminal Law (Human Trafficking) Act 2008, for instance, the territorial, nationality and passive personality principles can be exercised. The scope is therefore much wider than the Modern Slavery Act 2015 in the UK as the legislation also covers cases where Irish nationals become the victims of this crime. The Criminal Justice Act 1994 as amended and the Criminal Justice (Illicit Traffic by Sea) Act 2008 allow the authorities to exercise jurisdiction over Irish and foreign ships that traffic narcotics. In addition, the flag principle is recognised for offences related to criminal organisations under the Criminal Justice Act 2006.[186] In summary, both jurisdictions appear to have sufficient legislative frameworks to facilitate cross-border law enforcement and criminal justice cooperation, and they amply reflect the relevant international and European standards.

4.7.2 Practical issues in cross-border cooperation

From a practical point of view, law enforcement stakeholders in both jurisdictions are of the view that the state of affairs in relation to cross-border cooperation is generally positive. In the UK, the main Central Authority for mutual assistance in criminal matters in England, Wales and Northern Ireland is the Home Office which receives and transmits requests for mutual legal assistance in criminal matters.[187] In the Republic of Ireland, the Minister for Justice and Equality is formally designated as the Central Authority[188] although the Department of Justice and Equality performs this function in practice. The arrangement, therefore, is similar to that in the UK, including Northern Ireland, apart from the fact that, whilst the UK does not require requests to be made through diplomatic channels, the Republic requires this for States which are not formally designated for the purpose of mutual assistance under the 2008 Act.[189]

It takes a certain amount of time (sometimes a very long time) to receive, transmit and execute formal requests for mutual assistance in criminal matters, and some frustrations were expressed by the law enforcement officers in both jurisdictions as this often results in delays in criminal investigations. Therefore, careful consideration seems to be given beforehand in deciding exactly what the law enforcement officers wish to achieve. Another example of formal cooperation between the two jurisdictions is the adoption of the Inter-Governmental Agreement on Police Co-operation[190] which provides for a range of functions

186 S 72.

187 Home Office, *supra* n 162, 4. In Scotland, the Crown Office is designated as the Central Authority, and HMRC is the Central Authority for tax and fiscal matters.

188 The 2008 Act, s 8.

189 Department of Justice and Equality, *Mutual Legal Assistance in Criminal Matters: A Guide to Irish Law and Procedures* (2008), 4. The EU Member States are regarded as designated States.

190 Agreement between the Government of the United Kingdom of Great Britain and Northern Ireland and the Government of Ireland on Police Co-operation (April 2002).

designed to improve cross-border law enforcement in the island of Ireland. These include the facility for police officers from Northern Ireland to apply for posts in An Garda Síochána and vice versa. It also provides for the organisation of an annual cross-border conference; training on cross-border policing; appointment of expert groups to review the existing arrangements; and joint investigations.

Whilst these and other formal arrangements for cross-border cooperation are respected, it was discovered that a more informal approach to cross-border cooperation is facilitated regularly. Frontline officers and prosecutors have their own contacts and can simply pick up the phone to ask questions and exchange information. They also have regular face-to-face meetings as not everything can be done through emails and phone calls. The key to successful cross-border cooperation is the ability to build a good personal/working relationship, and it is important to highlight that the law enforcement communities in both jurisdictions have been able to do just this. There are examples of good practice to illustrate this. In 2014, An Garda Síochána and the PSNI conducted a joint drug trafficking operation that targeted one particular criminal group which resulted in the seizure of cannabis worth over £3 million (€3.8 million) as well as the arrest of 9 gang members at various locations in Dublin and County Meath.[191] In March 2013, HMRC, the CAB and Revenue, Irish Tax and Customs jointly conducted *Operation Loft* in which 10 raids were conducted across the island of Ireland, resulting in the recovery of 40,000 litres of illegal fuel.[192] These and other examples demonstrate that the law enforcement communities in both jurisdictions work well together. This resonates well with the point raised by Beare that informal cooperation is likely to produce more rewarding results.[193]

There are other ways to facilitate cross-border cooperation. For example, one of the 9 OCTF sub-groups, the Cross-Border Fuel Fraud Enforcement Group, includes representatives from the Republic of Ireland.[194] This ensures direct communication and facilitation of good working relationships. Staff exchanges also take place regularly within the law enforcement communities between both jurisdictions.[195] Interestingly, these are governed by legislation in the Republic of Ireland, namely the Garda Síochána (Police Co-Operation) Act 2003. However, such exchanges do not seem to be common for Revenue, Irish Tax and Customs.[196] Finally, both An Garda Síochána and the PSNI published a joint *Cross-Border Policing Strategy* in 2010 which builds on existing practical and strategic cooperation and identifies a number of key strands of work that can strengthen

191 PSNI and An Garda Síochána, *supra* intro n 12, 14.
192 BBC News Online, 'Major Cross-Border Operation against Illegal Fuel Trade' available at <www.bbc.co.uk/news/uk-northern-ireland-21766952>.
193 Margaret Beare, 'Shifting Boundaries: Between States, Enforcement Agencies and Priorities' in Hans-Jorg Albrecht and Cyrille Fijnaut (eds.), *The Containment of Transnational Organised Crime: Comments on the UN Convention of December 2000* (IUSCRIM 2002), 189.
194 Northern Ireland Affairs Committee, *supra* intro n 10, 42 (Ev. 6).
195 Interviews with Garda officers, *supra* ch 3 n 7.
196 Interviews with Revenue, Irish Tax and Customs, *supra* ch 3 n 133.

cooperation. Paragraph 2.1 provides for the establishment of joint tasking and co-ordination groups. Paragraph 2.5 sets out a mandate for a proactive multi-agency immigration strategy for the policing of the borders between An Garda Síochána, the PSNI, the UK Border Agency and the Irish Naturalisation and Immigration Service. In addition, Paragraph 3.1 calls for an examination of legislation with a view to putting forward proposals to respective departments that would enhance current cross-border crime fighting functions. Other measures include intelligence sharing, cross-border communication and enhanced training.[197] One example of good practice in this regard is the establishment of the Cross-Border Tobacco Fraud Enforcement Group, consisting of An Garda Síochána, the PSNI, HMRC, Revenue, Irish Tax and Customs and the NCA.[198]

Whilst formal and informal cross-border law enforcement cooperation appears to work well, some issues have been identified. Cross-border surveillance is one such example. In Europe, this is facilitated by the Schengen *Acquis* as noted earlier. Article 40 permits authorised cross-border surveillance and in urgent cases it also allows surveillance of up to 5 hours without prior authorisation. Article 41 touches upon hot pursuit. The UK has opted in to Article 40 but not Article 41. The central government has recently endorsed Article 40 as it provides an effective arrangement compared to formal mutual legal assistance which is slow and time-consuming.[199] In contrast, the Republic of Ireland opted in to neither of these provisions. In relation to customs cooperation, the UK decided not to be part of the hot pursuit provision of the Naples II Convention and the Irish government has opted out of hot pursuit, cross-border surveillance and covert investigation.[200] Effective communication and coordination may mean that UK law enforcement officers no longer need to continue with surveillance in the Republic of Ireland as that task may be taken up by their Irish counterparts instead (and vice versa). However, in extremely urgent circumstances, where communication or coordination is not possible, it might be helpful to have an option of continued surveillance for a limited period. Whilst it is important to respect State sovereignty in implementing measures against transnational organised crime, approximation of national laws in this area can further facilitate an integrated approach. A similar argument can be raised for the EIO regime. Whilst the UK decided to opt in to this instrument, the Republic has chosen not to do so for the reason that it is contrary to Irish law and practice.[201]

Another point to be noted is the reluctance of An Garda Síochána to take an active part in JITs despite the existence of domestic legislation. Whilst the PSNI

197 Paras 4.1–6.1.

198 Dáil Éirann Debate, Written Answer 169, 'Illicit Trade in Tobacco' (54483/13), 18 December 2013.

199 House of Commons European Scrutiny Committee, *The UK's Block Opt-Out of Pre-Lisbon Criminal Law and Policing Measures* (October 2013), paras 346–349.

200 Customs and Excise (Mutual Assistance) Act 2001.

201 Dáil Éireann Debate 166, col. 23939/14, 4 June 2014.

supports establishment of JITs for transnational organised crime,[202] the same level of enthusiasm is not apparent from An Garda Síochána. Many officers did not see the need for this facility as they regarded the current arrangements between the two jurisdictions as sufficient.[203] Normally, cases with a cross-border element are dealt with through informal parallel investigations by the PSNI and the Garda with, or through the formal execution of mutual legal assistance requests such as transfer of evidence. The fact that the island of Ireland is based upon the common law tradition also facilitates smoother cooperation compared to other European jurisdictions. However, it has been pointed out that this policy only works properly when both parties have an interest in an investigation.[204] Without mutual interest, it becomes difficult to deploy additional resources across the border. In addition, investigators are naturally keen to guard their intelligence as much as possible but they would have to involve other stakeholders if JITs were set up, potentially causing problems in terms of data protection, for instance.[205] It was also acknowledged that JITs take time to establish in practice[206] and this might discourage law enforcement authorities from doing so. This can be contrasted with cross-border customs cooperation as it has been discovered that HMRC and Revenue, Irish Tax and Customs proactively establish JITs with HMRC based upon the Naples II Convention.[207]

Interestingly, this sentiment by An Garda Síochána is reflected in the utilisation of one of the EU agencies charged with promoting cross-border law enforcement cooperation: Eurojust.[208] In 2014, a total of 17 requests for assistance were received by Eurojust from the Irish law enforcement community.[209] In contrast, the UK transmitted 107 requests in the same year.[210] The Irish National Member of Eurojust participated in only 5 coordination meetings and organised none in 2014. This can be compared to the 40 meetings participated in and 22 organised by the UK National Member.[211] This demonstrates the difference in attitude towards law enforcement cooperation despite sharing the common law tradition. In particular, preference for more information cooperation seems to be stronger in the Republic of Ireland compared to the UK, including Northern Ireland.

Finally, the importance of human rights protection for suspects and defendants in the cross-border context must be emphasised. One pertinent issue relates to the use of special investigative techniques such as cross-border surveillance and

202 Interviews with PSNI officers, *supra* ch 3 n 3.
203 Interviews with Garda officers, *supra* ch 3 n 7.
204 Interview with a PSNI officer, *supra* ch 3 n 3.
205 Interviews with Garda officers, *supra* ch 3 n 7.
206 Northern Ireland Affairs Committee, *supra* n 170, 119 (EV. 79).
207 Interviews with Revenue, Irish Tax and Customs, *supra* ch 3 n 133.
208 [2009] OJ L 138/14.
209 Eurojust, *Eurojust Annual Report 2014*, 10.
210 Ibid.
211 Ibid., 16.

interception of communications. Whilst the usefulness of these measures should be emphasised, if they were to be implemented in the island of Ireland in the future, the relevant human rights norms and principles elucidated elsewhere (e.g. legality, proportionality and necessity) must be strictly adhered to. This is all the more important as the legislative frameworks on special investigative techniques, including their authorisation, are different between the two jurisdictions and this can create protection gaps. Another dimension to this issue is the extra-territorial applicability of human rights law. This has, for instance, been recognised when a State has effective control of a territory abroad.[212] More importantly, international human rights law also applies when State agents have control over individuals.[213] In applying this principle to the present discussion, the UK and the Republic of Ireland could be held liable if their law enforcement authorities utilised special investigative techniques in each other's jurisdiction which did not meet the requisite standards.[214] So, for instance, in *Liberty and Others v United Kingdom*,[215] the ECtHR found a violation of the right to privacy when the UK intercepted communications exchanged with organisations in the Republic of Ireland because the relevant domestic law at that time was not sufficiently clear or accessible to the general public (foreseeability).

Another area is the grounds for refusal in relation to mutual legal assistance as noted above. Under the Criminal Justice (Mutual Assistance) Act 2008 in the Republic of Ireland, mutual legal assistance 'shall' be refused if the Minister of Justice and Equality considers, amongst other things, that such assistance might contravene the ECHR.[216] This mandatory nature of refusal certainly enhances the human rights protection of suspects and defendants although an argument may be made that such a decision should be left to the judiciary. The lack of a similar provision under the UK's Crime (International Co-Operation) Act 2003 raises a concern as wide discretion can be exercised by the law enforcement authorities without being challenged in a court of law. A similar reasoning should apply to

212 General Comment No. 31 (Nature of General Legal Obligation on State Parties to the Covenant) of the Human Rights Committee, CCPR/C/21/Rev.1/Add.13 (2004), para 10; *Loizidou v Turkey*, App no 15318/89 (1995); *Cyprus v Turkey*, App no 25781/94 (2001), para 78; and *Bankovic v Belgium*, App no 52207/99 (2001).

213 *Al-Skeini v United Kingdom*, App no 55721/07 (2011), paras 135–137. See also *Medvedyev and Others v France*, App no 3394/03 (2010).

214 Marko Milanovic, 'Human Rights Treaties and Foreign Surveillance: Privacy in the Digital Age' (2015) 56 *Harvard International Law Journal* 81, 111; Ian Brown, 'The Feasibility of Transatlantic Privacy-Protective Standards for Surveillance' (2014) 22 *International Journal of Law and Information Technology* 1, 7; Ian Brown and Douwe Korff, 'Foreign Surveillance: Law and Practice in a Global Digital Environment' (2014) *European Human Rights Law Review* 243, 246–248; and Ilina Georgieva, 'The Right to Privacy under Fire – Foreign Surveillance under the NSA and the GCHQ and Its Compatibility with Art. 17 ICCPR and Art. 8 ECHR' (2015) 31 *Utrecht Journal of International and European Law*, <www.utrechtjournal.org/articles/10.5334/ujiel.cr>.

215 *Supra* n 57.

216 S 3.

where he/she is satisfied that there is a risk that the administration of justice will be impaired.[1] Non-jury trials in the context of terrorism came to be known as 'Diplock trials' in this jurisdiction (and are still widely referred to as such) because it was Lord Diplock's report into emergency procedures in Northern Ireland in 1972 that recommended this arrangement.[2] The single-judge 'Diplock courts' were subsequently introduced under the Northern Ireland (Emergency Provisions) Act 1973 in an attempt by the UK government to deal with the intimidation of witnesses by paramilitary groups and the perceived subversion of jury decisions along sectarian lines. Significant improvements in the security situation in the mid-2000s led the then Secretary of State for Northern Ireland Peter Hain to propose a programme of security normalisation within which the abolition of the Diplock trials was an important part.[3] However, the continuing risk of obstruction of justice through jury intimidation and tampering was recognised by the Northern Ireland government, and this led to the enactment of the aforementioned legislation. The relevance of this legislation in relation to organised crime is evident because of the clear link between terrorism and organised crime in Northern Ireland noted throughout this book. Indeed, the Secretary of State for Northern Ireland clearly envisaged the application of the Act to cases that involved organised crime.[4]

Another important aspect of the 2007 Act is the anonymity of jurors. During the consultation stage of the legislation, protection of the anonymity of jurors was supported by Lord Carlisle, the reviewer of the terrorism legislation in the UK:

> I am strongly of the view that a principle of anonymity for jurors in Northern Ireland would give considerable reassurance, and would be proportionate to risk. In addition, there should be some courts where more serious cases could be tried with the jury entirely unseen from the public seating areas. If jurors could attend court, knowing that their names, addresses and occupations were unknown to the defence and their connections, and that in serious cases their faces were not observable from the public seating, that would provide considerable reassurance. I see no difficulty about this. Each juror could simply be referred to by number when they came to take their jury oath.
>
> I believe that the anonymisation of jurors and associated steps for their protection would diminish the risk of perverse verdicts.[5]

1 S 1.

2 *Report of the Commission to Consider Legal Procedures to Deal with Terrorist Activities in Northern Ireland* (1972), Cm 5185. See further John Jackson and Sean Doran, *Judge without Jury: Diplock Trials in the Adversarial System* (Oxford University Press 1995).

3 Northern Ireland Office, *Replacement Arrangement for the Diplock Court System: A Consultation Paper* (August 2006), 4.

4 Hansard col. 895 (13 December 2006).

5 Northern Ireland Office, *supra* n 3, 23.

The Northern Ireland Office supported this position, and the 2007 Act amended the Juries (Northern Ireland) Order 1996 to strengthen anonymity for jurors. They are now identified by numbers, which allows their personal identification to be protected.

There are a couple of issues of note in relation to the 2007 Act. First, it provides for limited judicial scrutiny of decisions made by the DPP. They cannot be questioned in any court of law except on the grounds of dishonesty, bad faith or other exceptional circumstances (including a lack of jurisdiction or error of law), or on the ground that there has been an infringement of a Convention right.[6] It is therefore evident that the DPP enjoys wide discretion, and that options for addressing his/her accountability are limited – a concern also expressed by the UN Human Rights Committee.[7] Whilst the Human Rights Act 1998 should be able to play an important role in safeguarding the rights of defendants, a greater degree of judicial scrutiny over the DPP's decisions is desirable in order to enhance and maintain the legitimacy of non-jury trials.[8] In this regard, it makes sense for a certificate to be issued by a judge. Although this was recommended by the Northern Ireland Human Rights Commission during the consultation stage,[9] this did not materialise. As was cogently argued by the Committee on the Administration of Justice (CAJ), an NGO based in Northern Ireland, such a change is also needed in order to boost public confidence in law enforcement.[10]

Another pertinent issue is jury anonymity and its implication for the right to a fair trial. In *Re McParland*,[11] the defendants argued that there was interference with fairness because the identities of jurors were withheld and they could not challenge their suitability. In acknowledging that the right to be informed of jurors' identities was not covered by Article 6 of the ECHR, the High Court of Northern Ireland eventually held that:

> The argument that knowing nothing about a proposed juror inevitably compromises the right to a fair trial under Article 6 neglects, in our opinion, the safeguards that a properly regulated system of trial already provides. It also unwarrantably concentrates on the parties' opportunity to dictate the composition of the jury as the sole guarantor of a fair trial.

6 S 7(1). An unsuccessful challenge was made, for example, in *Re Brian and Paula Arthurs* [2010] NIQB 75.

7 *Concluding Observations of the Human Rights Committee: United Kingdom of Great Britain and Northern Ireland*, CCPR/C/GBR/CO/6 (2008), para 17.

8 Jackson has further argued that the practice of allocating cases to a non-jury trial in Northern Ireland, although significantly reformed, still exemplifies the continued dominance of the security approach over a due process approach. John Jackson, 'Many Years on in Northern Ireland: The Diplock Legacy' (2009) 60 *Northern Ireland Legal Quarterly* 213, 215.

9 Northern Ireland Human Rights Commission, *Replacement Arrangements for the Diplock Court System: Response of the Northern Ireland Human Rights Commission to the Consultation by the Northern Ireland Office* (October 2006), para 7.

10 CAJ, *CAJ's Commentary to the Northern Ireland Office on 'Non-Jury Arrangements in Northern Ireland'* (March 2013), 8.

11 [2008] NIQB 1.

This decision affirms the importance of protecting juries from intimidation and tampering and of balancing the rights of all parties involved.

In addition to the 2007 Act, there is a provision under the Criminal Justice Act 2003 whereby an application may be made for a non-jury trial if there is a risk of jury tampering.[12] This also includes cases where a trial starts with a jury but is dismissed during the proceedings upon discovery of jury tampering.[13] One of the reasons for the existence of this arrangement is the need to protect a jury from organised criminals.[14] The National Crime Squad, the predecessor to SOCA, was particularly supportive of trial without jury for organised crime.[15] The annual cost related to the protection of juries is estimated to be around £4.5 million,[16] and this also suggests that jury tampering continues to pose a problem within the British criminal justice system. This cost aspect was said to be another reason for the utilisation of a non-jury trial under this Act.[17]

There are two criteria which must be satisfied in order to utilise this arrangement under the 2003 Act. The first is that a judge must be satisfied that there is evidence of a 'real and present danger' that jury tampering would take place.[18] Examples of evidence of 'real and present danger' include:

(a) a case where the trial is a retrial and the jury in the previous trial was discharged because jury tampering had taken place,
(b) a case where jury tampering has taken place in previous criminal proceedings involving the defendant or any of the defendants,
(c) a case where there has been intimidation, or attempted intimidation, of any person who is likely to be a witness in the trial.[19]

The second is when, despite the existence of measures which could be taken to prevent jury tampering, the likelihood of this occurring is 'so substantial as to make it necessary in the interests of justice for the trial to be conducted without a jury'.[20] Compared to the aforementioned 2007 Act, therefore, the threshold for the use of a non-jury trial is much higher under the 2003 Act.

12 Pt 7.
13 S 46.
14 Evidence given by Sir Ian Blair, the then Deputy Commissioner of the Metropolitan Police, in Home Affairs Committee, *Criminal Justice Bill: Second Report of Session 2000–2003*, 54 (Ev 14).
15 Ibid., 121.
16 *Criminal Bar Quarterly*, Issue 1 (March 2010), 10. See also *R v T* [2009] EWCA Crim 1035, where it was stated that protection of jury can range between £1.5 million at the lower end of the scale for the duration of 6 months involving 32 police officers and £6 million for the same amount of time involving 82 officers.
17 Liz Campbell, 'The Prosecution of Organised Crime: Removing the Jury' (2014) 18 *International Journal of Evidence and Proof* 83, 88.
18 S 44(4).
19 S 44(6).
20 S 44(5).

Whilst a jury trial is a fundamental aspect of the British criminal justice system, it has been recognised that the defendant's right in this regard can be restricted when the jury is compromised. This was recognised by Lord Bingham in *R v Comerford*:[21]

> The proper functioning of the jury is crucial to the fair and effective conduct of the trial.
>
> . . .
>
> But all these rules and procedures are rendered of little effect if the integrity of an individual juror, and thus of the jury as a whole, is compromised. Such a compromise occurs when any juror, whether because of intimidation, bribery or any other reason, dishonours or becomes liable to dishonour his or her oath as a juror by allowing anything to undermine or qualify the juror's duty to give a true verdict according to the evidence.

In *R v Guthrie and Others*,[22] a case involving fraud and money laundering, the Court of Appeal further recognised that the involvement of organised violent crime is one relevant factor in deciding whether or not to start a trial without jury.

It is worth mentioning that a non-jury trial does not automatically lead to a violation of the right to a fair trial. In the cases of *Twomey and Cameron v United Kingdom*[23] and *Guthrie v United Kingdom*,[24] the ECtHR held that there was no right under Article 6 to be tried before a jury as each State enjoys considerable freedoms in choosing the types of criminal justice procedures.[25] One of the key issues in these cases was the fact that the decision to proceed with a non-jury trial under the 2003 Act was made based upon undisclosed materials, thus potentially affecting equality of arms. However, as these undisclosed materials did not concern the applicants' guilt or innocence and the 2003 Act afforded sufficient safeguards for them, the ECtHR concluded that a non-jury trial did not contravene Article 6.[26]

When asked whether a non-jury trial was appropriate for cases that involved organised crime, the Recorder of Belfast and a judge of the High Court found this to be acceptable, provided that sufficient safeguards existed to protect the rights of defendants.[27] The Parliamentary Northern Ireland Affairs Committee also shares this view.[28] Having said this, it was also recognised that reliance on trial without jury under the 2003 Act must remain the decision of 'last resort',[29] thus

21 [1998] 1 Cr App Rep 235.

22 [2011] EWCA Crim 1338.

23 App no 67318/09 (2013).

24 App no 22226/12 (2013).

25 Para 30.

26 See also *Kavanagh v Ireland* before the UN Human Rights Committee. Communication No 89/1998, CCPR/C/71/D/819/1998 para 10.1.

27 *Supra* ch 3 n 5.

28 Northern Ireland Affairs Committee, *supra* intro n 10, 22.

29 *R v J, S, M* [2010] EWCA Crim 1755.

highlighting its exceptional nature. In practice, a non-jury trial under this Act is rare for organised crime.[30] Campbell opines that this is due in part to the high threshold set by the 2003 Act.[31] In addition, given the culture of fear noted elsewhere in the book, proving jury intimidation and tampering might be difficult. In relation to the creation of a special court for organised crime, such as the one in the Republic (discussed below), the stakeholders generally did not see any need for this as they regard the current arrangements to be sufficient.[32]

Another point to emphasise is the relationship between the 2007 Act and the 2003 Act. Section 50 of the 2003 Act as amended by the 2007 Act states that a non-jury trial under the former does not apply to terrorism cases. The current arrangements therefore create a two-tier system whereby different criteria and sets of safeguards are applied depending on whether organised crime is committed by paramilitary or non-paramilitary groups. This does raise a question of fairness, particularly when the crimes committed are exactly the same and the sophisticated and dangerous nature of groups are also similar. An argument may therefore be made that all cases of organised crime, regardless of the types of entities which commit them, should be dealt with in a single piece of legislation, the 2003 Act in particular, as it has the higher threshold. A similar point was expressed by the Northern Ireland Human Rights Commission.[33]

In addition to the exclusion of a jury, there are some immediate steps which the UK and Northern Ireland could take to prevent jury tampering. The Criminal Justice (Northern Ireland) Order 1996 has created an offence of jury intimidation, similar to the offence under the Criminal Justice and Public Order Act 1994 in England and Wales, with a term of 5 years' imprisonment. Intimidation of witnesses attracts the same level of penalty as noted earlier in the book. In addition, the 2007 Act imposes a penalty of up to 2 years' imprisonment for disclosure of jury information.[34] Given the need to tackle the culture of fear prevalent in Northern Ireland, the efficacy of these punishments is open to question. By way of comparison, jury and witness intimidation in the Republic of Ireland attracts 10 years' imprisonment.[35] Although the deterrent effect must be carefully examined, increasing the penalty regime would at least send a clear message to the criminals that they would face severe consequences for intimidating and tampering with the jury. This in turn would boost public confidence in the fight against transnational organised crime.

30 Interview with the Recorder of Belfast, *supra* ch 3 n 5. Also a case worth mentioning is *R v Clarke and Anor* [2010] NICC 7, concerning tiger kidnapping. In this case, McCloskey J (and subsequently upheld by the Court of Appeal) recognised the existence of jury intimidation and proceeded to try the case without jury.

31 Campbell, *supra* n 17, 88–89.

32 Interviews with the Recorder of Belfast and a High Court judge, *supra* ch 3 n 5; and interview with a defence lawyer, *supra* ch 4 n 41.

33 *Supra* n 9, 4.

34 S 10.

35 Criminal Justice Act 1999, s 41.

In the Republic of Ireland, jury trial is protected by Article 38.5 of the Constitution which provides that 'no person shall be tried on any criminal charge without a jury'. However, Article 38.3 of the Constitution also stipulates that special courts may be established for the trial of offences in cases where it may be determined that the ordinary courts are inadequate to secure the effective administration of justice and the preservation of public peace and order. Section 35(2) of the Offences Against the State Act 1939 further permits the government to issue proclamations establishing special courts. The current SCC was brought into being in this way in 1972. It consists of 13 members (5 High Court, 3 Circuit Court and 5 District Court judges). Although the Irish government justified the reintroduction of the Court in 1972 on the basis of the paramilitary threat of terrorism, the Supreme Court has upheld the use of the SCC for organised crime where it is believed that juries will be prevented from dispensing justice.[36] In October 2015, the Minister of Justice and Equality Frances Fitzgerald announced the creation of the second SCC in order to deal with the backlog of cases and prevent unnecessary delay.[37] Its composition will be smaller than the first one, with only 7 judges involved (3 High Court, 2 Circuit Court and 2 District Court judges).

The SCC has jurisdiction over 'scheduled offences' set out in the Offences Against the State (Scheduled Offences) Order 1972 unless the DPP directs otherwise in a specific case or over cases where the DPP certifies that in his/her opinion the ordinary courts are an inadequate means of administering justice.[38] Among others, the offences related to explosives, firearms, malicious damage and unlawful organisations (terrorist groups) are included. The scope of 'scheduled offences' was extended by Section 8 of the Criminal Justice (Amendment) Act 2009 so that offences that involve criminal organisations (e.g. participating in criminal organisations or committing offences for such organisations) will go to the SCC unless the DPP directs otherwise.[39] The passing of this legislation was said to be influenced by the killing of Roy Collins in Limerick by criminals involved in organised crime.[40] The Minister of Justice and Equality also emphasised the need to prosecute and punish organised crime more swiftly and she felt this could be achieved by the establishment of the second SCC. The usefulness of the SCC is also recognised by the law enforcement community.[41] In particular, intimidation of juries was said to have been prevented more effectively because of this Court. It should further be emphasised that the SCC is able to address the organised crime-terrorism nexus. Unlike Northern Ireland, the SCC regime does not create a two-tier system and therefore is much simpler.

36 *DPP v Quilligan* [1986] IR 495.

37 Department of Justice and Equality, <www.justice.ie/en/JELR/Pages/PR15000556>.

38 Ss 36 and 46(1).

39 S 8.

40 Alan Greene, 'Shielding the State of Emergency: Organised Crime in Ireland and the State's Response' (2011) 62 *Northern Ireland Legal Quarterly* 249, 256.

41 Interviews with Garda officers, *supra* ch 3 n 7; and interviews with public prosecutors, *supra* ch 3 n 16.

However, a number of criticisms have been raised against the SCC. During the drafting stage of the Criminal Justice (Amendment) Act 2009, a group of 133 practising lawyers published a letter[42] setting out their objections to the abolition of jury trial. For instance, they felt that the legislation was passed without sufficient research and evidence, and proper debate in the Dáil. They also cast doubt on the reliability of opinion evidence provided by the Garda officers to establish the existence of a criminal organisation. Further, other non-governmental stakeholders stressed that intimidation could be adequately managed by a trial judge deciding in a particular instance to waive the use of a jury in response to a particular threat,[43] and that the SCC might be counterproductive in practice as it makes martyrs of convicted people and projects an image that they are treated differently to others.[44] Finally, a lack of transparency in the procedure has been raised as a concern.[45]

Despite these criticisms, the establishment of the SCC in Ireland was upheld as constitutional in the past.[46] In addition, in the recent case of *Donohoe v Ireland*,[47] which concerned opinion evidence provided by a senior Garda officer before the SCC, the ECtHR was satisfied that in the circumstances of this case where the officer's evidence was not the sole or decisive evidence grounding the applicant's conviction, sufficient procedural safeguards were in place for the SCC to protect the right to a fair trial. This decision, however, should be treated with caution as it has emphasised the importance of observing the relevant principles such as the duty to disclose evidence, equality of arms and adversarial proceedings.[48] If these and other relevant principles are not respected, then the SCC may be found to be breaching the right to a fair trial in the future.

In this regard, there are several issues to be considered further. For instance, the DPP's discretion in certification was held to be in breach of human rights standards in the past.[49] A major problem, as Campbell argues, is that a prosecutor holds the power to limit a constitutional right to a jury trial.[50] Unfortunately, the DPP's powers cannot be scrutinised by the judiciary under the current regime, and an amendment was recommended by the Irish Human Rights Commission[51]

42 *Irish Times*, 'Leading Lawyers Call for Bill on Gangs to Be Withdrawn' (3 July 2009).

43 Interviews with defence lawyers, *supra* ch 3 n 71; interview with an ICCL representative, *supra* ch 3 n 14; and interview with the CAJ, *supra* ch 4 n 77. See also Irish Human Rights Commission, *Observations on the Criminal Justice (Amendment) Bill 2009*, 6; and ICCL, *Combating Organised Crime and Respecting the Rule of Law: Human Rights Based Alternatives to the Criminal Justice (Amendment) Bill 2009*, 5.

44 Interview with a defence lawyer, ibid.; and Greene, *supra* n 40, 259–260.

45 Ibid.

46 *Kavanagh v Ireland* [1996] 1 IR 348, 354.

47 App no 19165/08 (2013).

48 See further *Rowe and Davis v the United Kingdom*, App no 28901/95 (2000).

49 *Kavanagh v Ireland*, *supra* n 26.

50 Campbell, *supra* n 17, 91.

51 Irish Human Rights Commission, *Observations on the Criminal Justice (Amendment) Bill 2009*, 6–7.

and the Law Reform Commission.[52] It has further been argued that the DPP's decision ought to be based on the merits of the individual case rather than on the preconceived statutory assumption that persons charged with scheduled offences should be sent to the SCC.[53] The Committee to Review the Offences Against the State Acts 1939–1998 stated succinctly that 'this distinction does not provide a sufficiently clear and transparent basis for depriving an accused of the right to jury trial to which he or she is otherwise prima facie constitutionally entitled'.[54] As noted earlier, however, the inherent characteristics of organised crime, regardless of whether it is carried out to subvert the constitution or for reasons of greed or the desire to build status, will always provide a reasonable case for the measured use of multi-judge, non-jury courts on an emergency basis.[55] A problem here, as expressed by Greene, is that 'Ireland is now in a state of de facto permanent emergency as regards organised crime'.[56] This, he continues, is contrary to the very notion of 'emergency' which must be exceptional and temporary. This is an important point as the notion of emergency can encourage States to retain and exercise extra powers and restrict human rights, and the current arrangement in the Republic may be regarded as a clear example of this.

In practice, there have not been very many cases tried before the SCC. According to the Irish Court Service, there were 33 cases before the SCC in 2014, compared to 26 in 2013 and 22 in 2012.[57] It is also important to acknowledge that not all of these cases have involved organised criminal groups. The relatively small number of cases may be due to the inability of the SCC to process enough cases each year, thereby prompting the announcement of the Minister of Justice and Equality noted above. On the other hand, it seems reasonable to argue that the majority of organised crime cases are indeed tried in ordinary courts. In fact, the DPP exercises her powers in a restrained matter in practice[58] as she is not generally in favour of trying organised crime cases before the SCC.[59] This raises the question as to the necessity of the SCC regime in prosecuting and punishing organised crime; an amendment to the relevant legislation (i.e. 2009 Act) to this effect should be considered.

52 Law Reform Commission, *Report on Jury Service* (April 2013), 95.

53 *Report of the Committee to Review the Offences Against the State Acts 1939–1998 and Related Matters* (2002). paras 9.57 and 9.64.

54 Ibid.

55 See further Peter Charleton and Paul McDermott, 'From Diplock Courts to Jury Courts?' (2000) 111 *CIJL Yearbook* 16.

56 Greene, *supra* n 40, 264.

57 *Court Service Annual Report 2014*, 58; and Court Service Archive, *Special Criminal Court 2008-2013*, <www.courts.ie/Courts.ie/library3.nsf/f0e0a24268c0a3da80256da500428fb8/7c5017c5469b4aac8025774c0057b3b3?OpenDocument>.

58 Campbell, *supra* n 17, 92.

59 Fergal Davis, *The History and Development of the Special Criminal Court 1922–2005* (Four Courts Press 2007), 151.

5.3 Evidential issues

There are several evidential issues that should be highlighted. In relation to witness intimidation during criminal proceedings, some measures have been introduced in both jurisdictions. Article 20 of the Criminal Justice (Evidence) (Northern Ireland) Order 2004 makes provision for the admissibility of the previous oral and documentary statements of witnesses who do not wish to give evidence through fear. In addition, Article 23 allows admission of prior statements inconsistent with a witness's testimony for the purpose of proving its truth. Similarly, Section 16 of the Criminal Justice Act 2006 in the Republic of Ireland stipulates the admissibility of a statement of a witness where the witness: a) refuses to give evidence; b) denies making the statement; or c) gives evidence which is materially inconsistent with it provided that the defence can cross-examine the witness. These measures are in line with Article 24 (Protection of Witnesses) of the UNTOC, and their usefulness has been confirmed.[60] At the same time, the desirability for more effective witness protection was also expressed so that there would be no need to rely on Section 16.[61]

From a human rights perspective, the use of such evidence may have a negative impact on the defendant's right to cross-examine a witness. For instance, in *Unterpertinger v Austria*[62] the applicant argued that conviction solely based on the statements made to the police breached his right to cross-examine under Article 6(3)(d) of the ECHR, and the ECtHR upheld the violation. There are a number of important principles which have emerged from the jurisprudence in relation to the right to cross-examination. To begin with, as noted in Chapter 1, the ECtHR has maintained the position that admissibility of evidence is a matter for domestic courts to decide, and that its task is to determine whether the proceedings taken as a whole are fair.[63] As with many other issues, therefore, a wide margin of appreciation is recognised. As to the examination of witnesses, it has been held that the defendant must be given an 'adequate and proper' opportunity to challenge and question them. An interesting case in this regard is *Luca v Italy*[64] which concerns the reliance on depositions made at an earlier stage of criminal investigations. In recognising the need to rely on depositions, particularly where a witness refuses to testify in public due to a fear of reprisal by mafia-type organisations, the ECtHR stated that admission of such evidence does not in itself result in a violation of the right to cross-examine, provided that the defendant is afforded an adequate and proper opportunity to challenge it.[65]

60 Interview with the Deputy DPP, *supra* ch 3 n 35.

61 Department of Justice and Equality, *White Paper on Crime Consultation, Third Discussion Document, Organised and White Collar Crime* (April 2011), 37; and interviews with defence lawyers, *supra* ch 3 n 71.

62 App no 9120/80 (1986).

63 *Supra* ch 1 n 180. See further *Ludi v Switzerland*, *supra* ch 1 n 145, para 43; and *Vidal v Belgium*, App no 12351/86 (1992), para 33.

64 App no 33354/96 (2001).

65 Ibid., para 40.

However, if such depositions are the sole or decisive evidence used for conviction, this would breach this right.[66] Similar reasoning has been applied to the use of anonymous witnesses where the interests of the defendant are outweighed by the need to ensure the safety of the witnesses.[67]

Another important matter is disclosure of evidence. This is essential for ensuring a fair trial for the suspects of organised crime.[68] The duty to disclose evidence is stipulated in the Criminal Procedure and Investigations Act 1996 (as amended) in the UK. One of the difficulties in relation to organised crime is that the intelligence gathered is often of a sensitive nature, and this requires the law enforcement communities in both jurisdictions to protect their sources as well as the means and methods of intelligence gathering. Consequently, the prosecutorial authorities may decide that they do not wish to disclose certain evidence. In the UK, so-called public interest immunity (PII) can be granted by the court for this purpose under the 1996 Act and the Criminal Procedure Rules 2005.[69] The CPS in England and Wales has issued guidance on PII to ensure that its prosecutors comply with relevant legislation and human rights.[70] In Northern Ireland, in addition to the *Code for Prosecutors*[71] which includes a section on disclosure, the PPS has produced a comprehensive and detailed *Disclosure Manual* which provides guidance on handling highly sensitive material and PII.[72] These are complemented by the *Attorney General's Guidelines on Disclosure*.[73] The need for PII has also been recognised by the judiciary. For instance, the UK's House of Lords held that:

> Circumstances may arise in which material held by the prosecution and tending to undermine the prosecution or assist the defence cannot be disclosed to the defence, fully or even at all, without the risk of serious prejudice to an important public interest. The public interest most regularly engaged is that in the effective investigation and prosecution of serious crime, which may involve resort to informers and under-cover agents, or the use of scientific or operational techniques (such as surveillance) which cannot be disclosed without exposing individuals to the risk of personal injury or jeopardising the success of future operations. In such circumstances some derogation from the golden rule of full disclosure may be justified but such derogation must

66 Ibid.

67 *Doorson v The Netherlands*, App no 20524/92 (1996), para 74. See also *Kostovski v The Netherlands*, App no 11451/85(1989); *Windisch v Austria*, App no 12489/86 (1990); and *Al-Khawaja and Tahery v United Kingdom*, App nos 26766/05 and 22228/06 (2011).

68 *Rowe and Davis v United Kingdom*, *supra* n 48.

69 Pt 25.

70 CPS, *Chapter 8: The Sensitive Material Schedule*, <www.cps.gov.uk/legal/d_to_g/disclosure_manual/disclosure_manual_chapter_8>.

71 PPS, *Code for Prosecutors* (Revised 2008).

72 Interviews with the PPS, *supra* ch 4 n 114.

73 It was published in 2005 and applies to England, Wales and Northern Ireland.

> always be the minimum derogation necessary to protect the public interest in question and must never imperil the overall fairness of the trial.[74]

A similar arrangement exists in the Republic of Ireland under 'public interest privilege'.[75] The duty to disclose is recognised in the Irish Constitution,[76] and the right to a fair trial is generally regarded as a superior constitutional right compared to the community's right to prosecute.[77] However, prevention and detection of crime has been identified as an example of public interest which can be weighed against the right to a fair trial.[78] This is particularly the case for so-called 'informer privilege' whereby the identity of an informer is protected. The Supreme Court in this regard affirmed that this privilege is of ancient origin and is essential for the prevention and detection of crime.[79] McGrath argues that judges have no discretion in balancing the public interest in relation to this informer's privilege, thus making it absolute[80] – a point also upheld by the Supreme Court.[81] The DPP in the Republic has guidance for public interest privilege under the 'Disclosure' section of the *Guidelines for Prosecutors*. If he decides not to disclose evidence, then the defendant can challenge this before the court.[82] It is worth highlighting that a so-called 'innocence at stake' exception is recognised in this jurisdiction. Simply put:

> if upon the trial of a prisoner the judge should be of opinion that the disclosure of the name of the informant is necessary or right in order to show the prisoner's innocence, then one public policy is in conflict with another public policy, and that which says that an innocent man is not to be condemned when his innocence can be proved is the policy that must prevail.[83]

It is important to add that withholding evidence is not an automatic violation of the right to a fair trial. It was recognised that entitlement to disclosure is not an absolute right as competing interests, such as the protection of witnesses and means and methods of intelligence gathering, must be carefully considered and balanced.[84] However, it is essential that sufficient procedural safeguards, bearing in mind the requirement for adversarial proceedings and equality of arms,

74 *R v H* [2004] UKHL 3, para 18.
75 Liz Heffernan, *Legal Professional Privilege* (Bloomsbury 2011), 9.
76 Arts 38 and 40. See also *DPP v McKevitt* [2005] IECCA 139.
77 *D v DPP* [1994] 2 IR 465, 475.
78 *Breathnach v Ireland (No. 3)* [1993] 2 IR 458; *Skeffington v Rooney and Others* [1997] 1 IR 22; and *McDonald v RTE* [2001] 1 IR 355.
79 *DPP v Special Criminal Court* [1999] 1 IR 60, 87.
80 Declan McGrath, *Evidence* (Thompson Round Hall 2005), 607.
81 *DPP v Special Criminal Court, supra* n 79, 87.
82 Para 9.24 of the *Guidelines for Prosecutors* (2010).
83 *Marks v Beyfus* (1890) 25 QBD 494 at 498.
84 *Rowe and Davis v United Kingdom, supra* n 48 paras 60–62.

should be afforded with judicial oversight.[85] This was recently confirmed in the aforementioned cases of *Twomey and Cameron v United Kingdom* and *Guthrie v United Kingdom*. In these cases, the ECtHR concluded that the Criminal Justice Act 2003 contained sufficient safeguards to maintain the applicants' right to a fair trial. Similarly, the position of the Irish Supreme Court and the Court of Appeal has been that Article 38 of the Constitution and Article 6 of the ECHR are not necessarily breached when Garda officers claim privilege for their opinion evidence provided that it is not the sole evidence.[86] This reasoning was followed in *Donohoe v Ireland* although this decision has been met with some criticism, such as that the ECtHR simply accepted the domestic practice at face value without any in-depth analysis through the application of relevant principles.[87]

In practice, it seems that an application for PII or public interest privilege is common in relation to serious crimes, including organised crime in Northern Ireland and the Republic of Ireland. One difficulty which has been identified by the law enforcement communities and judges in both jurisdictions is the protection of witnesses during criminal investigation and proceedings. They confirmed that sometimes they must stop criminal prosecutions and proceedings in order to protect the right to life of informants and/or witnesses rather than disclosing their identities to the defence. A related point is the existence of a so-called 'innocence at stake' exception that was noted above. This exception can put the life of informants at risk and under such circumstances the prosecution would generally be discontinued.[88] These practices demonstrate that prosecutors and judges carefully consider the human rights of relevant individuals involved in the criminal proceedings and balance competing interests.

Another interesting issue related to evidence is the use of intercepts in court. At present, evidence collected from interception is not admissible in court in the UK.[89] The UK government has commissioned a Privy Council review[90] led by Sir John Chilcot with the terms of reference being to advise on whether a regime to allow the use of intercepted material in court could be devised. The Chilcot Report, regarded as the most authoritative on intercept evidence, raised a number of risks in allowing such evidence to be used,[91] including the exposure of sensitive materials and sources of intelligence as well as the means and methods of intelligence gathering. Ultimately, the report concluded that the use of intercept

85 Ibid. See also *Doorson v The Netherlands*, *supra* n 67; *Jasper v United Kingdom*, App no 27052/95 (2000); and *A and Others v United Kingdom*, App no 3455/05 (2009).

86 *DPP v Kelly* [2006] 3 IR 115; *DPP v Binead* [2007] 1 IR 374; and *DPP v Donnelly and Murphy* [2012] IECCA 78.

87 Colin King, 'Belief Evidence and Informer Privilege: Revisited in Strasbourg' (2014) 18 *International Journal of Evidence and Proof* 340.

88 Guidelines for Prosecutors, *supra* n 82, 43.

89 RIPA, s 17.

90 Privy Council, *Review of Intercept as Evidence: Report to the Prime Minister and the Home Secretary* (January 2008).

91 Ibid., ch 4.

evidence in criminal trials should be used in order to effectively combat serious and organised crime, provided that it utilised a robust legal model based in statute and was compatible with the ECHR. This was also supported by the Parliamentary Joint Committee on Human Rights.[92] The use of intercept evidence does not automatically result in a violation of Article 6. In this regard, the relevant principles highlighted previously are equally applicable (opportunity to challenge, equality of arms, adversarial proceedings, etc.).[93]

The prospect of using intercept evidence drew mixed responses in Northern Ireland. Some respondents from the PSNI, SOCA and the PPS felt that the benefits that might result from using this method (e.g. an increase in the number of successful prosecutions and the ability to target the senior members of organised crime groups) outweighed the risks.[94] However, it was also pointed out that intercept materials are not necessarily 'the magic bullet' for dealing with organised crime. There are limits to its effectiveness because, for instance, there is a difficulty in identifying who is speaking and what is being discussed. Criminals also use coded language to avoid getting arrested. Consequently, the reliability of intercept evidence can be called into question. In the end, a High Court judge stated that there is no lacuna or need to press for the use of intercept evidence in practice as the prosecution can use other reliable evidence.[95]

In the Republic of Ireland, whilst the Interception of Postal Packets and Telecommunications Messages (Regulation) Act 1993 does not specifically prohibit the use of intercept evidence in court, it is not relied upon as a matter of practice.[96] Garda officers seem to prefer this facility to be used only for intelligence-gathering purposes.[97] The reasons are similar to those raised above, including a difficulty in identifying the actual speakers; a risk of alerting criminals about the means and methods of intelligence gathering; and a possible negative impact on public confidence in law enforcement. In any event, there also does not appear to be a pressing need to rely on intercept evidence in relation to organised crime in the Republic. One anomaly, however, is that the use of intercept evidence obtained abroad may be admissible in both jurisdictions.[98] Whilst judges have discretion not to admit such evidence in practice, there does not seem to be a justification for this separate treatment. An argument therefore could be made to examine this issue further in order to promote consistency in law enforcement.

Finally, there is an additional dimension to the use of opinion evidence. In relation to the existence of 'unlawful organisations' within the meaning of the

92 Joint Committee on Human Rights, *Counter-Terrorism Policy and Human Rights: Prosecution and Pre-Charge Detention, Twenty-fourth Report of Session 2005–06.*

93 See, in particular, *Schenk v Switzerland*, *supra* ch 1 n 181.

94 Interviews with PSNI officers, *supra* ch 3 n 3 and ch 4 n 1; interviews with SOCA officers, *supra* ch 4 n 39; and interviews with the PPS, *supra* ch 4 n 114.

95 Interview with a High Court judge, *supra* ch 3 n 5.

96 Privy Council, *supra* n 90, 33; Justice, *Intercept Evidence: Lifting a Ban* (June 2006), 56–57.

97 Interviews with Garda officers, *supra* ch 3 n 7.

98 *DPP v Kinsella* (unreported); and *R v P* [2001] 2 WLR 463.

Offences Against the State Act 1939 as amended (terrorist organisations), opinion evidence must come from officers not below the rank of Chief Superintendent.[99] This was put in place to establish trust and credibility in such evidence.[100] In contrast, under the Criminal Justice Act 2006 as amended by the Criminal Justice (Amendment) Act 2009, opinion evidence in relation to the existence of 'criminal organisations' can be given by 'any' Garda officer. It is important to note that opinion evidence in this context is more limited than the Offences Against the State Acts as it is not admissible to prove that a particular defendant was in any way connected with criminal organisations.[101] However, this provision still leaves the possibility of opinions being given by officers who do not possess sufficient experience and knowledge of transnational organised crime. It is therefore desirable that evidence is given by high-ranking officers with sufficient experience. This would also maintain consistency in law enforcement.

5.4 Sentencing

A major concern expressed by the law enforcement communities in Northern Ireland and the Republic of Ireland was that the penalties imposed for organised crime are too lenient. For example, it appears that the sentences imposed in Northern Ireland for fiscal/excise fraud are generally lower than in England and Wales.[102] Between 2002 and 2012, there were only 4 prosecutions for fuel fraud that resulted in custodial sentences (ranging from a few months to 2.5 years), with the majority of criminals receiving suspended sentences or fines.[103] The Assistant Chief Constable of the PSNI also stated that suspended sentences for fuel fraud seem to be the norm in Northern Ireland,[104] and the Parliamentary Northern Ireland Affairs Committee expressed the view that the punishment regime for this crime did not serve as a strong deterrent.[105] The same picture emerges in the Republic of Ireland according to Revenue, Irish Tax and Customs.[106] In relation to drug offences, a total of 1,732 penalties were imposed by the Dublin Circuit Court in 2013.[107] Of these, only 311 involved custodial sentences.[108] Similarly, in Northern Ireland, the available crime statistics reveal that, of 1,718 penalties for drug offences in 2014, custodial sentences were imposed in 238 cases.[109] Further, in the aforementioned *Matyas Pis* case,[110] the defendant received

99 Offences against State (Amendment) Act 1972, s 3(2).
100 *DPP v Kelly*, *supra* n 86.
101 Interview with a defence lawyer, *supra* ch 3 n 71.
102 Northern Ireland Affairs Committee, *supra* intro n 10, 21.
103 Ibid., 39 and 95.
104 Ibid., 74.
105 Ibid., 22.
106 Interviews with Revenue, Irish Tax and Customs, *supra* ch 3 n 133.
107 *Court Service Annual Report 2014*, 57.
108 Ibid.
109 Department of Justice, *Northern Ireland Conviction and Sentencing Statistics 2014*, 20.
110 *Supra* ch 4 n 167.

3 years' imprisonment for human trafficking offences (18 months on remand followed by 18 months on licence). It is understandable that individual mitigating circumstances such as a guilty plea and the defendant's previous good character are normally taken into consideration in sentencing. It is also important to acknowledge that imprisonment is not the only punishment available to judges. However, a question can be raised as to whether these sentences are effective and serve as a strong deterrent. The lighter punishments in the island of Ireland can also make it more vulnerable to forum shopping and the concentration of criminal activities as stressed earlier, and this would certainly go against the aim of creating a hostile environment for criminals.

A few more points on sentencing should be highlighted. According to defence lawyers, the courts seem to be reluctant to impose heavy custodial sentences upon offenders at the lower end of the food chain even if they have actually committed crimes.[111] In addition, HMRC has argued that large confiscation orders are sometimes viewed as mitigation against custodial sentences rather than being in addition to them, and this was also pointed out by the DPP.[112] This goes against Section 163(4) of the POCA which provides that 'the court must leave the confiscation order out of account in deciding the appropriate sentence for the defendant'.[113] Further, many law enforcement officers in both jurisdictions also recognised a difficulty in prosecuting and punishing leaders or bosses of criminal organisations. In the end, the question raised by the law enforcement community in general was whether the serious nature of organised crime is understood by the judiciary.

In contrast, the judiciary in both jurisdictions does not necessarily share similar concerns, and this highlights a different perception of the current state of affairs. The Recorder of Belfast and a judge of the High Court have stated that the sentences passed are generally appropriate as judges have to take various factors, including aggravating and mitigating circumstances, into consideration.[114] The judge of the High Court and the SCC in Ireland also pointed out that discretion is important so that judges can address the various issues on a case-by-case basis.[115] Further, a Crown Court judge also made the important point that a sentence reflects the quality of evidence.[116] This is the reason why sentences for cigarette and fuel smuggling seem to be lower. This means that the law enforcement community also has an important role to play by presenting high-quality evidence if they want to see an appropriate sentence passed.

111 Interviews with defence lawyers, *supra* ch 3 n 71 and ch 4 n 41. See also Campbell, *supra* intro n 33, 168.
112 Interviews with HMRC officers, *supra* ch 3 n 6; and Northern Ireland Affairs Committee, *supra* intro n 10, 95.
113 The Sentencing Guidelines Council in England and Wales also makes this point clear in *Sentencing for Fraud: Definitive Guidelines*, 14.
114 *Supra* ch 3 n 5.
115 *Supra* ch 4 n 64.
116 Interview with a Crown Court judge, *supra* ch 3 n 5.

There is a possibility for the DPP in Northern Ireland to refer unduly lenient sentences to the Court of Appeal within 28 days of the original judgment.[117] According to the PPS, the power of the DPP is exercised only exceptionally in a small percentage of cases.[118] This suggests that the majority of the sentencing decisions are regarded as appropriate by prosecutors. It should be mentioned in this regard that, of 2,591 criminal convictions secured before the Crown Court in 2013, 26 cases were considered by the DPP for referral.[119] Also, the DPP's reference generally applies to indictable offences (before the Crown Court), and a difficulty arises when particular conduct is a 'hybrid' offence (i.e. an offence that may be tried either on indictment or summarily) although the Secretary of State may include these offences through statutory instruments.[120]

It is important to recognise here that the Northern Ireland government has taken some steps to rectify this problem for some forms of organised crime. For instance, fiscal/excise fraud under Section 170 of the Customs and Excise Management Act 1979 was not previously referable to the Court of Appeal. This changed with the adoption of the Criminal Justice Act 1988 (Review of Sentencing) Order (Northern Ireland) 2013 which came into force in December 2013. A similar action was taken in relation to trafficking for labour exploitation by the Criminal Justice (Northern Ireland) Act 2013. These are examples of good practice and demonstrate the commitment of Northern Ireland to make this jurisdiction a hostile environment for criminals to operate in.

In the early part of 2015, the Department of Justice in Northern Ireland issued a consultation on unduly lenient sentences and published a report in September 2015 summarising the responses received.[121] In this report, the Department recognised the need to make offences of public concern referable through statutory instruments. In this regard, it stated that the offences of slavery and forced labour would be added to the list in line with the arrangements made in England and Wales.[122] However, it fell short of endorsing that all cases tried in the Crown Court, including hybrid offences, should be made referable due to the potential business and policy impact on the work of the DPP and the Court of Appeal.[123] This may be contrasted with the recent developments in England and Wales where both the Attorney General and Solicitor General acknowledged the shortcomings

117 Criminal Justice Act 1988, pt IV as amended.

118 Interviews with the PPS, *supra* ch 4 n 114.

119 Department of Justice, *The Law on Unduly Lenient Sentences: A Consultation Paper* (February 2015), 6 and 22.

120 One recent example is the Criminal Justice Act 1988 (Reviews of Sentencing) Order 2006, and relevant offences included are production/supply of controlled drugs, possession of controlled drugs with intent to supply and trafficking for sexual exploitation.

121 Department of Justice, *The Law on Unduly Lenient Sentences: Report on the Department of Justice Consultation* (September 2015).

122 Ibid., 14. See the Criminal Justice Act 1988 (Reviews of Sentencing) Order 2014 applicable in England and Wales.

123 Ibid., 17.

in the current system and expressed their willingness to modify it.[124] This is another example where devolution may impact on actions taken against transnational organised crime.

In the Republic of Ireland, the DPP can also refer unduly lenient sentences to the Court of Criminal Appeal within 56 days of the original judgment.[125] The length of period is therefore longer, and this is a better model as it allows the DPP to consider cases more carefully. There is a rate of approximately 30 referrals annually (most of which are not organised crime).[126] Similar to Northern Ireland, the Court of Criminal Appeal will not intervene unless it can be shown that there has been a substantial departure from what could be regarded as the appropriate sentence.[127] Also, the DPP can only refer sentences imposed upon conviction on indictment although hybrid offences which are tried before the Circuit Court are not explicitly excluded from consideration.[128] This means that summary conviction, which applies to offences including fiscal/excise fraud, is not referable in this jurisdiction. In 2006, the Law Reform Commission published a report entitled *Consultation Paper on Prosecution Appeals from Unduly Lenient Sentences in the District Court*. After carefully examining arguments for and against allowing appeals from the District Court, the Commission recommended that a procedure should be introduced into Irish law to appeal against unduly lenient sentences that are imposed in the District Court.[129] This reform could strengthen the sentencing regime for organised crime and respond to the public opinion that the government should take a tougher stance to combat organised crime.[130] The sentiment in the Republic is clearly different from that in Northern Ireland. In any event, a judge of the High Court and the SCC stated that the Court of Criminal Appeal can be active in increasing sentences (up to 50 per cent, applying to all cases).[131] The frequency and percentage therefore are higher in this jurisdiction than in Northern Ireland. Whilst this may demonstrate the willingness of upper courts to increase sentences, it also shows that trial judges are sometimes too lenient when it comes to sentencing.

Some of these issues can be addressed through the creation of clear sentencing guidelines for organised crime which would enhance consistency in sentencing and public confidence in the criminal justice systems. In this regard,

124 Jacqueline Beard, *Review of Unduly Lenient Sentences, House of Commons Library Briefing Paper* (October 2015).

125 Criminal Justice Act 1993, s 2 as amended.

126 Interviews with public prosecutors, *supra* ch 3 n 16. For example, in 2014 there were 31 applications lodged and 36 applications were heard. Of those heard, 23 were successful and 11 were refused with 2 applications struck off or withdrawn. Office of the DPP, *Annual Report 2014*, 52–53.

127 *DPP v Byrne* [1995] 1 ILRM 279.

128 Department of Justice (2015), *supra* n 121, 20.

129 Consultation Paper, 95.

130 Red C, *supra* ch 4 n 14.

131 *Supra* ch 4 n 64.

a review of the existing guidelines (or the creation of new ones where crimes were not sufficiently understood) was recommended by the law enforcement community in Northern Ireland. In England and Wales, the Sentencing Council publishes sentencing guidelines on various crimes to allow judges to achieve consistency in sentencing and to facilitate public understanding on the issue.[132] Some of the relevant guidelines are for drug offences,[133] fraud[134] and sexual offences (which includes a part on trafficking for sexual exploitation).[135]

However, currently there is no equivalent body in Northern Ireland. Whilst the courts can rely on the guidelines produced by the Sentencing Council for England and Wales, these are secondary; those developed by the Court of Appeal in Northern Ireland take precedence.[136] It has been recognised that the Court of Appeal guidelines are a very effective way of sending a clear message to the lower courts and of structuring judicial sentencing.[137] Without casting doubt on the ability of the Court of Appeal to provide effective guidance in many cases, one of the difficulties is that without comprehensive guidelines that govern all cases at all levels, there is the risk that inconsistent sentences continue to be imposed by trial judges in Northern Ireland. This can be exacerbated by a degree of subjectivity reflected in sentences depending on how factors such as the 'public interest' or the 'interests of justice' are interpreted by individual judges. One defence lawyer also made the important point that there can be no guidance until an issue is taken up by the Court of Appeal,[138] and this creates the possibility that some of the new/emerging forms of criminality do not receive immediate and appropriate attention. In addition, a lack of published guidelines prevents members of the general public from gaining a better understanding of the subject matter as they do not generally possess sufficient skills in legal research and analysis. This can have an impact on their confidence in law enforcement. All of these point to the conclusion that it is desirable to have clear, published guidelines for organised crime in Northern Ireland.

It is important to mention a couple of recent developments on sentencing in this jurisdiction. The Department of Justice in Northern Ireland initiated a consultation on a Sentencing Guidelines Mechanism in October 2010 in response to the Hillsborough Castle Agreement.[139] The need to achieve greater consistency and transparency was highlighted during consultation. The Northern Ireland Assembly also commissioned research on comparative sentencing guidelines

132 Sentencing Council, <http://sentencingcouncil.judiciary.gov.uk>.
133 *Drug Offences: Definitive Guidelines* (2012).
134 *Sentencing for Fraud: Definitive Guidelines* (2009).
135 *Supra*, ch 3 n 42.
136 *Attorney General's Reference (Number 1 of 2008)*, *Gibbons and Others* [2008] NICA 41, para 44.
137 Interview with a High Court judge, *supra* ch 3 n 5.
138 Interview with a defence lawyer, *supra* ch 4 n 41.
139 Department of Justice, *Consultation on a Sentencing Guidelines Mechanism* (October 2010), and *Summary of Responses* (March 2011).

mechanisms which examined the role of various sentencing guidelines and bodies and suggested a number of issues for consideration.[140] Alongside this, the Lord Chief Justice of Northern Ireland set up a Programme of Action on Sentencing that sought to introduce new guidelines for a range of offences identified in the consultation.[141] Crimes such as fiscal/excise fraud, human trafficking and slavery/forced labour were mentioned. A sub-group to draft some guidelines was set up and is continuing its work at the time of writing. These are positive developments which can strengthen action against transnational organised crime.

In the Republic of Ireland, there is also no Sentencing Council. The appellate courts have begun to formulate general sentencing guidance and, in some instances, specific guidelines but not in the area of organised crime. This lack of guidance may be mitigated to some extent by the fact that a serious offence committed as part of, or in furtherance of, the activities of a criminal organisation is statutorily treated as an aggravating factor.[142] In this way, the potential for organised crime to attract higher sentences is greater than in Northern Ireland, and this can send a strong message to criminals that they would face serious consequences for committing organised crime. However, clear guidelines on organised crime are still desirable for the reasons stated earlier.

It should be mentioned that discussions on sentencing guidance have been taking place for some time in this jurisdiction. In 1996, the Law Reform Commission recommended the introduction of sentencing guidelines on crime generally in order to achieve consistency in sentencing.[143] In 2003, the Working Group on the Jurisdiction of the Courts, chaired by Justice Fennelly of the Supreme Court, also recognised the need to develop a system of objective guidance for sentencing judges at all levels and called for a further independent study.[144] Subsequently, the Department of Justice and Equality published a *White Paper on Crime, Discussion Document No. 2: Criminal Sanctions* in 2010 as part of a consultation process. Many of the responses received were in favour of the creation of a sentencing council and guidelines for clarity, coherence and the building of public confidence.[145]

In order to address some of these issues, the judiciary has established an online platform known as the 'Irish Sentencing Information System'[146] which provides

140 Northern Ireland Assembly, *Comparative Research into Sentencing Guidelines Mechanisms* (2011).

141 Sentencing Working Group, *Monitoring and Developing Sentencing Guidance in Northern Ireland: A Report to the Lord Chief Justice* (June 2010); and *Report by the Lord Chief Justice's Sentencing Group* (December 2012).

142 Criminal Justice Act 2006, s 74 as inserted by the Criminal Justice (Amendment) Act 2009.

143 Law Reform Commission, *Report on Sentencing* (1996).

144 Working Group on the Jurisdiction of the Courts, *The Criminal Jurisdiction of the Courts* (2003), 172.

145 *White Paper on Crime Consultation Process: Criminal Sanctions, Overview of Written Submission Received* (August 2010), 6 and 11.

146 ISIS, *Irish Sentencing Information System* <www.irishsentencing.ie>.

information on sentencing to judges. This can also be accessed by the general public. However, concerns have been expressed about its long-term sustainability.[147] There is also currently no guidance on organised crime listed on this website. More recently in 2013, the Law Reform Commission stated that the aforementioned Information System could be supplemented by a dedicated body to formulate sentencing guidelines.[148] In particular, it highlighted the limitations inherent in relying upon guidance issued by the Court of Criminal Appeal, such as the insufficient volume of sentencing appeals and a case-by-case approach, as this could potentially lead to inconsistency.[149] When asked if there should be a body like the Sentencing Council in Ireland, a judge of the High Court and the SCC stated that clearer guidelines for serious offences were indeed desirable and revealed that a similar system to the Sentencing Council is currently being developed which is a welcome development.[150] If established, this could enhance action against transnational organised crime.

5.5 Confiscation of criminal proceeds/asset recovery

In the UK, including Northern Ireland, the main law that governs confiscation of criminal proceeds is the POCA as amended,[151] which provides the authorities with the powers to freeze and confiscate criminal proceeds and imposes an obligation on financial and other related institutions to disclose suspicious transactions. This is in conformity with Article 12 of the UNTOC as well as the relevant EU instruments explored previously. There are two types of confiscation stipulated under this legislation: 1) conviction-based confiscation; and 2) non-conviction-based civil asset recovery. With respect to the former, a confiscation order can be issued by the court in separate proceedings if it is found that the defendant has benefited from his/her criminal conduct.[152] A court could establish, on the balance of probabilities, whether a defendant had benefited from a 'criminal lifestyle'. This could be established through convictions from one or more 'lifestyle offences' listed under the Schedules. Under Schedule 5, offences such as drug, people and arms trafficking; money laundering; and fiscal/excise fraud are included.[153] It is therefore evident that the offences explored in this book are covered by the POCA. There are normally two important considerations in any such process. The first is a calculation of the amount of 'criminal benefit' that the offender has accumulated through his or her illegal activities. The second is

147 *White Paper on Crime Consultation Process, supra* n 145, 12.
148 Law Reform Commission, *supra* ch 3 n 75, 35 and 40.
149 Ibid.
150 *Supra* ch 4 n 64.
151 Most recently by the Serious Crime Act 2015.
152 Ss 6 (England and Wales), 92 (Scotland) and 156 (Northern Ireland). See CPS, *Proceeds of Crime Guidance: Confiscation and Ancillary Orders – Post POCA 2002*; and PPS, *supra* n 71, 27–28.
153 Schs 2 and 4 contain identical lists for England, Wales and Scotland.

the 'available amount' which the state can realistically recover through the imposition of a court ordered confiscation order.[154] According to Bullock, the calculations based on these two principles do not offer a fair representation of the profit generated by crime but rather can be viewed as a product of complex relationships between the outworkings of the POCA; the discretion of law enforcement officials; organisational restrictions; and informal communication between the defence and prosecution.[155] If a confiscation remains unpaid, the person responsible will be liable for a default sentence of imprisonment ranging from 6 months to 14 years depending on the amount of criminal proceeds that are involved. In any event, the Recorder of Belfast confirmed that conviction-based confiscation is enforced rigorously in Northern Ireland.[156]

Another type of confiscation is non-conviction-based confiscation, also known as civil (asset) recovery, generated from unlawful conduct under Part 5 of the POCA. One of the driving factors for establishing such a measure is the need to tackle serious and organised crime,[157] and its usefulness in this regard has been recognised.[158] This can be instituted against property worth more than £10,000 through civil proceedings before the High Court if it is satisfied that the alleged unlawful conduct occurred to the civil standard of the 'balance of probabilities'.[159] From such a perspective, there is no requirement for a person to be convicted of a criminal offence before their property can be seized, with civil recovery said to operate *in rem* (against the property) rather than *in personam* (against the person). This regime can therefore be viewed as an escalation of approaches that attempt to deter criminal enterprise by removing the profit incentive and providing an opportunity to pursue the criminal gains of 'the upper echelons of organised crime gangs seen to be beyond the reach of the criminal law'.[160] According to the Attorney General in England and Wales, the following is a non-exhaustive list of circumstances where civil asset recovery is regarded as appropriate:

- the only known criminality is overseas, and there is no extra-territorial jurisdiction to pursue a criminal case in the courts of England and Wales or Northern Ireland

154 Karen Bullock, 'Criminal Benefit, the Confiscation Order and the Post-Conviction Confiscation Regime' (2014) 62 *Crime Law and Social Change*, 45, 62.
155 Ibid.
156 Interview with the Recorder of Belfast, *supra* ch 3 n 5.
157 See, for instance, Kenneth Murray, 'A Square Go: Tackling Organised Crime Where It Doesn't Want to be Tackled' (2013) 16 *Journal of Money Laundering Control* 99; and Peter Sproat, 'To What Extent Is the UK's Anti-Money Laundering and Asset Recovery Regime Used against Organized Crime?' (2012) 12 *Journal of Money Laundering Control* 134.
158 Casella, *supra* ch 1 n 155; Jeffrey Simser, 'Perspectives on Civil Forfeiture' in Simon Young (ed.), *Civil Forfeiture of Criminal Property: Legal Measures for Targeting the Proceeds of Crime* (Edward Elgar 2009), 20.
159 Proceeds of Crime Act 2002 (Financial Threshold for Civil Recovery) Order 2003.
160 Colin King, 'Civil Forfeiture and Article 6 of the ECHR: Due Process Implications for England and Wales and Ireland' (2014) 34 *Legal Studies* 371, 373.

- there is no identifiable living suspect who is within the jurisdiction or realistically capable of being brought within the jurisdiction
- proceeds of crime can be identified but cannot be linked to any individual suspect or offence
- a law enforcement authority considers that an investigation could not generate sufficient evidence to create a realistic prospect of conviction
- a criminal investigation has been conducted but the prosecuting authority considers that there is insufficient evidence to create a realistic prospect of conviction
- a prosecution has been conducted but has not resulted in a conviction.[161]

According to SOCA officers, civil recovery investigations normally involve more than one predicate offence and take into account a number of relevant factors such as intelligence, cash seizures and tax offences as well as people who may be affected.[162] It is also worth pointing out that over 95 per cent of civil recovery in Northern Ireland was previously conducted by SOCA.[163] This underscores the importance and relevance of the work carried out by nationwide agencies in this jurisdiction.

Some important issues should be highlighted on this matter. To begin with, the available statistics cast some doubt on the effectiveness of the current confiscation regime in Northern Ireland. In 2014, a total of £2.02 million was said to have been confiscated through confiscation orders.[164] However, whether this constitutes strong evidence of effectiveness is not clear. Approximately £4.5 million was confiscated a few years earlier in 2012,[165] and this may be an indication that the criminals are increasingly becoming more sophisticated in hiding their proceeds. In addition, there is no evidence to suggest that organised crime has declined in the past few years. On the contrary, various forms of organised crime continue to increase. The quantity of drugs seized is steadily increasing[166] which suggests that they are becoming more readily available to the general public. The result of drug prevalence surveys conducted in Northern Ireland seems to confirm this as, for example, the life-time use of cannabis in the country has increased.[167] All of this suggests that the confiscated amount does not represent an accurate reflection of profits generated from organised crime.

161 Asset Recovery Powers for Prosecutors: Guidance and Background Note 2009, <www.gov.uk/guidance/asset-recovery-powers-for-prosecutors-guidance-and-background-note-2009>.
162 Interviews with SOCA officers, supra ch 4 n 39.
163 Ibid.
164 OCTF, *supra* intro n 9, 15.
165 OCTF, *Annual Report and Threat Assessment 2012*, 19.
166 OCTF, *supra* intro n 9, 18.
167 From 16.8 per cent (2002–2003) to 24 per cent (2010–2011). See also Department of Health, Social Services, and Public Safety, *A Framework for Reducing Alcohol and Drug Related Harm in Northern Ireland 2011–2016*, 11–20 for a detailed discussion of the impact of illegal drugs in Northern Ireland.

In addition, there are some issues related to civil recovery. In the recent case of *Perry v Serious Organised Crime Agency*,[168] the UK Supreme Court held that the High Court had no jurisdiction to make property freezing orders/civil recovery orders in relation to property held outside the UK. From the point of view of law enforcement, if they did not have the power to freeze criminal proceeds located abroad, this would undermine their action against money laundering and organised crime. This concern was raised by the UK government,[169] eventually leading to the enactment of the Crime and Courts Act 2013 under which the High Court in England and Wales may issue an order against property held abroad if, among other grounds, a crime has taken place wholly or partly in the UK and/or a defendant is present in this jurisdiction.[170]

The human rights aspect of civil asset recovery is also worth expanding on in the UK context. As explained in Chapter 1, the ECtHR has upheld civil recovery as generally being in compliance with the ECHR. UK jurisprudence also supports this position. In *Serious Organised Crime Agency v Gale*,[171] the appellant claimed that the application of the civil standard in determining the existence of criminal proceeds, particularly in the context of his acquittal in Portugal, was a breach of Article 6(2) of the ECHR (presumption of innocence). The appeal was dismissed by the Supreme Court on the grounds that the POCA proceedings were not a 'direct sequel' or 'a consequence and the concomitant' of any criminal proceedings, thereby adopting similar reasoning to the ECtHR.

There is another dimension to the presumption of innocence. In the often-cited case of *Phillips v United Kingdom*,[172] the applicant argued that Section 4 of the Drug Trafficking Act 1994, which related to the assumptions made by the court that any property held by a convicted person within the preceding 6 years represented criminal proceeds,[173] breached the presumption of innocence. The ECtHR began by holding that the purpose of the confiscation proceedings was not to determine the applicant's guilt (as he had been convicted previously), and therefore that the presumption of innocence did not apply.[174] It continued by emphasising that there were sufficient procedural safeguards in place (public/open hearing, disclosure of the prosecution's case and an opportunity to rebut such an assumption on the balance of probabilities).[175] Regardless of this technical distinction between civil and criminal, it has been cogently argued that civil

168 [2012] 3 WLR 379.

169 Crime and Courts Bill: Supplementary Memorandum Submitted by the Home Office, <www.publications.parliament.uk/pa/cm201213/cmpublic/crimeandcourts/memo/m15.htm>.

170 It is important to note, however, that this new rule is still subject to *lex situs* of the jurisdiction where assets are located.

171 [2011] UKSC 49.

172 *Supra* ch 1 n 153.

173 The equivalent provisions can be found in POCA (s 160 for Northern Ireland).

174 Para 35.

175 Paras 43–47.

recovery is criminal in nature and therefore that it should be regarded as a criminal mechanism.[176]

More importantly in Northern Ireland, the ability to carry out civil recovery has been placed in doubt, and this is another area in which devolution has had a tangible impact. The National Crime Agency (Limitation of Extension to Northern Ireland) Order 2013 restricted the NCA to carrying out civil recovery functions in Northern Ireland only in relation to non-transferred offences (e.g. immigration and customs offences) and closely connected transferred offences.[177] To illustrate this with an example, the NCA could investigate fuel laundering, which is a non-transferred offence. In addition, it could simultaneously investigate a transferred offence of money laundering that is connected closely to this offence. In reality, it was discovered that the NCA has not addressed the latter types of offences bearing in mind the political environment.[178] In the light of this, the PPS has been attempting to fulfil the civil recovery function in this jurisdiction. It has, however, admitted that it had no experience in using these civil recovery powers as these had been exercised previously by SOCA;[179] other issues, including a lack of resources and training, are hampering more effective implementation of civil recovery.[180] It was also pointed out that, unlike the CPS in England and Wales, the PPS enjoys no indemnity against claims for costs in the event of a failed attempt to recover assets by these means.[181] All of these circumstances have made Northern Ireland more vulnerable to money laundering and other criminal activities. The potential risk of inconsistent implementation of civil recovery was also expressed as a concern by the law enforcement community in this jurisdiction.[182] A workable compromise was suggested by some representatives of the Policing Board that would allow the NCA to conduct civil recovery in relation to all forms of organised crime in addition to reserved matters such as immigration and taxation.[183]

The limited nature of the NCA's powers should be put in the context of Northern Ireland's history. The responses to terrorism since the time of the Troubles have led to strong political opposition to the UK's national agencies operating in this jurisdiction, and this has spilled over into the area of organised

176 Anthony Gray, 'Forfeiture Provisions and the Criminal/Civil Divide' (2012) 15 *New Criminal Law Review* 32; and Michelle Gallant, 'Civil Processes and Tainted Assets: Exploring Canadian Models of Forfeiture', in Colin King and Clive Walker (eds.), *Dirty Assets: Emerging Issues in the Regulation of Criminal and Terrorist Assets* (Ashgate 2014), 165–181.

177 Sch 25.

178 Interviews with SOCA officers, *supra* ch 4 n 39.

179 Northern Ireland Affairs Committee, *supra* intro n 10, 24.

180 Ibid.

181 Ibid.

182 Interviews with SOCA officers, *supra* ch 4 n 39; interview with the Head of the PSNI Organised Crime Branch, *supra* ch 4 n 1; and interview with a Crown Court judge, *supra* ch 3 n 5.

183 Interviews with the Policing Board, *supra* ch 4 n 78.

crime. Indeed, it has been discovered that there has been strong opposition on the part of some political parties against the NCA operating in Northern Ireland. One example of this can be seen in the rejection by the Assembly of a consent motion tabled by the Ulster Unionist Party in February 2013 for the purpose of legislating for the NCA.[184] The key issue is the local control or accountability over policing as agreed in the Belfast Good Friday Agreement 1998 which was approved by a referendum and the bilateral UK-Ireland Treaty.[185] The Northern Ireland Policing Board was established to facilitate these key elements of the Agreement. As expressed by the CAJ, transparency and effective accountability are essential elements in ensuring that the policing activities comply with relevant human rights standards, and the NCA model would go against the current arrangement in place.[186]

Fortunately, this situation has been addressed by the Crime and Courts Act 2013 (National Crime Agency and Proceeds of Crime) (Northern Ireland) Order 2015. Under this legislation, the NCA became fully operational in Northern Ireland as of May 2015. The precondition for the coming into force of this order was the consent of the Northern Ireland Assembly. A consent motion was tabled in January 2015 and approved in the following month.[187] This is a significant development as the political community in Northern Ireland explicitly recognised the importance of the NCA's work in relation to serious crimes, including organised crime. Although it is important to recognise some opposition and concerns expressed in terms of the NCA itself,[188] this consent motion also shows that it is possible to seek some common ground and obtain cross-community support.

In practice, the NCA officers are now able to exercise the powers of a constable, address assets located overseas and conduct civil asset recovery. Their functions are therefore in line with other parts of the UK, and this will facilitate a more robust and consistent UK-wide approach to transnational organised crime. In terms of the accountability of the NCA in Northern Ireland, whilst the Home Secretary remains ultimately responsible for its operation, the NCA's work is now scrutinised by the Northern Ireland Policing Board.[189] The relevant codes and guidance applicable to PSNI officers are also relevant to NCA officers operating in this jurisdiction.[190] In addition, the Police Ombudsman for Northern

184 Northern Ireland Assembly, Private Members Debates 4 February 2013 <www.theyworkforyou.com/ni/?id=2013-02-04.6.23>.

185 CAJ, *Briefing Paper to Members of Legislative Assembly on the National Crime Agency* (February 2013), 5.

186 Ibid.

187 Explanatory Memorandum to the Crime and Courts Act 2013 (National Crime Agency and Proceeds of Crime) (Northern Ireland) Order 2015.

188 See the Debates on the Draft Order in the Northern Ireland Assembly, <http://aims.niassembly.gov.uk/officialreport/report.aspx?&eveDate=2015/02/03&docID=221589>.

189 Police (Northern Ireland) Act 2000 as amended, s. 33A.

190 Ibid., ss 52(10)(A) and (10)(B).

Ireland is able to examine complaints related to NCA officers.[191] Local accountability, therefore, has been enhanced through this legislation, thereby respecting the devolution arrangement and addressing the concerns expressed by the CAJ to a greater extent. The Director-General of the NCA and the Home Secretary must also consult the Minister of Justice for Northern Ireland, and the Northern Ireland Assembly is to be kept informed of the NCA's work.[192] In summary, a substantial improvement in relation to civil recovery is evident in Northern Ireland.

In the Republic of Ireland, like the UK, there are two types of confiscation. The first type is ordered after conviction under the Criminal Justice Act 1994. It is worth pointing out that Irish proceeds of crime legislation are often used as a template for other States, including the UK, as the Irish legislation predates others.[193] One interesting aspect of asset recovery is the existence of procedural differences; these are dependent on the types of crimes committed. Drug trafficking entails enhanced confiscation; for other crimes, the DPP has to prove that any benefit was generated solely as a result of a crime for which one is convicted.[194] For example, if a person is charged with multiple offences and convicted of just one of them, the court can issue an order for this convicted offence but not the others. This is different for drug trafficking where confiscation applies to all criminal activities connected to this offence. When asked whether this anomaly should be rectified, one prosecutor stated that it should be.[195] Certainly, it is difficult to see reasonable grounds for separate treatment as this can send the wrong message to the general public as well as criminals that some organised crime offences are less serious than drug offences. Further, under Section 19 of the 1994 Act, a person can be imprisoned if he/she does not pay the amount ordered by the court[196] although it appears that imprisonment happens only in exceptional cases.[197]

The second type is non-conviction-based civil recovery which is stipulated under the Criminal Assets Bureau Act 1996 and the Proceeds of Crime Act 1996. Civil recovery orders may be made against property worth at least €13,000 which is deemed to constitute proceeds of crime. As with the UK, the civil standard of proof applies in relation to recovery proceedings.[198] Opinion evidence of senior

191 The 2015 Order, sch 1.

192 Explanatory Memorandum, *supra* n 187.

193 Liz Campbell, 'The Recovery of "Criminal" Assets in New Zealand, Ireland and England: Fighting Organised Crime in the Civil Realm' (2010) 41 *Victoria University of Wellington Law Review* 15, 18.

194 Ss 4–8 for drug trafficking and s 9 for other offences.

195 Interview with a public prosecutor, *supra* ch 3 n 16.

196 The length ranges from 45 days to 10 years, depending on the amount stipulated in an order.

197 Fachtna Murphy and Barry Galvin, 'Targeting the Financial Wealth of Criminals in Ireland' (1999) *Irish Criminal Law Journal* 133, 142.

198 S 8.

police officers or officers of Revenue, Irish Tax and Customs is admissible in the application of these orders if the High Court is satisfied that there are reasonable grounds for that belief.[199] King has highlighted the concern that the use of opinion evidence, which has traditionally been a tool used for prosecuting terrorist offences, is a clear example of criminal law powers being deployed within the civil confiscation regime.[200] Further, like the UK's Crime and Courts Act 2013, the 1996 Act as amended by the Proceeds of Crime (Amendment) Act 2005 covers proceeds and property held abroad, provided that the suspect is domiciled, resident or present in Ireland, or that any part of the crime takes place within its jurisdiction.[201] It is evident that the Irish legislative framework is more advanced than that of the UK in this regard and generally is in line with international and European standards.

In terms of the effectiveness of the Irish legislative frameworks, the CAB, which consists of officers from An Garda Síochána, Revenue, Irish Tax and Customs and the Department of Social, Community and Family Affairs,[202] argued strongly that it was both fair and highly effective.[203] Many officers recounted the unacceptable situation prior to the enactment of the Act when criminals were able to flaunt their illicit wealth through the acquisition of desirable properties, sports cars and other forms of affluent living. It also seems that good safeguards are in place. Judicial scrutiny is provided by a specialist judge in the High Court, and it has been confirmed that the system is generally efficient.[204] One of the reasons for this seems to be that relevant agencies within the CAB work together well and this has ensured consistency in confiscation of criminal proceeds. This has also been confirmed externally.[205] It should be noted here that in *Gilligan v Criminal Assets Bureau*, the submission that the 1996 Act violated the Constitution by interfering with the judicial function and infringing the guarantees on private property rights was rejected by the Supreme Court.[206] This also suggests that the civil recovery regime thus far has been regarded as constitutional and generally compliant with human rights in the Republic of Ireland.

Whilst it seems evident that the Republic of Ireland has been proactive in tracing and confiscating criminal proceeds compared to the past, similar issues exist in this jurisdiction. In 2014, criminal assets worth €1.186 million were

199 Ibid.

200 Colin King, 'Using Civil Processes in Pursuit of Criminal Law Objectives: A Case Study of Non Conviction Based Asset Forfeiture' (2012) 16 *International Journal of Evidence & Proof*, 337, 347.

201 Campbell, *supra* intro n 33, 206.

202 Criminal Assets Bureau Act 1996 as amended.

203 Interview with Garda officers, *supra* ch 3 n 7.

204 Interview with a High Court judge, *supra* ch 3 n 17.

205 Theodore S. Greenberg, *et al.*, *Stolen Asset Recovery: A Good Practice Guide for Non-conviction Based Asset Forfeiture* (World Bank/International Bank for Reconstruction and Development 2009), 158.

206 [2001] IESC 82.

seized.[207] This figure can be compared with €2.764 million in 2012,[208] €2.011 million in 2011[209] and €3.051 million in 2010.[210] These statistics therefore do not provide clear evidence that criminal assets in the Republic are confiscated effectively. Some frustrations were expressed in this regard,[211] which once again highlights the sophisticated nature of organised crime operations as well as the need to have a more robust system of detection, freezing and confiscation of criminal proceeds.

In addition, human rights concerns have also been raised in relation to civil recovery in the Republic of Ireland. Some scholars have pointed out that the current Irish system prioritises the needs of the State over the rights of individuals to due process.[212] In particular, a problem arises when someone is found innocent of criminal charges and yet his assets are pursued on the same allegation and evidence, potentially negating or contradicting the outcome of the criminal proceedings.[213] The use of the lower burden of proof (balance of probabilities) and additional powers granted to the law enforcement authorities in civil proceedings are problematic in this regard.[214] In the end, those in possession of property are in effect punished through deprivation even though the purpose of civil proceedings are *in rem*.[215] Having said this, it is open to question whether this is a problem created by the judiciary as its job is to apply the current law. It then seems reasonable to argue that a wider political debate on the desirability of civil recovery is needed in order to be able to address these concerns.

5.6 Cross-border dimensions of criminal proceedings and confiscation of criminal proceeds

In addition to the investigation and prosecution of organised crime, there are certain important issues in relation to criminal proceedings and confiscation of criminal proceeds in the cross-border context. To begin with, trial *in absentia* becomes a possibility for criminals located abroad. Among others, the Framework Decision on EAW envisages a possibility of executing a sentence or a detention order imposed by a decision rendered *in absentia*,[216] and therefore both jurisdictions may be in a position to facilitate this in relation to organised crime. In order to enhance the human rights protection of the defendants, however, the

207 Office of the DPP, *Annual Report 2014*, 55.
208 Office of the DPP, *Annual Report 2012*, 60.
209 Office of the DPP, *Annual Report 2011*, 58.
210 Office of the DPP, *Annual Report 2010*, 66.
211 Interviews with Garda officers, *supra* ch 3 n 7.
212 Michelle Gallant and Colin King, 'The Seizure of Illicit Assets: Patterns of Civil Forfeiture in Canada and Ireland' (2013) 42 *Common Law World Review* 91, 96.
213 Ibid., 97.
214 Ibid., 103.
215 Ibid.
216 Art 5(1).

Framework Decision provides that they should be given the opportunity of a retrial.[217] Section 20 of the Extradition Act 2003 in the UK incorporates this but goes further than the Framework Decision as judges are additionally required to determine whether the individuals concerned have the right to legal assistance and cross-examination. The European Arrest Warrant Act 2003 in Ireland also contains a similar provision.[218] The Framework Decision was amended[219] to increase the procedural safeguards for the convicted criminals by including trial *in absentia* as a ground for refusal. The human rights protection is further enhanced by the ECHR. In *Colozza v Italy*,[220] for instance, it was held that there would be a breach of Article 6 unless the waiver of his right to be present was established unequivocally. This means that the accused must be notified of the charges (including reasons for them) against him and expressly waive his right to appear.[221]

There are a few cases of trial *in absentia* and extradition in both jurisdictions. In *Bohm v Romania*,[222] the applicant successfully argued that retrial was not automatic in Romania as there was judicial discretion, and therefore that the practice did not comply with Section 20 of the Extradition Act 2003.[223] In the Republic of Ireland, the Supreme Court in *Minister of Justice, Equality and Law Reform v Sliczynski*[224] decided not to return the applicant as he was not notified of the time and place of his original trial and the relevant judicial authority in Poland did not provide an undertaking in writing that the person would be retried. Another interesting case is *Minister of Justice and Equality v Gherine*[225] where the execution of an EAW issued by Italy was refused by the High Court as the applicant was convicted *in absentia* for drug offences and the Irish authorities were not properly informed. These cases demonstrate that the judges do in fact carefully examine the issue of trial *in absentia* connected to extradition and apply respective legislation appropriately in order to safeguard the rights of suspects or defendants.

Admissibility of evidence obtained outside of their jurisdictions is another important issue. The UK's Criminal Justice (International Co-operation) Act

217 Ibid.

218 S 45 amended by the Criminal Justice (Miscellaneous) Act 2009.

219 Council Framework Decision 2009/299/JHA of 26 February 2009 amending Framework Decisions 2002/584/JHA, 2005/214/JHA, 2006/783/JHA, 2008/909/JHA and 2008/947/JHA, thereby enhancing the procedural rights of persons and fostering the application of the principle of mutual recognition to decisions rendered in the absence of the person concerned at the trial, [2009] OJ L 81/24.

220 App no 9024/80 (1985).

221 Para 28. See also *Brozicek v Italy*, App no 10964/84 (1989); and *Zana v Turkey*, App no 69/1996/688/880 (1997).

222 [2011] EWHC 2671 (Admin).

223 See also *Beretki v Harghita Law Court Romania* [2012] EWHC 336 (Admin); and *Wawrzyczek v Poland* [2015] EWHC 2854 (Admin).

224 [2008] IESC 73.

225 [2012] IEHC 536.

2003[226] and the Criminal Justice (Mutual Assistance) Act 2008[227] of the Republic of Ireland facilitate mutual identification, collection and exchange of evidence with foreign States, and these are broadly in line with the relevant international and regional standards on mutual legal assistance in criminal matters. In terms of human rights principles, the same rules highlighted throughout this book should apply in the cross-border context. Therefore, a starting point is that each State is entitled to decide on admissibility of evidence obtained abroad but must ensure overall fairness in criminal proceedings.

A few important issues have emerged over the course of time in relation to admissibility of evidence. For instance, in the landmark case of *A and Others v Secretary of State for the Home Department (No. 2)*, it was established that evidence obtained as a result of torture is inadmissible.[228] This was recently affirmed by the ECtHR in *Othman (Abu Qatada) v Others v United Kingdom*.[229] However, a slightly different approach has been taken in relation to evidence obtained as a result of ill-treatment short of torture. For instance, in *Gäfgen v Germany*, it was held that admission of evidence obtained through ill-treatment would result in a violation of the right to a fair trial only if the breach of Article 3 had a bearing on the outcome of the proceedings (e.g. conviction or sentence).[230] Put differently, if such evidence does not have any bearing on the outcome, then this might not lead to a breach of the right to a fair trial. This principle has been cogently criticised by scholars as unjustifiable[231] and an undermining of the absolute prohibition enshrined in Article 3 of the ECHR.[232]

Another pertinent issue is the transfer of criminals to face justice in another jurisdiction. To begin with, the extradition arrangements (e.g. EAWs) as well as pertinent principles, such as *non-refoulement*, must be observed. In modern times, however, some States have relied on irregular rendition and abduction to bring suspects into their jurisdiction to stand trial. This is made possible in certain jurisdictions under the controversial doctrine of *male captus bene detenus* (wrongly captured, properly detained). This allows the domestic court to exercise jurisdiction over an accused person regardless of how that person came into its jurisdiction. For instance, in the often-discussed case of *United States v Alvarez-Machain*,[233] the defendant, who was accused of killing an agent of the US Drug Enforcement Administration in Mexico, was forcibly brought into the US. The US Supreme

226 Chs 2 and 3.

227 Pt 7.

228 [2005] UKHL 71. See also *Harutyunyan v Armenia, Supra* ch 1 n 184; *Levinta v Moldova*, App no 17332/03 (2009).

229 *Supra* ch 1 n 164.

230 *Supra*, ch 1 n 184, para 178. See also *Jalloh v Germany, supra* ch 1 n 184.

231 See, for instance, Jackson and Summers, *supra* ch 1 n 183, 163–169.

232 Rosemary Pattenden, 'Evidence Obtained by Inhuman Treatment in Violation of Article 3 – European Court of Human Rights' (2009) 13 *International Journal of Evidence and Proof* 58, 61.

233 504 US 655 (1992).

Court affirmed that procedural safeguards satisfied the due process requirements. However, the courts in the UK can set aside criminal proceedings as abuse of process under such circumstances. Lord Bingham of the House of Lords in *R v Horseferry Road Magistrates' Court, ex parte Bennett*,[234] emphasised in this regard that:

> When it is shown that the law enforcement agency responsible for bringing a prosecution has only been enabled to do so by participating in violations of international law and of the laws of another state in order to secure the presence of the accused within the territorial jurisdiction of the court, I think that respect for the rule of law demands that the court take cognisance of that circumstance.
>
> . . .
>
> Since the prosecution could never have been brought if the defendant had not been illegally abducted, the whole proceeding is tainted.

From a human rights perspective, the doctrine of *male captus bene detentus* does not always result in a violation. Hence, in *Öccalan v Turkey*,[235] the ECtHR recognised that:

> Inherent in the whole of the Convention is the search for a fair balance between the demands of the general interest of the community and the requirements of the protection of the individual's fundamental rights. As movement about the world becomes easier and crime takes on a larger international dimension, it is increasingly in the interest of all nations that suspected offenders who flee abroad should be brought to justice. Conversely, the establishment of safe havens for fugitives would not only result in danger for the State obliged to harbour the protected person, but also tend to undermine the foundations of extradition.

The Court continued that '(an) arrest made by the authorities of one State on the territory of another State, without the consent of the latter, affects the person concerned's individual rights to security under the right to liberty and security', and the consent can be regarded as a form of international cooperation.[236] To put it simply, this line of reasoning suggests that forcible abduction can be justified as long as there is consent by both parties. Whilst this decision raises concerns, additional principles have been emerging. In the cases of *Nashiri v Polana*[237] and *Husayn v Poland*,[238] the ECtHR recognised the responsibility of Poland in allowing

234 [1994] 1 AC 42.
235 App no 49221/99 (2005).
236 Ibid., paras 86, 88 and 93–99.
237 App no 287611/11 (2015).
238 App no 7511/13 (2015).

the transfer of applicants to the US for the purposes of secret detention and interrogation. In particular, it held that its actions breached Article 3 (due to the risk of the applicants being subjected to torture and ill-treatment), Article 5 (risk of further undisclosed detention) and Article 6 (risk of flagrant denial of justice). These are important principles which must be borne in mind in relation to treating suspects and defendants of transnational organised crime.

In addition, transfer of criminal proceedings is relevant in the cross-border context. As noted in Chapter 3, the Criminal Jurisdiction Act 1975 (Northern Ireland) and the Criminal Law (Jurisdiction) Act 1976 (Republic of Ireland) make the transfer of criminal proceedings possible for terrorism-related offences. Apart from this, there is no clear statutory basis to facilitate a transfer of proceedings. The UK does this on a discretionary or case-by-case basis[239] whilst the Republic of Ireland seems less willing to do this.[240] Both States are not parties to the European Convention on the Transfer of Criminal Proceedings in Criminal Matters 1972[241] and both entered a reservation to Article 21 of the European Convention on Mutual Assistance in Criminal Matters 1959 which touches upon this issue. The reasoning behind this is the belief that a criminal proceeding should take place where the major part of a crime has been committed.[242] This reflects the fundamental principle of territoriality explored in Chapter 1. Article 21 (Transfer of Criminal Proceedings) of the UNTOC merely obliges States to 'consider' this option, and therefore both States are not strictly in breach of this international obligation. As stressed previously, however, there is scope to consider amending the respective legislation to include organised crime in order to strengthen their action.

If extradition or transfer of criminals from their jurisdictions is not possible, then the principle of *aut dedere aut judicare* should be observed. The UK does not have specific legislation that enshrines the principle although prosecution is permitted for crimes such as international crime, hijacking and terrorism.[243] In the Republic of Ireland, the Extradition Act 1965 as amended,[244] allows prosecution only when extradition of Irish nationals is not permitted because of a lack of reciprocal arrangements with other States.[245] In addition, similar to the UK, the Republic can prosecute serious crimes.[246] However, the positions of both

239 Home Office, *supra* ch 4 n 162, 44.

240 Implementation Review Group, *Country Review Report of Ireland under the United Nations Convention against Corruption* (2015), 232.

241 ETS No. 73.

242 Home Office, *supra* ch 4 n 162, 44.

243 *The Obligation to Extradite or Prosecute*, A/CN.4/579 and Add. 1–4 (2007), 25. For discussion of the principle, see *R v Bow Street Metropolitan Stipendiary Magistrate, ex parte Pinochet Ugarte*, [2000] 1 AC 61. In *R v Zardad*, [2007] All ER (D) 90, the defendant was prosecuted for torture he committed in Afghanistan.

244 Extradition (Amendment) Act 1994.

245 The Obligation to Extradite or Prosecute, *supra* n 243, 15.

246 Ibid.

governments in relation to organised crime remain unclear. As signatories to the UNTOC, they should consider implementing this principle in order to ensure that criminals are properly punished.

Further, transfer of sentenced criminals raises interesting issues. This allows UK and Irish nationals convicted abroad to serve their sentences back home. Alternatively, the UK and Irish authorities are able to transfer criminals within their jurisdictions to serve their sentences abroad. The key reasons for the existence of this arrangement are the rehabilitation and reintegration of offenders.[247] Article 17 of the UNTOC and the European Convention on the Transfer of Sentenced Persons 1983[248] are important in this regard. At the domestic level, the relevant legislative frameworks are the Repatriation of Prisoners Act 1984 in the UK and the Transfer of Sentenced Persons Act 1995 in the Republic of Ireland. Such transfers largely depend on the existence of transfer agreements with foreign States.[249] However, transfer requests appear to be made regularly between the UK and the Republic. In 2014, for instance, a total of 24 requests for transfer into the Republic were made by the UK (4 from Northern Ireland) and 22 requests were made within this jurisdiction for transfer to the UK (8 to Northern Ireland).[250] The total number of transfers made with the UK (420) since 1995 is far greater than any other States in the world, including the EU Member States and US.[251] This suggests that the level of cross-border cooperation is strong between the two jurisdictions.

An interesting issue is whether the sentences imposed abroad can be converted once criminals are returned to their home countries. Both the UK and the Republic of Ireland made a declaration not to do this when ratifying the aforementioned European Convention,[252] thereby supporting the continuation of the original sentences imposed by foreign States. Neither the Repatriation of Prisoners Act 1984 nor the Transfer of Sentenced Persons Act 1995 provide for conversion. However, a different approach was recognised by the House of Lords in *R v Secretary of State for the Home Department, ex parte Read*.[253] This case concerned a prisoner sentenced to 12 years' imprisonment in Spain for counterfeiting currency. The same offence would have attracted a much lower sentence if convicted in the UK but the UK government's intention was to maintain this sentence.

247 Jamil Mujuzi, 'Transferring Sentenced Persons (Offenders) to the United Kingdom: Highlighting Some of the Human Rights Issues the Courts Have Had to Deal with' (2014) 1 *State Practice and International Law Journal* 73, 75.

248 ETS No. 112. The United Kingdom and the Republic of Ireland ratified this instrument in 1985 and 1995 respectively.

249 Foreign and Commonwealth Office, *Transfer Home for Prisoners Abroad* (March 2014), 3.

250 Department of Justice and Equality, *Report on the Operation of the Transfer of Sentenced Persons Acts* (2014), 5. It is important to stress that these do not apply exclusively to organised crime.

251 Ibid., 6.

252 See the Full List of Reservations and Declarations, <www.coe.int/en/web/conventions/full-list/-/conventions/treaty/112/declarations?p_auth=IrbDA8B4>.

253 [1988] 3 WLR 948.

The House of Lords held that where the court in a sentencing State imposes a sentence longer than what is prescribed under English law, then the Home Secretary has the power to change it to the English maximum.[254] Apart from this case, there are a few instances where the sentences have been changed.[255] Similarly, in the Republic of Ireland, the 1995 Act was amended by the Transfer of Sentenced Persons (Amendment) Act 1997 which now allows the High Court to convert the original sentences imposed by foreign States. Whilst it is important to acknowledge that the perceptions of the seriousness of crimes are influenced by the cultural, political, social and legal underpinnings of each State, such conversion does affect the spirit of international law enforcement cooperation as well as the principle of mutual recognition if exercised frequently.

Another important issue is the consent of prisoners to be transferred. Article 3 of the European Convention stresses the significance of this, and it is important to ensure that transfer is not used as a means of deporting foreign criminals.[256] However, the stance on consent has changed over the course of time. For instance, the Additional Protocol to the European Convention 1997[257] allows transfer of sentenced persons without consent when the sentence includes expulsion or deportation after completing their imprisonment or when criminals flee sentencing States. The EU Council Framework Decision 2008/909/JHA[258] further permits the transfer of prisoners without consent more broadly. Whilst the UK is part of this Framework Decision,[259] the Republic of Ireland is not, although the Irish government is currently considering the Transfer of Sentenced Persons and Transfer of Execution of Sentences Bill in order to transpose this instrument.[260] From the point of view of law enforcement, different approaches can affect cross-border cooperation.

In terms of the human rights safeguards surrounding the transfer of sentenced criminals, the aforementioned Framework Decision provides for grounds for non-enforcement which include the breach of the *ne bis in idem* principle and judgment *in absentia*.[261] This unfortunately is far from satisfactory as the obligations are not

254 Para 25.

255 *Re Abdur Rashid Khan* [2006] EWHC 2826 (QB); *R v Hull* [2011] EWCA Crim 1261; and *Samantha Orobator v Governor of HMP Holloway and Secretary of State for Justice* [2010] EWHC 58 (Admin), cited in Mujuzi, *supra* n 247, 79–80.

256 UNODC, *Handbook on the International Transfer of Sentenced Persons* (2012), 33.

257 ETS No. 167.

258 Council Framework Decision 2008/909/JHA of 27 November 2008 on the application of the principle of mutual recognition to judgments in criminal matters imposing custodial sentences or measures involving deprivation of liberty for the purpose of their enforcement in the European Union, [2008] OJ L 327/27.

259 2014/858/EU: Commission Decision of 1 December 2014 on the notification by the United Kingdom of Great Britain and Northern Ireland of its wish to participate in acts of the Union in the field of police cooperation and judicial cooperation in criminal matters adopted before the entry into force of the Treaty of Lisbon and which are not part of the Schengen *Acquis* [2014] OJ L 345/6.

260 See Government Legislation Programme Spring/Summer Session 2015.

261 Art 9.

mandatory as the term 'may refuse' suggests. Having said this, the UK Supreme Court has taken an important step by interpreting this Decision to include non-discrimination:

> Nothing in this Framework Decision should be interpreted as prohibiting refusal to execute a decision when there are objective reasons to believe that the sentence was imposed for the purpose of punishing a person on the grounds of his or her sex, race, religion, ethnic origin, nationality, language, political opinions or sexual orientation, or that that person's position may be prejudiced on any one of those grounds.[262]

The human rights protection is further strengthened by the ECHR. The principle of *non-refoulement* is a case in point. Whilst this principle may not be relevant to British and Irish nationals wishing to serve their sentences back home, it becomes important when they are to serve their sentences abroad. In addition to the death penalty and its implication for Article 3 in the aforementioned case of *Soering*, the principle is also held to apply in the contexts of life imprisonment without parole[263] and poor prison conditions overseas.[264] Further, the right to private and family life might come into play if these criminals already have an established home and family in the UK or the Republic of Ireland. For instance, in *Mehemi v France*, the applicant, who was convicted of drug trafficking, successfully argued that his expulsion to Algeria and permanent exclusion from France breached his right to private and family life due to his strong ties with his family there.[265] Whilst these human rights principles are often discussed in the context of extradition or deportation, their relevance to the sentencing stage and beyond is evident, and the UK and the Republic of Ireland are bound by them.

Although a refusal to provide mutual assistance in relation to sentencing on human rights grounds is reasonable, this once again has implications in terms of mutual respect and recognition. Administration of justice can also be called into question if criminals are not punished properly. One way to mitigate this difficulty is to execute sentences imposed abroad. This is similar to the *aut dedere aut judicare* principle. Although the UK does not have specific legislation on this, it has decided to be bound by the aforementioned Council Framework Decision 2008/909/JHA. This makes it possible to at least execute sentences imposed by other Member States in addition to transferring sentenced criminals. In contrast, the Republic of Ireland enacted the Transfer of Execution of Sentences Act 2005. In addition to EU Member States and those of the Council of Europe, this

262 *HH v Deputy Prosecutor of the Italian Republic, Genoa*; *PH v Deputy Prosecutor of the Italian Republic, Genoa*; and *F-K v Polish Judicial Authority* [2012] UKSC 25.

263 *Kafkaris v Cyprus*, App no 21906/04 (2008); and *Vinter and Others v United Kingdom*, Applications nos 66069/09, 130/10 and 3896/10 (2013).

264 *Enea v Italy*, App no 74912/01 (2009); *Kudła v Poland*, App no 30210/96 (2000); and *Dougoz v Greece*, App no 40907/98 (2001).

265 *Supra* ch 1 n 163.

legislation allows the Minister of State to designate other States to facilitate execution of sentences.[266] This is a better model as the existence of legislation enhances legality and clarity. In any event, this arrangement can ensure that criminals are appropriately punished.

Finally, one issue is worth pointing out in terms of confiscation of criminal proceeds. Whilst there does not seem to be any problem facilitating cross-border tracing and confiscation of criminal proceeds between the UK (including Northern Ireland) and the Republic of Ireland, the CAB highlighted some difficulties in facilitating international cooperation with other States. When the CAB transmits a mutual legal assistance request for evidence, for instance, the information it gains cannot be used in the civil environment as many States do not recognise non-conviction-based civil recovery.[267] Whilst this problem can be circumvented by obtaining prior authorisation from other States in this regard or by asking them to provide an expert witness, these do not materialise in practice.[268] This does not seem to be a problem between Northern Ireland and the Republic as it is common practice for officers from HMRC and the PSNI in Northern Ireland to give evidence in civil recovery cases in the Republic and vice versa.[269]

An important facility to alleviate this problem is the Camden Asset Recovery Inter-Agency Network (CARIN), which is an informal network of asset recovery offices and agents. The name comes from the Camden Court Hotel in Dublin where the first meeting was held in 2003. Whilst it originally involved 5 European States with asset recovery legislation for the purpose of comparing good practice, membership has grown to 53 States and 9 international organisations.[270] This appears to facilitate coordination and dialogue among members to strengthen their asset recovery capability[271] and can be regarded as an example of good practice. In addition, the Minister of Justice and Equality recently published the Criminal Justice (Mutual Assistance) (Amendment) Bill which aims to strengthen cross-border cooperation with other EU Member States. When enacted, it will incorporate the Council Framework Decision 2006/783/JHA on mutual recognition of confiscation orders. In summary, in looking at cross-border issues related to criminal proceedings and confiscation of criminal proceeds, it seems reasonable to argue that some important international and European standards have been incorporated into the legislative frameworks of both the UK (and Northern Ireland) and the Republic of Ireland. However, some variations and gaps are recognised in certain areas, and this once again highlights the difficulty of promoting the principles of approximation and mutual recognition at the national level.

266 S 5.
267 Interviews with Garda officers, *supra* ch 3 n 7.
268 Ibid.
269 Ibid.
270 Europol, *CARIN Information Leaflet*.
271 Interviews with Garda officers, *supra* ch 3 n 7.

5.7 Conclusion

This chapter has considered key issues relevant to criminal proceedings and the confiscation of criminal proceeds of transnational organised crime. Despite the existence of some variations, both jurisdictions generally have legislative frameworks and procedures in place to bring criminals to justice and confiscate their criminal proceeds. Similar to investigation and prosecution, some important international and European standards are incorporated which once again demonstrates that both the UK (including Northern Ireland) and the Republic of Ireland pay attention to them. However, a number of concerns, human rights implications in particular, have been identified in areas such as the use of non-jury trials for organised crime and evidential matters. Whilst the current systems in Northern Ireland and the Republic of Ireland have been ruled to comply with human rights and constitutional principles, there still remains the possibility that they will be held liable if they do not fully observe them in the future. Sentencing also raises an issue as the law enforcement bodies do not always regard the sentences passed as appropriate. Although it is important to respect judicial independence and discretion, it is not clear whether the current practice provides an effective deterrent in both jurisdictions. It also raises a question as to whether the serious nature of transnational organised crime is sufficiently understood by the judiciary.

A few more points should be highlighted. The present study demonstrates the impact of devolution on action against transnational organised crime. The arrangements under the Justice and Security (Northern Ireland) Act 2007, the sentencing guidelines as well as the operation of the NCA are examples of this. Like Scotland, therefore, Northern Ireland has begun to show its own initiative in implementing action against transnational organised crime. Whether this will lead to effective prevention and suppression remains to be seen as varied responses by England and Wales, Northern Ireland and Scotland can lead to negative consequences such as forum shopping and the concentration of criminal activities in a particular jurisdiction or jurisdictions. In addition, whilst both jurisdictions do seem to have decent legislative frameworks to facilitate cross-border cooperation, certain areas such as the transfer of criminal proceedings and the principle of *aut dedere aut judicare* are not yet widely recognised and implemented. In summary, it is reasonable to conclude that, although both Northern Ireland (as well as the UK) and the Republic of Ireland have taken important steps to implement international and European standards in tackling transnational organised crime, there is scope for improvement.

Conclusion

This book has examined the law enforcement responses to transnational organised crime in the island of Ireland based upon a research project entitled 'North–South Irish Responses to Transnational Organised Crime'. After identifying the relevant international and regional standards designed to enhance individual and collective responses stipulated in the UNTOC and EU law, the book proceeded to present the case studies of Northern Ireland and the Republic of Ireland. It analysed the key issues identified as part of the said research project, such as substantive criminal laws on core offences; special investigative techniques; prosecutorial guidance on organised crime; obstruction of justice; non-jury trial; evidential matters; sentencing; and confiscation of criminal proceeds. These have been supported by the overarching themes of cross-border cooperation and the protection of human rights.

A number of key conclusions have been reached. First, it is clear that many important standards have been incorporated by both jurisdictions. This indicates that legislators as well as law enforcement officials regard them as useful in combating transnational organised crime. The Republic of Ireland seems to have been more willing to incorporate the UNTOC into domestic legislation than the UK. However, the UK has been more willing to abide by the EU measures as Ireland has exercised its option of opting out more often. The varied implementation of obligations established by the UNTOC and EU law in practice means that the principle of State sovereignty operates strongly in action against transnational organised crime. Despite this, the value of the UNTOC and EU law should not be underestimated as it has also been demonstrated that they are gradually producing positive results on the ground.

It is also important to acknowledge the inherent weaknesses of these standards in terms of the protection of human rights. A lack of sufficient attention to human rights is counterproductive as this can affect the legitimacy of measures implemented, leading to a loss of public confidence in law enforcement. The international community missed an important opportunity in this regard as the UNTOC does not contain sufficient human rights obligations. Some progress has been made in relation to EU law with the legally binding nature of the EU Charter of Fundamental Rights as well as some instruments that are applicable to the victims and perpetrators of transnational organised crime. Despite this, it is clear that the EU and Member States must do more to integrate a human rights approach into their action against transnational organised crime. All this means that international and regional human rights law continue to play an important role, and it has been shown that important norms and principles on law enforcement have emerged over the course of time, many of which are equally applicable to action against transnational organised crime.

At the national level, there is no doubt that Northern Ireland and the Republic of Ireland have been making good progress in tackling organised crime, both in terms of legislative frameworks and law enforcement practice. The examples of good practice in both jurisdictions, such as the multi-agency approach in Northern Ireland and stronger punishment regimes in the Republic, have been highlighted throughout this book. One of the important aspects analysed has been the devolution of policing and criminal justice in Northern Ireland. It has been demonstrated that devolution has had some impact on the formulation of some statutory frameworks related to transnational organised crime and their enforcement. Although nothing negative has emerged yet, there still remains a risk of promoting fragmented, rather than integrated, responses within the UK in areas such as the definitions of substantive offences, prosecution guidelines and sentencing. These can make Northern Ireland more vulnerable to criminal activities. It is therefore important that Northern Ireland continues its efforts to coordinate its responses with the rest of the UK.

In relation to cross-border cooperation between the two jurisdictions, which is another important focus of this book, the current state of affairs seems generally positive. Once again, important international and regional standards are being observed by both jurisdictions. In addition to formal arrangements established by respective legislation, frontline law enforcement officers regularly facilitate an informal approach which seems to work quite well in the island of Ireland. This cannot be done without a high level of mutual respect and trust, and their efforts in establishing and maintaining positive working relationships should be recognised. However, the differences in attitude towards certain measures is also revealing, such as on JITs and cross-border surveillance. Therefore, despite the shared history, culture and common law tradition, State sovereignty is dominant in cross-border law enforcement cooperation as well.

As to the human rights dimension of action against transnational organised crime in Northern Ireland and the Republic of Ireland, the current measures seem to be generally in compliance with the relevant norms and principles. Despite concerns expressed by scholars and the human rights community, their domestic courts as well as the ECtHR have so far upheld the validity of measures, including special investigative techniques, civil asset recovery and non-jury trials. The law enforcement agencies in both jurisdictions also seem to take human rights seriously although this is more evident in Northern Ireland. Having said this, the situation may change in the future as a degree of uncertainty remains. In this regard, the lack of legislative frameworks and rigorous judicial oversight that has been identified in this book may be held to breach the principle of legality, accountability and other important norms. Before this happens, it is desirable that both the UK, including Northern Ireland, and the Republic of Ireland address them sufficiently through legislative and other means.

Finally, it is clear that law enforcement responses alone are not sufficient in preventing and suppressing transnational organised crime. Despite their ongoing efforts in this regard, it is a fact that organised crime continues to flourish in both jurisdictions. A more holistic approach which also tackles its multi-faceted nature is therefore needed. Of particular importance in this regard are the dynamics of supply and demand. Organised criminal groups will continue to provide goods, services and even people through illegal markets as long as there is a strong demand for them in the island of Ireland. Education and awareness-raising which target the general public, the business sector and the media are therefore needed. Whilst publication of annual reports and threat assessments may enhance their understanding to an extent, a more community-based approach would widen opportunities to reach out to the relevant audience. This means that public authorities other than the law enforcement agencies must take an active part in designing and implementing a more effective prevention strategy. The participation of civil society organisations with relevant expertise and experience should also be sought. This truly multi-agency approach would strengthen action against transnational organised crime in the island of Ireland.

Selected bibliography

Armada I, 'The European Investigation Order and the Lack of European Standards for Gathering Evidence: Is a Fundamental Rights-Based Refusal the Solution?' (2015) 6 *New Journal of European Criminal Law* 8

Bassiouni MC, 'The Penal Characteristics of Conventional International Criminal Law' (1983) 15 *Case Western Reserve Journal of International Law* 27

Bassiouni MC, *International Extradition: United States Law and Practice* (Oceana Publications 1987)

Bassiouni MC, 'Universal Jurisdiction for International Crimes: Historical Perspectives and Contemporary Practice' (2001) 42 *Virginia Journal of International Law* 81

Beare M, 'Shifting Boundaries: Between States, Enforcement Agencies and Priorities' in Albrecht H-J and Fijnaut C (eds.), *The Containment of Transnational Organised Crime: Comments on the UN Convention of December 2000* (IUSCRIM 2002)

Beittel JS, *Mexico: Organized Crime and Drug Trafficking Organizations* (US Congress Research Service 2015)

Blackwell JM, 'The Costs and Consequences of US Drug Prohibition for the People of Developing Nations' (2014) 24 *Indiana International and Comparative Law Review* 665

Blake D and Finlaw J, 'Marijuana Legalization in Colorado: Lessons Learned' (2014) 8 *Harvard Law and Policy Review* 359

Blakesley CL, 'United States Jurisdiction over Extraterritorial Crime' (1982) 73 *Journal of Criminal Law and Criminology* 1109

Block L, 'Combating Organised Crime in Europe: Practicalities of Police Cooperation' (2008) 2 *Policing: A Journal of Policy and Practice* 74

Brown I, 'The Feasibility of Transatlantic Privacy-Protective Standards for Surveillance' (2014) 22 *International Journal of Law and Information Technology* 1

Brown I and Korff D, 'Foreign Surveillance: Law and Practice in a Global Digital Environment' (2014) *European Human Rights Law Review* 243

Bruinsma G and Bernasco W, 'Criminal Groups and Transnational Illegal Markets' (2004) 41 *Crime, Law and Social Change* 79

Bullock K, 'Criminal Benefit, the Confiscation Order and the Post-Conviction Confiscation Regime' (2014) 62 *Crime Law and Social Change* 45

Calderoni F, *Organized Crime Legislation in the European Union* (Springer 2010)

Campbell L, 'The Recovery of "Criminal" Assets in New Zealand, Ireland and England: Fighting Organised Crime in the Civil Realm' (2010) 41 *Victoria University of Wellington Law Review* 15

Campbell L, *Organised Crime and the Law: A Comparative Analysis* (Hart 2013)

Campbell L, 'The Prosecution of Organised Crime: Removing the Jury' (2014) 18 *International Journal of Evidence and Proof* 83

Cape E and Hodgson J, 'The Right to Access to a Lawyer at Police Stations: Making the European Union Directive Work in Practice' (2014) 5 *New Journal of European Criminal Law* 450

Carnegie AR, 'Jurisdiction over Violations of the Laws and Customs of War' (1963) 39 *British Yearbook of International Law* 402

Casella S, 'The Case for Civil Forfeiture: Why In Rem Proceedings are an Essential Tool for Recovering the Proceeds of Crime' (2008) 11 *Journal of Money Laundering Control* 8

Cassese A, 'Is the Bell Tolling for Universality? A Plea for a Sensible Notion of Universal Jurisdiction' (2003) 1 *Journal of International Criminal Justice* 589

Caulkins JP *et al.*, 'High Tax States: Options for Gleaning Revenue from Legal Cannabis' (2012–2013) 91 *Oregon Law Review* 1041

Charleton P and McDermott P, 'From Diplock Courts to Jury Courts?' (2000) 111 *CIJL Yearbook* 16

Chu YK, *The Triads as Business* (Routledge 2008)

Cohen AK, 'The Concepts of Criminal Organisation' (1977) 17 *British Journal of Criminology* 97

Connolly J, *National Drug Intervention, What Works* (Health Research Board 2011)

Cressey D, *Theft of the Nation* (Harper Collins 1969)

Davis F, *The History and Development of the Special Criminal Court 1922–2005* (Four Courts Press 2007)

Dickinson ED, 'Codification of International Law: Part II: Jurisdiction with Respect to Crime' (1935) 29 *American Journal of International Law Supplement* 435

Edwards A and Gill P (eds.), *Transnational Organised Crime: Perspectives on Global Security* (Routledge 2005)

Fichera M, 'The European Arrest Warrant and the Sovereign State: A Marriage of Convenience?' (2009) 15 *European Law Journal* 70

Fijnaut C, 'Organized Crime: A Comparison Between the United States of America and Western Europe' (1990) 30 *British Journal of Criminology* 321

Gallant M, 'Civil Processes and Tainted Assets: Exploring Canadian Models of Forfeiture' in King C and Walker C (eds.), *Dirty Assets: Emerging Issues in the Regulation of Criminal and Terrorist Assets* (Ashgate 2014)

Gallant M and King C, 'The Seizure of Illicit Assets: Patterns of Civil Forfeiture in Canada and Ireland' (2013) 42 *Common Law World Review* 91

Georgieva I, 'The Right to Privacy under Fire – Foreign Surveillance under the NSA and the GCHQ and Its Compatibility with Art. 17 ICCPR and Art. 8 ECHR' (2015) 31 *Utrecht Journal of International and European Law* <www.utrechtjournal.org/articles/10.5334/ujiel.cr>

Gilbert G, *Aspects of Extradition Law* (Martinus Nijhoff Publishers 1991)

Gray A, 'Forfeiture Provisions and the Criminal/Civil Divide' (2012) 15 *New Criminal Law Review* 32

Greenberg TS *et al.*, *Stolen Asset Recovery: A Good Practice Guide for Non-conviction Based Asset Forfeiture* (World Bank/International Bank for Reconstruction and Development 2009)

Greene A, 'Shielding the State of Emergency: Organised Crime in Ireland and the State's Response' (2011) 62 *Northern Ireland Legal Quarterly* 249

Harding C, 'The Offence of Belonging: Capturing Participation in Organised Crime' (2005) *Criminal Law Review* 690

Heffernan L, *Legal Professional Privilege* (Bloomsbury 2011)

Helenius D, 'Mutual Recognition in Criminal Matters and the Principle of Proportionality: Effective Proportionality or Proportionate Effectiveness?' (2014) 5 *New Journal of European Criminal Law* 349

Hillyard P, 'The Normalisation of Special Powers from Northern Ireland to Britain' in Scraton P (ed.), *Law, Order and the Authoritarian State: Readings in Critical Criminology* (Open University Press 1987)

Hughes CE and Stevens A, 'What Can We Learn from the Portuguese Decriminalisation of Illicit Drugs?' (2010) 50 *British Journal of Criminology* 999

Jackson J, 'Many Years on in Northern Ireland: The Diplock Legacy' (2009) 60 *Northern Ireland Legal Quarterly* 213

Jackson J and Doran S, *Judge without Jury: Diplock Trials in the Adversarial System* (Oxford University Press 1995)

Jackson J and Summers S, *The Internationalisation of Criminal Evidence: Beyond the Common Law and Civil Law Traditions* (Cambridge University Press 2012)

Joossens L, *Smuggling, the Tobacco Industry and Plain Packs* (Cancer Research UK 2012)

Joossens J *et al.*, *How Eliminating the Global Illicit Cigarette Trade Would Increase the Tax Revenue and Save Lives* (International Union against Tuberculosis and Lung Disease, 2009)

Kaplan D and Dubro A, *Yakuza: Japan's Criminal Underworld* (University of California Press 2003)

King C, 'Using Civil Processes in Pursuit of Criminal Law Objectives: A Case Study of Non Conviction Based Asset Forfeiture' (2012) 16 *International Journal of Evidence & Proof* 337

King C, 'Civil Forfeiture and Article 6 of the ECHR: Due Process Implications for England and Wales and Ireland' (2014) 34 *Legal Studies* 371

King C, 'Belief Evidence and Informer Privilege: Revisited in Strasbourg' (2014) 18 *International Journal of Evidence and Proof* 340

Klerks P, 'The Network Paradigm Applied to Criminal Organisations: Theoretical Nitpicking or a Relevant Doctrine for Investigators? Recent Developments in the Netherlands' in Edwards A and Gill P (eds.), *Transnational Organised Crime: Perspectives on Global Security* (Routledge 2005)

Kugler M, Verdier T and Zenou Y, 'Organised Crime, Corruption and Punishment' (2005) 89 *Journal of Public Economics* 1639

Lee GD, *Global Drug Enforcement: Practical Investigative Techniques* (CRC Press 2004)

Leong A, *The Disruption of International Organised Crime* (Ashgate 2007)

Loftus B and Goold B, 'Covert Policing and the Invisibilities of Policing' (2011) 12 *Criminology & Criminal Justice* 278

Mangiaracina A, 'A New and Controversial Scenario in the Gathering of Evidence at the European Level: The Proposal for a Directive on the European Investigation Order' (2014) 10 *Utrecht Law Review* 113

Marin L, 'The European Arrest Warrant and Domestic Legal Orders: Tension between Mutual Recognition and Fundamental Rights: The Italian Case' (2008) 15 *Maastricht Journal of European and Comparative Law* 473

Mass S, 'The Dilemma of the Intimidated Witness in Federal Organised Crime Prosecution: Choosing among the Fear of Reprisal, the Contempt Powers of the

Court, and the Witness Protection Programme' (1981–1982) 50 *Fordham Law Review* 582

McClean D, *International Co-operation in Civil and Criminal Matters* (Oxford University Press 2002)

McGrath D, *Evidence* (Thompson Round Hall 2005)

McIllwain JS, 'Organized Crime: A Social Network Approach' (1999) 32 *Crime, Law and Social Change* 301

Milanovic M, 'Human Rights Treaties and Foreign Surveillance: Privacy in the Digital Age' (2015) 56 *Harvard International Law Journal* 81

Mitsilegas V, 'The Constitutional Implications of Mutual Recognition in Criminal Matters in the EU' (2006) 43 *Common Market Law Review* 1277

Montaldo S, 'Directive 2014/42/EU and Social Reuse of Confiscated Assets in the EU: Advancing a Culture of Legality' (2015) 6 *New Journal of European Criminal Law* 195

Mujuzi J, 'Transferring Sentenced Persons (Offenders) to the United Kingdom: Highlighting Some of the Human Rights Issues the Courts Have Had to Deal with' (2014) 1 *State Practice and International Law Journal* 73

Murphy F and Galvin B, 'Targeting the Financial Wealth of Criminals in Ireland' (1999) *Irish Criminal Law Journal* 133

Murray K, 'A Square Go: Tackling Organised Crime Where It Doesn't Want to be Tackled' (2013) 16 *Journal of Money Laundering Control* 99

Obokata T, *Trafficking of Human Beings from a Human Rights Perspective: Towards a Holistic Approach* (Martinus Nijhoff Publishers 2006)

Obokata T, *Transnational Organised Crime in International Law* (Hart 2010)

Obokata T, 'Key EU Principles to Combat Transnational Organised Crime' (2011) 48 *Common Market Law Review* 801

Paoli L, 'The Paradoxes of Organised Crime' (2000) 37 *Crime, Law and Social Change* 51

Paoli L, *Mafia Brotherhood: Organised Crime, Italian Style* (Oxford University Press 2003)

Paoli L, 'Italian Organised Crime: Mafia Associations and Criminal Enterprises' (2004) 6 *Global Crime* 19

Paoli L and Fijnaut C (eds.), *Organised Crime in Europe: Concepts, Patterns and Control Policies in the European Union and Beyond* (Springer 2006)

Pattenden R, 'Evidence Obtained by Inhuman Treatment in Violation of Article 3 – European Court of Human Rights' (2009) 13 *International Journal of Evidence and Proof* 58

Reuter P, *Options for Regulating New Psychoactive Drugs: A Review of Recent Experiences* (UK Drug Policy Commission 2011)

Rollins J, Wyler L and Rosen S, *International Terrorism and Transnational Crime: Security Threats, U.S. Policy, and Considerations for Congress* (Congressional Research Service 2010)

Sambei A, *Civil Forfeiture (Confiscation in Rem): Explanatory and Impact Study* (Council of Europe 2012)

Schalken T and Pronk M, 'On Joint Investigation Teams, Europol and Supervision of and Their Joint Actions' (2002) 10 *European Journal of Crime, Criminal Law and Criminal Justice* 78

Schloenhardt A, 'Organised Crime and the Business of Migrant Trafficking: An Economic Analysis' (1999) 32 *Crime, Law and Social Change* 203

Seddon T, 'Drug Policy and Global Regulatory Capitalism: The Case of New Psychoactive Substances (2014) 25 *International Journal of Drug Policy* 1019

Simonato M, 'Directive 2014/42/EU and Non-Conviction Based Confiscation: A Step Forward on Asset Recovery?' (2015) 6 *New Journal of European Criminal Law* 213

Simser J, 'Perspectives on Civil Forfeiture' in Young S (ed.), *Civil Forfeiture of Criminal Property: Legal Measures for Targeting the Proceeds of Crime* (Edward Elgar 2009)

Spapens T, 'Joint Investigation Teams in the European Union: Article 13 JITs and the Alternatives' (2011) 19 *European Journal of Crime, Criminal Law and Criminal Justice* 239

Sproat P, 'To What Extent Is the UK's Anti-Money Laundering and Asset Recovery Regime Used against Organized Crime?' (2012) 12 *Journal of Money Laundering Control* 134

Stevenson KM *et al.*, *Barriers to Asset Recovery: An Analysis of Key Barriers and Recommendations for Action* (The International Bank for Reconstruction and Development/The World Bank 2011)

Van den Wyngaert C, *The Political Offence Exception to Extradition* (Kluwer Law International 1980)

Van Hout M-C and Brennan R, 'Curiosity Killed M-Cat: Post Legislative Study on Mephedrone Use in Ireland,' (2012) 19 *Drugs: Education, Prevention and Policy* 156

Varese F, *The Russian Mafia: Private Protection in a New Market Economy* (Oxford University Press 2001)

Vettori B, *Tough on Criminal Wealth: Exploring the Practice of Proceeds from Crime Confiscation in the EU* (Springer 2006)

Weyembergh A, 'The Functions of Approximation of Penal Legislation within the European Union' (2005) 12 *Maastricht Journal of European and Comparative Law* 149

Williams P, 'Organising Transnational Crime: Networks, Markets and Hierarchy' in Williams P and Vlassis D (eds.), *Combating Transnational Crime: Concepts, Activities and Responses* (Frank Cass 2001)

Williams P and Godson R, 'Anticipating Organized and Transnational Crime' (2002) 37 *Crime, Law and Social Change* 311

Winstock A and Wilkins C, *'Legal Highs': The Challenges of New Psychoactive Substances* (Transnational Institute 2011)

Winter LB, 'The EU Directive on the Right to Access to a Lawyer: A Critical Assessment' in Ruggerri S (ed.), *Human Rights in European Criminal Law: New Developments in EU Legislation and Case Law After the Lisbon Treaty* (Springer 2015)

Wise EM, 'The Obligation to Extradite or Prosecute' (1993) 27 *Israel Law Review* 268

Woodiwiss M, 'Transnational Organised Crime: The Strange Career of an American Concept' in Beare M (ed.), *Critical Reflections on Transnational Organized Crime, Money Laundering and Corruption* (University of Toronto Press 2003)

Woodiwiss M, 'Transnational Organised Crime: The Global Reach of an American Concept' in Edwards A and Gill P (eds.), *Transnational Organised Crime: Perspectives on Global Security* (Routledge 2005)

Xanthopoulou E, 'The Quest for Proportionality for the European Arrest Warrant: Fundamental Rights Protection in a Mutual Recognition Environment' (2015) 6 *New Journal of European Criminal Law* 32

Zhang S and Chin KL, *Characteristics of Chinese Human Smugglers: A Cross-National Study* (U.S. Department of State 2003)

Zhang S and Chin KL, 'Snakeheads, Mules and Protective Umbrellas: A Review of Current Research on Chinese Organized Crime' (2008) 50 *Crime, Law and Social Change* 177 in law enforcement

Index